D0397390

Back from the Deep

Carl LaVO

BACK FROM THE DEEP

The Strange Story of the Sister Subs *Squalus* and *Sculpin*

NAVAL INSTITUTE PRESS
ANNAPOLIS, MARYLAND

Library of Congress Cataloging-in-Publication Data
LaVO, Carl, 1944–
Back from the deep : the strange story of the sister subs
Squalus and Sculpin / Carl LaVO.
p.   cm.
Includes bibliographical references (p.) and index.
ISBN 1-55750-507-1 (acid-free paper)
1. World War, 1939–1945—Naval operations—Subma-
rine.   2. World War, 1939–1945—Naval operations,
American.   3. Sailfish (Submarine)
4. Sculpin (Submarine)   I. Title.
D783.L38   1994
940.54'51—dc20   94-25853
                                                          CIP
Printed in the United States of America on acid-free paper ∞
3 5 7 9 8 6 4 2
First printing

Contents

To the late Leo Haggerty (USS Seafox*), who inspired me to write this book*

To my wife, Mary Anne Ferber, who never lost faith, giving me the encouragement and support to see this through

To my beloved daughter, Genevieve, in appreciation of her patience and understanding during the years I was locked away in my den finishing this book

and

To veterans of the Squalus/Sailfish *and the* Sculpin *who have helped me through those years.*

Preface

He laughs as he turns and
　　he'll dance until three
And he'll flourish that tattoo
　　down under his knee.
When the dancing is finished,
　　he'll talk until five,
Since with memories he lives,
　　with the ones who survived.
　　　　　G. M. SOLAN, M.D., "ROSE TATTOO"

During the 1930s and 1940s, thousands of officers
and enlisted men made the 200-mile journey from the
national submarine training school in New London,
Connecticut, to Portsmouth, New Hampshire, where
mysterious black boats awaited them on the Piscataqua River. The births and the deaths of two of
those vessels—the twin submarines USS *Sculpin* (SS-
191) and USS *Squalus/Sailfish* (SS-192)—occupy a special niche in Portsmouth's history.

These submarines were built by the U.S. Navy in
the late 1930s in an era of great uncertainty about
submarine safety. Between 1921 and 1939, twenty-
two boats from Japan, England, France, Italy, and the
United States were lost in peacetime accidents, claiming 1,096 lives. The mortality rate escalated sharply
during World War II. By 1945, more than 40,000
submariners had perished on 1,100 boats worldwide.

For the United States, 374 officers and 3,131
enlisted men were lost on 52 submarines—the highest
fatality rate of any branch of the service. American

casualty lists after the war showed that six submariners died for every nonsubmariner killed in action.

Submarine volunteers and the Navy always have realized the great risks to be assumed. Only once—in 1939 in the Atlantic Ocean off New Hampshire—has a crew been rescued from a submarine disaster at great depth. And during World War II, only a handful of survivors lived to tell about American submarines lost in battle. The underseas sailors who never came back vanished completely. But a few did return from the list of presumed dead, and counted among them are surviving crewmembers of the *Squalus* and the *Sculpin*.

Today, the *Sculpin* lies a twisted hulk in a nameless patch of the Central Pacific, five miles down in the perpetual darkness of the ocean floor. All that remains of the *Squalus* (known as the *Sailfish* during the war) is her salvaged bridge, enshrined in the Portsmouth Naval Shipyard. In the late spring of each year, townspeople gather around the memorial and recall the men who went to sea on the two boats. Occasionally, surviving veterans join them to tell of the triumph, tragedy, humor, and despair that shaped their lives for eight years on three continents, two oceans, and in one war. For them, it is a revival of a very special brotherhood honed from tense years at war, a time when these men were unlike the crews of any other naval vessels.

They were the soul of the "Silent Service," as the wartime submarine navy came to be known. They are today a legion steeped in honor, tightly bound with a strong sense of pride and general reluctance to discuss wartime experiences with outsiders. So mysterious were their comings and goings during the war that occasionally their unmarked submarines were mistaken for the enemy and bombed by friendly forces. For years after the war, the nation knew little of the sacrifice of these men. But they never objected, never claimed to be owed anything. Rather, they remained within the code of their service long after the war.

This is the true story of those who sailed the *Sculpin* and the *Squalus/Sailfish* through seven incredible years that wove a strange destiny for the survivors of both boats.

Acknowledgments

I am grateful to the following, who aided me in editing portions of the rough draft of this book:

Joseph Tucker, *Sailfish* lieutenant; George Brown, *Sculpin* lieutenant, the only officer to survive captivity; Carl Bryson, Gerald McLees, and Jud Bland, *Squalus* survivors; Aaron Reese, *Sailfish-Sculpin* veteran; Lester Bayles and Larry Macek, *Sailfish* veterans; George Rocek, Edwin Keller, and Billie Minor Cooper, *Sculpin* survivors; and Arthur G. McIntyre, the senior American officer held captive in Ashio in 1945.

Also a note of appreciation to Michael Talbot, the Australian author who assisted me in my Albany-Perth research; Capt. Frank Wheeler, an Annapolis classmate of *Sailfish* captain Robert Ward; Mark Gatlin, acquisitions editor at the NIP who was enthusiastic and supportive from the beginning; Therese Boyd, superb copyeditor who fine-tuned the manuscript for me; my father, a veteran of the destroyer USS *Halford*, who gave me a feel for the Pacific war; and my wife, Mary Anne, who made significant contributions to the direction of the manuscript and helped sharpen the overall story. I couldn't have done it without her.

Back from the Deep

PART ONE

The Short Life of the *Squalus*

Out of the deep, the oily black deep,
Returned from the limbo of doom,
Comes a cargo of men, white silent men,
Back from a watery tomb.

WILLIAM E. BABER, "SUBMARINE" (1943)

The Survivors

Capt. Robert E. M. Ward and two lookouts ducked, putting their backs to the force of 50-foot breakers. With undiminished fury, the waves knocked them against the bridge coaming and then flung them backwards against the periscope sheers. Wind-driven bullets of seawater blistered their eyes and chiseled relentlessly at their faces. Still, they fixed their stares into binoculars that butted sharply against their eye-sockets, bruising them in the wild motions of the boat. Although Ward clenched a towel around his neck, he could not stem the flow of frigid water beneath his rubberized parka, high-waisted pants, and wool sweater. Shuddering, he followed the bow's unbroken line to where it disappeared in an inky fog.

At 16 minutes to midnight and four years after the bodies of her first crew were removed from her wreckage, his boat, the *Sailfish*, struggled to make headway against a typhoon. There were no markings of any kind to identify the submarine, the former *Squalus*, as the "ghost ship" of the American fleet. Without running lights, she was completely hidden in the frenzy of the night 300 miles southeast of Tokyo Bay. Sustained winds of 50 knots produced a hell's chorus of moans and screams on the bridge. Breakers buried the boat's deck, smashing against the bulwark of the bridge fairwater, which stood like a statue in the sea. The cigar-shaped pressure hull groaned, the underlying frame tortured by the storm. The vessel corkscrewed on a crest, tilting precariously. Her propellers spun free, snorting a geyser of spray, as the bow plunged like a rollercoaster into the trough, crushing the ocean with 1,450 tons of black steel. She then leaped upward as another heavy swell coiled in the dark, cascading in a thunderous, charcoal-gray blur at Ward and his men.

The captain strained to recognize what he knew was out there amid the monstrous smudges of motion. "Do you see anything?" he shouted, cupping his hands to the ear of the quartermaster, the man with the best night vision on the boat. But neither he nor the officer of the deck could make out a thing, much less a black wall of steel perhaps three times the length of the *Sailfish*.

Below them, eight officers and sixty-two enlisted men stood at battle stations in seven watertight compartments. For them, this was the beginning of a perilous, 10,000-mile voyage in which the submarine would be on her own for nearly two months. The crew had confidence in their new skipper. But above all, they believed their vessel would persevere. In some ways, the *Sailfish* seemed transcendent. No matter how difficult the circumstances, she always managed to make it back to port. Others in the Navy had assumed for years she would not survive the war. But as the weeks and months passed, inevitably she did come back to bases in Java, Australia, and Pearl Harbor—fiercely battered but intact. It was nothing short of amazing in view of the breakdown of one of her captains, her ill-fated rescue mission to embattled Corregidor, and the scandalous failure of her torpedoes in that first year of combat. So certain was Japan that the infamous boat was a casualty of its destroyers that it broadcast the news in English in hopes of further demoralizing U.S. forces in a war that was already going badly for them.

Yet, here she was on December 3, 1943, preparing to make an unthinkable attack on three enemy aircraft carriers, a cruiser, and two destroyers in a storm of prodigious strength. The *Sailfish* accelerated on an intercept course, singling out the largest ship by radar reckoning alone. The submarine struggled in the typhoon to gain on the target, 3,000-plus yards to the east. On the bridge, Ward wondered about the feasibility of an attack at such range. Would the torpedoes maintain accurate depth control as they crossed massive waves and deep troughs? Would they detonate prematurely from the buffeting they would take en route? Was the trajectory plotted by radar accurate? Visual contact would help, if only to identify the ship. But in these conditions, that was impossible.

The skipper cursed his luck as the storm threatened to foil his chance to become the first submarine commander to sink such a large enemy warship single-handedly. It would be a glorious redemption for the troubled *Sailfish*, making her tenth war patrol. Her orders were to head northwest from Pearl Harbor nearly 3,000 miles to a position off Tokyo Bay, where she would lie in wait to interdict Japanese commerce and warships on the main shipping lanes. The boat was one of dozens on patrol between the coast of Japan and Truk Atoll, 2,000 miles to the south, where the *Sailfish*'s twin sister, the *Sculpin* also lay in wait.

To submariners, the two boats were a story unto themselves. Among the oldest fleet subs in the war, they had followed each other around the Pacific for years. It was the *Sculpin* that miraculously located the missing *Sailfish* (when she was known as the *Squalus*) and helped rescue her trapped crew 240 feet down on the Atlantic Ocean floor off New Hampshire in 1939. After the Japanese attack on Pearl Harbor and capture of the Philippines, the two boats were among a combined force of fewer than fifty capable of waging a counteroffensive in the vast Pacific. But by late 1943, more than 100 were doing battle.

The *Sculpin*'s mission on November 5, 1943, was to voyage to the imposing volcanic islands of Truk, Japan's heavily fortified naval base. The United States was about to launch the first major counteroffensive of the war—retaking the Gilbert Islands 1,400 miles southeast of Truk. Worried that the enemy would sortie reinforcements from Truk or Japan, U.S. commanders counted on the submarines to intercept and sink any that tried. Subsequently, the *Sculpin* was dispatched from Pearl to Truk a few days before the *Sailfish* embarked for Japan. Others took up position between the two.

The *Sculpin* was to serve as the flagship of a three-submarine attack force. On November 29, she was ordered to assemble her "wolfpack" for a sweep to the northwest of Truk. But the boat never responded to the broadcast, apparently lost in action.

This would have been devastating news to Ward and the *Sailfish* crew, many of whom had acquaintances on the *Sculpin*. But they had no way of knowing. As it was, they were preoccupied with the latest intelligence radioed to the boat: A Japanese task force of six ships—a light carrier (*Zuiho*), two 22,250-ton escort carriers (*Chuyo* and *Unyo*), a cruiser (*Maya*), and two destroyers—had sailed from Truk, bound for Tokyo. So accurate was the information that the navigator of the *Sailfish* plotted the convoy's course and correctly predicted the boat would intercept it at midnight on December 3.

The convoy followed a high-speed zig-zag course in order to outmaneuver and outrun American boats. But as the ships entered the typhoon, they slowed. Due to mountainous seas, the task force commander on the *Zuiho* decided the sub danger had passed, allowing the ships to cease evasive maneuvers. Thus, at midnight on the third, as the *Sailfish* moved into position on their left flank, the carriers presented a single line of targets in close proximity to one another.

Still, Ward and his lookouts were unable to sight the warships. "I can't see a thing but blackness and water, with the water mostly in my face," the captain anguished into the bridge intercom linking him to the control center of the submarine below the conning tower. But the boat's radar operator maintained an electronic fix on the targets. He estimated their make and distance: A destroyer at 400 yards leading the convoy. Then possibly a cruiser, followed by a carrier or battleship, another carrier or battleship, and then something else beyond that. Each appeared to be separated by no more than 900 to 1,000 yards.

With the full thrust of her four diesel engines, the *Sailfish* slowly closed the distance between her and the closest large target. As the skipper contemplated the impossibility of a methodical attack, a green beacon suddenly pierced the night, blinking a message from one ship to another. Startled, Ward ordered a dive to 40 feet as he and the lookouts jumped through the conning tower hatch, dogging it behind them and sliding in a bound down the vertical stair rail to the control room. There a ship's electrician, the chief of the boat, auxiliarymen, and lookouts operating the bow and stern diving planes—a dozen men— awaited orders as Ward stripped off his weather gear and joined his executive officer at a small plotting table. The exec wore earphones, linking him to the conning tower where continuous target coordinates were fed to him and into a targeting computer; the boat was just deep enough to keep her radar mast above water.

At nine minutes past midnight, the primary target was 2,100 yards from the *Sailfish*, with her lead destroyer now moving away from the sub at 400 yards. Ward could hesitate no longer. In quick succession, he launched four torpedoes from the boat's forward firing tubes and then swung the craft around to bring the loaded stern tubes to bear.

At 16 minutes past midnight, the first and the fourth torpedoes detonated with a terrific rumble. Immediately, Ward took the submarine deep as two depth charges rained down on the boat from the destroyer, rocking the boat violently. But she escaped in the commotion, crossing under the target as nineteen additional depth charges exploded at greater distance. Ward and his crew worked calmly to reload the tubes for another attack, while staying submerged but close to the track of the convoy.

For the *Sailfish*, it was impossible to have foretold the strange twist of fate consummated in the storm. Above them, twenty-two survivors of the *Sculpin* were imprisoned on the carrier *Chuyo*. "A few of us were sitting on deck in a cramped hold below the waterline. When the first torpedo hit, we flew straight up about two or three feet in the air," recalled George Rocck (MoMM1c), a *Sculpin* motormac, part of the diesel engineering crew. "We cheered the blast even though we knew, if the carrier went down, we would probably never survive."

One torpedo hit the carrier's hull, just below the prisoners. The other seriously damaged the ship's propulsion. "We could sense the ship lost power and smoke filtered into our compartment," said Rocek. "We heard various alarms sound off and damage control men running and yelling. On deck below us, we could hear the frantic [Japanese] crew attempting to shore up the bulkheads with timber, but a heavy sea was running and nullifying the efforts of the damage control party. Soon we heard the bulkhead collapse and water pouring into the compartment below us. As the water rose to our compartment, we yelled and pounded on the locked hatch."

But no one came to their aid. They were trapped.

Now the rearmed *Sailfish* surfaced and set out once again to overtake and sink the carrier. In the savage night, fate had interlocked tragically for the last time for the crews of the two inseparable submarines.

The Volunteers

The late 1920s and early 1930s were perilous years for submarine navies throughout the world. Tragedy after tragedy riveted public interest:

1927   U.S. submarine *S4* sinks off Provincetown, Mass.; crew of 40 lost

1928   Italian sub *F14* sinks in the Adriatic; 31 lost
       French sub *Ondine* sinks off Portugal; 43 lost

1929   British sub *H47* sinks in the Irish sea; 21 lost

1931   British sub *Poseidon* sinks off the China coast; 20 lost
       Russian sub sinks in the Gulf of Finland; 50 lost

1932   British sub *M2* sinks off Portland, England; 60 lost
       British sub *H42* sinks off Gibraltar; 26 lost
       French sub *Promethee* sinks off Cherbourg; 62 lost

1935   Russian submarine *B3* sinks in the Baltic Sea; 55 lost

Newspapers and radios played up each disaster, heightening the public's perception of the underseas ships as a "coffin service." Yet teenagers like Gerald McLees and Carl Bryson, who would join the first crew on the doomed *Squalus* in 1939, hardly noticed.

By 1935, they were among tens of thousands of young men looking to the Navy as their only hope for a better life. Out of the rural South and Depression-wracked midsection of the country, men packed recruiting stations in small towns dotting the backwaters of America. For McLees and Bryson, it didn't matter what lay ahead in the military—even in something as mysterious and dangerous as a submarine. Anything was better than the life they had known.

McLees, a sandy-haired, rail-thin youngster with a sunny, open-faced disposition, was the son of a hard-pressed Kansas farmer who with his wife reared four children on a 360-acre ancestral homestead 65 miles southwest of Topeka. The remoteness of the farm—15 miles from the nearest town—and the ravages of insects and drought turned McLees off to farming despite his father's wishes. Although the family raised all their own food, they had few advantages and a doubtful future. "I went to a one-room school in a class of twelve—five boys and seven girls. . . . We had no money at all," he recalled.

A thousand miles to the east, in the foothills near Greenville, South Carolina, Bryson contemplated a life of toil in a large family of teamsters—a father, grandfather, and uncle who made a living driving wagons pulled by horses into the mountains to sell merchandise and haul out crops. A bright, stocky youth of medium height, he projected a serious demeanor born of hard work learned early in life. "I wasn't a child since 10 years old. I worked for wages since 12. I grew up in a hard work environment during the Depression. My last year in school at home, I worked 80 hours a week at a restaurant and went to school full-time," Bryson said.

By any measure, the formative years for both youths were the worst for the nation. For five years, it had faced the greatest natural and economic disaster it had ever known. The collapse of the stock market in 1929 began a seemingly endless cycle of hardship for the masses. Life savings evaporated in banking failures, and one out of every four Americans was unemployed.

Despite their poverty, the McLees didn't usually lack food, because they raised chickens, pigs, and cows, and grew corn and wheat. But that came to an end in the 1930s, as it did on other farms in what was to become the Dust Bowl. "You'd either have a drought and get no crops, or you would have a good crop started and the grasshoppers would come though and eat it all up. Or you would get a big hailstorm and it would knock everything down," said McLees. "People really had it tough."

McLees bolted, joining a migration of 3.5 million people who left their homes in the Great Plains during the 1930s. "For many of us, there was nothing to do at home. No jobs. So we left," he said. His route accidentally led to an enlistment office at a time when the Navy was recruiting many of its submarine volunteers from Kansas, Oklahoma, and Texas where conditions were so arduous. Initially, he and a friend set out to join the federal Civilian Conservation Corps (CCC), a public works program of Pres. Franklin Roosevelt's New Deal administration which was designed to end the Depression by putting people to work. But after hitchhiking 15 miles to the nearest town to apply, the two boys were turned down. "Since our folks weren't on relief or anything like that, we couldn't get in," said McLees. "So we hitched another 50 miles to Topeka to enlist. We were just two dumb country boys who had no more than 50 cents in our pockets. We got to the recruiting office in a big federal building just about four o'clock and the chief was getting ready to go home. We convinced him that we had no place to stay and would have to return home that afternoon. So he gave us a physical on the spot and I passed but my buddy didn't.

"I had no idea of going into the Navy. It just happened to be the first door we went into. I never thought about submarines when I joined. I didn't even know what a submarine was. I just wanted to get away from the farm."

A week later, his decision was reinforced aboard a Santa Fe passenger train bound for boot camp in San Diego. He stared forlornly at the ghastly scenery of his native Kansas flashing by: homes blistered silver-gray from incessant sandstorms. Fields laying fallow. Barbed wire fences drifted over by dunes. Starving livestock standing under the drooping canopies of dying trees. And hopeless people in hopeless towns, coping with the dust, dust everywhere. Like the other travelers aboard, he kept a wet towel over the lower part of his face so he could breathe amid the powdery dirt that floated into every inch of the passenger coach.

Half a continent away, Carl Bryson faced hard times of a different sort, intensified by a blight destroying the huge American chestnut forests that his family depended on for a living.

"The thing about my family, everybody worked," he said. "There were no negative thoughts in my family. They weren't on the welfare or the handout group. Everybody worked hard. My grandfather, my uncle, my dad. We were like peddlers. We would handle fruit, produce, things they needed in the mountains because you couldn't drive a car back there. But the majority of the money we earned was off chestnuts.

"I used to go with my grandfather up into the mountains in a wagon pulled by a mule. We'd ring a bell and the mountaineers would come from all over. They'd come with burlap bags filled with chestnuts. We would pay them one or two pennies a pound and load the wagon right down to the standards. Then we would resell them back home at a profit."

At the time, the late 1920s, American chestnut trees stretched in a nearly unbroken forest from Maine to Georgia, providing the greatest supply of staple food for both animals and people. The trees, valued also for their lumber, were magnificent, the "Sequoias of the East," soaring to heights of 100 feet with trunks four feet across. Yet, in the course of a few short years they all died from an incurable Oriental fungus, brought accidentally into the country through New York City. "It was a disaster, really," said Bryson, whose family fortune died with the trees. "All over the mountains you would see millions of skeletons of the dead trees. It was a horrible thing."

At 18, looking for a better livelihood he, like McLees, left home to join the CCC in Georgia, where he blasted out rock for roadbeds in a quarry on Lookout Mountain just across the border in Tennessee. The Corps had become a haven for men down on their luck. After several months of hard labor, he dropped by a Navy recruiting office in nearby Chattanooga to take an enlistment exam. "The fellow who examined me said I would have no problem enlisting but I would have to enlist through the recruiting station near my home. I was in the top group with the marks I made," Bryson recalled. Because of the Navy's career opportunities, a place where he could learn a trade, Bryson left the CCC and returned home to enlist. "I took another examination and I thought I was going in. The recruiter was a first class machinist's mate named Luke Durken, a submariner who I later served with. I found out he had a waiting list of 300 people. I said, 'How many do you send a day?' And he said about two or three a week. And I thought, 'Oh, my God. I'll never get into the Navy.' So he says, 'Go home and get a job. I'll get you in the Navy.'" It wasn't until more than a year later, in January of 1936, that the call came.

Bryson at first opted to go to pharmacist's mate school. But on arrival, medics were coping with an epidemic of spinal meningitis affecting the fleet. "A lot of people died. I didn't have the stomach for it so I went to machinist's mate school." Like McLees, Bryson hadn't contemplated submarine service as part of his enlistment. But his work ethic and high IQ perfectly suited him to undersea duty. "Two-thirds of my company were college graduates or had gone to college for two or three years. The Navy was looking for someone who would study and was devoted to duty. The Navy was your life then. It was a career, not like it was later during the war. I loved the Navy. I really did," said Bryson.

Both McLees, then stationed as a base mess cook in Hawaii, and Bryson, attached to the Norfolk, Virginia, naval base, became well acquainted with submariners, a major influence in their decisions to volunteer for the underseas boats. A number of factors attracted them. First was the independence of sub sailors, men who were not bound by the normal strictures enforced on other branches of the fleet. Submariners also got extra liberty. They had more responsibility and a better chance of promotion than on a large ship. And on a submarine, you were a member of the family, not part of some faceless horde on a battlewagon. From the skipper on down, there was a sense of mutual concern in the tight confines of the boats. Thus, a more relaxed camaraderie normally existed within sub crews. There was also the mystique of joining an elite cadre of men on secret missions, sailors who under no circumstances could discuss their operational orders. Another inducement was hazardous duty pay ($25–30 per month, later to become 50 percent of base pay). Enacted by Congress, it brought new prestige to the service. Last, the submarine crews were the best-fed sailors in the Navy.

But weighing against all of these advantages was one big tradeoff: No naval career was as dangerous. The men had to accept the fact that a submarine disaster at sea most likely would cost them their lives. No navy in the world had yet to rescue a crew trapped at great depth. Indeed, the entire history of submarines was punctuated with headline-grabbing tragedies. The thought of men drowning or suffocating while trapped in iron boats resulted in general revulsion to the service. Many a recruit, under pressure from his family, signed up for surface fleet duty, secure in the knowledge that at least he had a chance to swim away from a ship going down.

During World War II, those sentiments were even more pronounced as submarine losses mounted. Edwin Keller, a *Sculpin* veteran, deliberately deceived his family when he joined the Silent Service; he only told them that he had enlisted and would be attending school at a base in New London, Connecticut. Five days later, his uncle returned home and asked where he was going to school. "And I say, 'New London, Connecticut.' And he says, 'That's submarines, isn't it?' And I say, 'Yes.' And he says, 'My God, we talk you out of the tank corps and you go and join the coffin service!' But the way I saw it, it would be better for the enemy not to know where I was than to be on the battlefield with the enemy having me right in his sights. I had the foolish idea that I had a better chance of surviving in the submarine service."

Despite the pessimism associated with the boats, adventurous youths like Bryson and McLees continued to sign up for the all-volunteer service. They made up a rather small pool of recruits, one that had to meet exceedingly tough criteria. Each enlistee had to be studious, capable of committing to memory every one of the thousands of valves, gears, pipes, switches, and hatches inside the complex underseas warships. Each had to draw from memory accurate diagrams of more than thirty electrical, mechanical, and pneumatic systems in the boats. Each also had to train unerringly to perform not only his own specialty aboard but that of every other crewman. Thus, even the boat's cook had to be able to fire a torpedo, to start an engine, and to dive the submarine. That ability at times could spell the difference between disaster and safety for the vessel. This mechanical aptitude was only one characteristic of the "typical submariner" being sought by the Navy.

Adm. Charles A. Lockwood, a submarine pioneer from the World War I era who rose to commander-in-chief of the Pacific sub fleet during World War II, summed up in a postwar memoir the type of individual the Navy was looking for: "The tasks of diving, attack and surfacing take scores of interlocking motions by dozens of crewmen with split-second timing. But more is demanded than mere mechanical ability. The men of submarines—from captains to cooks—must have certain well-defined characteristics.

"They must be alert without being brittle; they must be interested in their shipmates without being nosy; they must appreciate food without being gluttons; they must respect privacy without being seclusive; they must be talkers without being gabby; and they must be friendly without being tail-waggers. They must, in short, be round pegs for very closely machined round holes. The wrong kind of a man aboard a sub, on a long cruise, can become an insufferable thorn in the sides of shipmates. He can, emotionally, cause almost as much damage as an enemy depth bomb.

". . . In no other branch of military service are men required to remain away from normal human contacts as long as submariners assigned to lengthy patrols that demand long hours—sometimes days— at depths far below the least glimmer of sunlight and far away from the natural feel and smell of natural air. Moreover, these conditions must be endured with good cheer in overcrowded, sometimes ill-smelling, dew-dripping, steel compartments. Those whose tempers or temperaments cannot stand the strain are soon eliminated."

Early on, it was obvious the Navy needed special facilities to screen and train the recruits. So in 1917—the very year the Navy launched its first government-built submarine, the *L-8*—it converted an obsolete ship coaling station on the Thames River near New London into a submarine base and school. From that time to the present, nearly all submarine officers and enlisted men have passed through New London, a historic ship-building town a few miles inland from Long Island Sound. The city, known for its foggy "British weather," lies among gently rolling hills, pasturelands, and sleepy country villages with colorful place names seemingly drawn from a J.R.R. Tolkien fantasy: Mystic. Dark Entry. Cow Shandy. Jangling Plains. Cos Cob. Moodus. Black Point. Voluntown. Uncasville.

The submarine school sits on a hillside overlooking the Thames and directly opposite the U.S. Coast Guard Academy and the Connecticut Women's College. The Thames flows downstream past New London on the opposite bank, and then empties into the sound six miles away. Although as many as 15,000 officers and men were stationed at the school and base in recent years, in the late 1930s only 200 were enrolled at a given time. The school's collection of World War I–era submersibles sat like fat, stubby whales at rest in their slips on the river. Clustered on a hillside overlooking the boats and the mile-wide river were the red-brick classrooms and dormitories of the submarine school, appearing like a tidy, upscale college. Only a large naval gun and two torpedoes poised on pedestals on the lawn signified the school's purpose.

The most dominant feature of the landscape, however, was a cylindrical tower reminiscent of the grain silos of McLees' native Kansas. Rising 140 feet near the river bank, the Submarine Escape Training Tank was topped by a large, octagonal cupola with windows around its circumference. A stairwell snaked around the exterior of the tank, from the cupola to the ground. The tank itself encompassed a vertical column of water, 118 feet deep and 18 feet wide. Approximately 240,000 gallons of purified water inside were steam-heated to 92°F. In order to qualify for submarines, McLees, Bryson, Keller, and all other volunteers before and after them were asked to enter at the bottom of the tank in their first week of schooling and make a free ascent 100 feet straight up through the middle to the surface.

As the recruits congregated at the base, the panorama of the escape tower, the serene campus, the submarines on the river, the broad Thames, and the colonial waterfront of New London mesmerized new arrivals. It was easy for them to imagine a time when tall-masted clipper ships linked New London to the rest of the world.

But the reverie wouldn't last long. Soon, many would be in the clutches of a man who ruled the school with a ruthless autocracy.

3

Spritz's Navy

"When I first arrived in New London," recalled Ed Keller, "I asked the guard where the barracks was. 'Oh, you're going to Spritz's navy,' he said with a grin, pointing to a building on the hillside. So I put my seabag on my back and went uphill to the barracks where I saw a chief torpedoman standing on the porch and I says to him, 'Where is Spritz's navy?' And he says, 'It's right here! Your hat is dirty. Your shoes are not shined. You're restricted for two days!!'"

The future *Sculpin* mate had come face to face with Chief Torpedoman Charles Spritz, the submarine navy's version of the marine master sergeant.

With a craggy scowl and guttural bellow one veteran described as ten octaves above a bullhorn, Spritz oozed authority. He stood six feet, two inches tall in impeccably crisp Navy blues with golden hash marks running the length of one sleeve. The emblems of the master sea diver, the torpedoman, and the crow of the chief petty officer (CPO) stood out plainly. His squarish face was accented by a large Roman nose, a cleft chin, and a huge mouth framing prominent, uneven teeth. Most noticeable were his coal-like eyes that bored holes in every enlistee. He was a man who seldom left the school and rarely fraternized. He didn't drink, didn't smoke. He never married, although

15

some said he once loved a British nurse who was killed during the V-2 bombing of London in World War II. Many were convinced that old Charlie had gone a little crazy after a deepsea diving accident in the 1930s. If one thing could be said with certainty about him, however, it was that he was the most despised person at the school, and perhaps in the entire underseas navy. To this former Bronx policeman the Navy entrusted an estimated 20,000 seamen who came to New London to become submarine sailors in the 1930s and 1940s.

"You men may have passed some tests wherever you come from," he snapped on the day of arrival. "But that don't mean you're going to make it here. You're just getting started."

Spritz issued a precise manifesto of expectations: Razor-sharp grooming in regulation clothing at all times. Daily work details. No smoking or talking while on assignment. Bunks made and personal effects stowed properly every morning. No standing, walking, sitting, or lying on the lawns anywhere on the base. Liberty one day each week, contingent on meeting Spritz's meticulous inspections and having no infractions on record.

In the 12 weeks the students spent at the base, Spritz blared axioms until they were fixed in the subconscious: "Around here there's only one daily prayer. You'll commit it to memory: 'O Lord, help us to keep our big mouths shut until we know what we are talking about!' . . . There is room for anything on a submarine—except a mistake! . . . Without teamwork, a submarine is no more than a bastard cousin to a foundering whale!"

From the beginning, the men came to loath Spritz, the omnipresent perfectionist. He had spies everywhere, some of whom brutalized students who got out of line. A yeoman toting a clipboard inevitably followed behind Spritz, noting infractions.

Spritz left the base once a month to do his banking and visit a relative. "He was afraid to go ashore because he thought someone would kill him. He was universally hated. The hatred was so widespread it was dangerous. The way he ran that place was like a concentration camp," said Bryson, who was an escape training instructor during the war. "Charlie always came to the tank parties. He felt safe there."

The reason for the hostility, said Bryson, was the constant haranguing the students would take and the punishment dealt out to those who violated the rules. "You have to remember that most of the men had already been in the Navy for some time. It was like going back to boot camp. They weren't going to take it."

Yet, they really had no choice. For a minor violation, said Keller, "you would have to take all the chairs out of one building and take them to another on a Monday and then line them up. Then on Wednesday, you would take them back. Transferring chairs was the normal punishment." But for more serious offenses, there was loss of liberty and extra duty. That meant extra work details after hours plus overnight confinement to the "Blue Room," an isolated barracks where every lightbulb inside was painted blue. In the supernatural glow, a sea-man had to answer roll call every hour on the hour throughout the night and then return to his normal barracks at 0500 for his workday.

Although most graduated from New London detesting Spritz, the teamwork he achieved was a major factor in the success of the boats in the days to come. Indeed, Keller said the experience "made me into somebody, a respectable man. He molded us into the discipline needed in the Navy." Wrote another veteran after the war, "To be sure, he instilled fear in those he commanded, but only that fear of making a mistake that could cost not only your life but all the lives of your ship-mates."

Although Spritz governed the daily routines of the recruits, other CPOs—mostly 20-year veterans of deepsea diving and submarines—provided the instruction and the encouragement, working closely with the students. Each class was divided into diving sections of perhaps six to eight students. One petty officer was paired up with each section for the entire training program.

The first task was to determine who was physically and mentally fit for submarine duty. On arrival, each student was led by two instructors into a dark room built to look like the bridge of a submarine. Pinpoints of light overhead represented stars, as if the boat were cruising at night. The instructors then asked if the student could see anything. After a period of eye adjustment, most began to distinguish the vaguely gray outlines of ships. But some couldn't, thereby becoming expendable.

By far the most physically demanding tests were in the submarine escape tower. After roll call in the first week, the students gathered in a room below the tower where a pressure chamber—a round, oversized barrel 20 feet long and 8 feet high—squatted on the floor. Painted gray and containing glass viewports, it was an imposing sight for the students lined up outside in swimsuits. An instructor opened the hatch and motioned the men inside, single-file, to two facing benches. He fol-lowed, squeezing between the men to the far end of the chamber while plopping a large pile of terrycloth robes on the floor next to him. Dog-ging the hatch, he faced the men grimly. "You're going to get fifty pounds of pressure. That's about three times the atmospheric pressure at sea level," he said, his voice booming off the walls of the chamber. "If you ever have to make an escape from a submarine, you will face this kind of pressure. If you can take it, you'll be all right for submarine work.

"As we start going down, remember to hold your nose with your left hand, and keep blowing. If you are suddenly in pain, raise your other hand as a signal to me. I'll immediately stop increasing the pressure inside the tank, and if you're in real trouble, you will be taken out of the tank. Okay, let's go!"

With dry mouths, the students sat anxiously as the chief banged the wall to signal those outside that the test had begun. Opening a valve protruding from the wall, he unleashed compressed air, which entered the chamber with a sharp hiss. All eyes were fixed on a large pressure dial on the bulkhead above the instructor. Abruptly, the hissing stopped.

"We're under two pounds of pressure per square inch," the instructor noted. "Two pounds doesn't sound like much. You probably don't feel anything yet. But all of us together couldn't open that hatch against two pounds. It equals about one ton.

"Don't forget now. Hold your nose and blow to clear your ears. Try also swallowing to clear them," he advised, knowing that those who couldn't were out of the program.

The students apprehensively eyed the pressure dial as the instructor again opened the pressure line. Ten, fifteen, twenty pounds.

A thermometer inside the chamber moved past 100°. Glistening with sweat, the men swallowed hard, popping their ears. The heat made it difficult to breathe, increasing the psychological strain. The chief studied the group, looking for signs of panic and making mental notes on any who seemed unduly distressed.

Twenty-five pounds. Thirty. Thirty-five. Forty. Forty-five. Fifty. There the pressure gauge held steady amid a sizzling 130°. The pressure simulated that which the men might experience at more than 100 feet deep. Despite their earlier trepidations, all passed the five-minute "descent." Quickly, the chief tripped a relief valve and the air rushed with a whoosh out of the room. Moisture in the air condensed, fogging the viewports. The men shivered in the sudden cold, grateful for the robes tossed to them. At ten pounds and again at five pounds, the pressure stabilized for a few minutes so the men could decompress to avoid the bends, the sometimes fatal scourge of deepsea divers.

The group exited the chamber greatly relieved. "We knew that if you could take that, it was no problem going through the [water-filled] tank," said McLees. They now faced the last of the physical tests—an ascent from the bottom of the escape tower, known informally as "the water works."

Since most of the men had been around water for a year or more in the Navy, there was at least a familiarity with diving. In addition, they had the reassurance of wearing Momsen lungs. Similar to inflatable, rubberized life vests, fitted around the neck and resting on the chest, the breathing devices were invented by then Lt. Cdr. Charles B. Momsen who was appalled at the loss of life in submarine accidents in which crews had no means of escape. Theoretically, the lungs enabled each person to exit a submarine from perhaps 200 feet deep and float to the surface. Each lung was inflated with oxygen before an ascent. A flexible tube ran from the lung, through a canister of carbon dioxide absorbent, to a mouthpiece. The chemical purified the air as a person breathed in and out through the mouthpiece. The key was not to panic, to rise slowly, and to stop at various stages to decompress to avoid the bends.

The students climbed the spiral staircase to the cupola at the top of the tower. There they entered a "roving bell," a metal chamber attached to a chain hoist which was lowered into the tank, first to the 18-foot and then to the 50-foot level. The men made two practice ascents from each level. For Bryson, it was a wonderful experience. "I dove in and swam down to the 50-foot level right away. When I was a kid, I learned to swim across the Saluda River [in North Carolina] under the water before I could swim across on top. My father taught me how to swim and he was a good swimmer."

At all times, the escape tank was manned by at least eight seasoned divers and instructors who worked in pairs. Most could hold their breath for several minutes at a time as they maneuvered around the tank. They worked out of air-filled vestibules on the sides of the win-dowless tank.

After the two uneventful shallow ascents, willing students returned to the ground by the stairs and entered the 100-foot ascent chamber, where the instructor-in-charge, a veteran deepsea diver, swung open a heavy watertight door. Instructors, mindful of two deaths in the tower in the early 1930s, realized this ascent posed the greatest risk. The group of students, the instructor, and an assistant ducked through the door into a lock built to look like the interior of a submarine. The chamber contained a hollow metal shaft that projected downward from the overhead, similar to a large stovepipe. Above this three-foot-wide "escape" pipe sat the tank's entire 240,000 gallons of water, sealed from the lock by a hatch at the top of the pipe. The floor was already flooded to ankle depth. As the students sloshed around, the instructor swung shut the compartment door, dogging it with the turn of a wheel. Then he checked to make sure all was in order.

"I'm going to flood the lock now—slowly," he announced, cracking a valve near the floor which released a stream of water. It rose steadily, bubbling up over the men's ankles, calves, thighs, past their waists and chests, automatically coming to a stop just below their arm pits. The level was just above the lower lip of the escape pipe. "We're under full pressure now," noted the instructor. The air trapped in the overhead of the lock had been compressed to 44 pounds per square inch—exerting enough force to prevent any more water from leaking in. At the same time, the hatch at the top of the escape pipe opened to the tank.

At the officer's direction, the students put on spring-loaded nose clips that would prevent them from accidentally breathing in water during their ascents. They also inserted the mouthpieces of their Momsen lungs. Then each ducked briefly underwater to test the devices. "Now charge up!" ordered the instructor, motioning to an air flask containing oxygen on the overhead above the men. Each in turn attached his lung to the flask and inflated the bag about half full.

Meanwhile, the instructor's assistant pulled a lever that released a yellow buoy from the top of the lock. This escape buoy shot rapidly to the surface of the tank, trailing behind an ascent rope tied to an eyebolt on the chamber. The students were told to wrap their feet around the line to keep themselves upright while using their hands as a brake to control the ascent. The Momsen lung tended to buoy the men too rapidly to the surface, and rising too quickly could cause the air in their bodies to expand, potentially bursting blood vessels in their lungs. Cupping his hands around the line, each student would float up until he reached a series of knots near the surface. At each knot, he was to breathe in and out of the Momsen lung while counting to ten slowly to decompress the air in his body. The students would be staged so that preferably none would ram the other on the way up. A tug of the rope at the bottom signaled those on the surface when each was coming up. Simultaneously, instructors at various levels and on the surface watched the progress of the ascent.

Assured that all was well, the instructors in the lock asked for a show of hands on who would like to go first. One by one, each student dropped below water and slid through the escape pipe. The first one out could see what appeared to be the deck of a stranded submarine below him. Gripping the line lightly between his legs and hands, and leaning out away from it, he began his ascent, concentrating on breathing slowly in and out of his Momsen. A small circle of greenish light illuminated the surface far above. Light also filtered into the tank from the illuminated vestibules on the sides of the tank and the roving bell. He could make out the caricatures of two mermaids painted on the sides of the tank. Instructors, gliding above and below him, gave the impression of flying, arms waving as they motioned to the students coming up the line. Reaching the first decompression knot at the 30-foot level, he stopped, counting slowly to ten, before moving on to the next, repeating the procedure. From one of the air-filled bells on the side of the tank, one instructor noticed a student gripping the line too tightly. In goggles and a nose clip, he swam over to set him right. After several minutes, the first student broke surface at the yellow buoy. Slipping off his nose clip and shutting the valves on his Momsen, he swam to the edge of the tank and stepped out onto a platform ringing the tank. From the warm cupola, he looked down triumphantly from the large windows to the submarine base, miniaturized by the height.

As the last student made it to the top without incident, there was a sense of general euphoria, because they knew they had made a simulated escape from a submarine. The experience gave them confidence they could make such an ascent at sea if needed—a factor that would come into play for McLees and Bryson a year later on the sunken *Squalus*.

For the next 11 weeks, the students were enmeshed in submarine training. For days, they went back and forth to classes while casting furtive glances to the submarines coming and going on the river. "I would think to myself, 'Tomorrow I am going to be on one of them.' And then when the day arrived, the hair on the back of my head stood up going aboard," recalled Keller.

The students concentrated on learning all aspects of the boats. It was a process that would turn the men into what was needed: electrician's mates, machinist's mates, torpedomen, radiomen, signalmen, cooks, gunner's mates, yeomen, and seamen. The regimen included in-depth study of submarine mechanisms, practice in simulators, and dives in training boats once a week in Long Island Sound. "There was a tremendous number of training devices," recalled Keller. "One room was exactly like the control room of a submarine. It was hooked up electrically to hydraulics which caused the room to move. You make one wrong move, and it tilted out of control. You had the illusion of the boat turning in the water. There was also an engine room for training. Bells would ring. A speed indicator would show the propellers turning. It was all very realistic."

A typical day consisted of four hours of classroom study in the morning, and four hours of instruction on the boats in the afternoon. Lectures and after-hours study assignments kept lights burning into the evening. The recruits were expected to devour such 200-page tomes as *Submarine, Diesel Engines, Electricity, Submarine Tactical Instructions, Storage Batteries,* and *Torpedoes.* In school laboratories, every man spent exhaustive hours tearing down and putting together practically every item making up a submarine. Diesel engines were dismantled and rebuilt. Motors and generators were rewound. Acid storage battery cells, each as tall as a man and used for underwater propulsion, were charged and discharged, and were observed emitting deadly chlorine gas if drenched by water—a constant concern on the boats. Torpedoes were taken apart, studied, and then put back together.

Every Monday the men took written tests; any who failed two exams were returned quietly to the surface fleet. "Every Monday morning, someone would be missing," said Keller. "You'd be told he went to a minesweeper, he went to a destroyer."

On the school's fleet of antiquated "O" and "R" boats from World War I, the students were divided into small groups for 10-minute dives. Under the watchful eyes of the regular crew, they experienced the deafening clatter and heat of the two diesel engines in each boat. They jumped at the explosive "ah-ooo-gah" of the Klaxon alarm just before diving, and were a bit edgy as crewmen cranked open huge Kingston valves to flood ballast tanks to start the boat down. They observed machinist's mates shutting down the noisy, air-breathing diesels while switching over to quiet motors, powered by the huge batteries at the bottom of the hull which accounted for nearly a fifth of each boat's weight. And they gathered around the helmsmen who stood before two oversized steering wheels at midships which controlled the stern and bow diving planes, giant mechanical wings deployed underwater to move the submarine up and down in the sea.

As the weeks rolled by, the groups practiced all shipboard operations, slowly taking control of the vessels. "Each group would have a number," said Keller. "Number 4, for instance, might be for the group learning to handle the bow planes of the sub. Number 5, the stern planes. Number 6, the helm. They had you rotating duties continuously. A subman, in order to qualify, had to know the submarine from one end to the other. Theoretically, every man aboard has to be able to do another man's job. You had to be able to start the engines in case chlorine gas from the batteries killed the engine crew, for instance."

In the end, Bryson graduated from diesel school, later to become a machinist's mate; McLees and later Keller became electrician's mates.

In September 1938, while Bryson was a student, one of the greatest storms to hit New England passed over New London. It had been nearly 70 years since the last big storm, so residents were completely unprepared. In fact, no warnings at all were issued north of New York City about a hurricane bearing up the East Coast on September 21. Two hundred miles off Long Island, it unexpectedly veered inland, pushing 18-foot breakers at the coast. Swimmers, seeking safety on 12-foot dunes, were swept away. Sustained winds of 120 MPH snapped telephone poles, toppled church steeples, and downed electric lines. Mammoth waves pounded the Connecticut shoreline, setting off seismographs as far away as California. Entire fishing fleets were lost. Trains were blown off their tracks. Houses were crushed and people killed by flying glass, bricks, and lumber. From the damage, meteorologists estimated wind velocity reached 250 MPH in some areas. Before the day was out, more than 700 people had perished throughout New England and 1,500 were injured.

In the middle of the storm, Bryson was about to take a well-earned liberty with a buddy. "I had a Ford bought for $45 in Hartford. The whole lot where the cars were parked at the end of the base was flooded. So my buddy and I devised a way to float it out of the lot. Then we had to get it started. So we pushed it up to the base behind the movie theater. Suddenly, a boxcar broke loose and ran down into the river, crashing through barriers where we had just been. Then the roof of the theater blew off. But we finally started the car and drove to the gate. There a marine told us to park the car and get in a truck. 'Not us,' we said. 'We're going on liberty.' To which he said, 'Not you?! You're on fire party. Liberty is canceled!!'"

New London was on fire. Flames stretched from a coal company on the riverfront to the downtown sector. Electricity was out and looters were having a field day. Throughout the night, men from the submarine school battled the blaze, finally bringing it under control by early dawn. For the next few weeks, as Bryson awaited orders following graduation, he was part of the relief effort in beachfront areas of New London. "No one had flood insurance back then. So the skipper of the base sent us sailors down there to do the dirty work—cutting up fallen trees, carrying out debris, and chlorinating cellars."

In the days to come, Bryson was attached to school submarine *R-4* where he saw brief duty. Meanwhile, the Navy began casting about for men to form the crews of huge, ultramodern submarines it was building in Portsmouth, New Hampshire. The boats were like no others, capable of operating in wartime off the Japanese coast from U.S. bases—if it came to that. Bryson, McLees, and other carefully chosen submariners from throughout the fleet—a mix of older veterans and top recruits— were asked to report to Kittery, Maine, in the fall of 1938. There, on the Piscataqua River, the nearly completed sister ships *Squalus* and *Sculpin* awaited them.

The Birth of Twins

Jud Bland and Lawrence Gainor could hardly believe it. In all their years in the submarine navy as career brown-baggers, whose wives and children followed them from yard to yard, trying to keep up with the men and their boats, neither had witnessed the launch of an underseas warship—let alone ride it down the ways.

But now, at 1525 on September 14, 1938, the two stood together on the deck of a black metallic whale, hidden from the outside world beneath the cavernous roof of Building 13 at the Portsmouth Naval Shipyard in Kittery, Maine. Below them, U.S. Navy submarine hull SS-192—310 feet long with a beam of 27 feet, and 11 months and 2 million man-hours in the making—was held aloft by a massive wooden cradle on a pair of heavily greased iron skids that trailed downhill toward the open end of the building and the Piscataqua River that divides Maine from New Hampshire. Hundreds of VIPs and yardworkers crowded around the 1,450-ton behemoth, gazing up at Gainor, Bland, and a handful of others standing at quarters in dress uniform, the nucleus of the boat's first crew. Colorful pennants fluttered overhead on an antenna wire strung from the bow to the stern, passing over the conning tower with a large "S 11" painted in white on each side.

The boat was one of only two submarines to be launched in Kittery in 1938. Thus, the area was alive with anticipation. On the New Hampshire side of the river, opposite the ways, thousands packed the shore of Pierce Island. Spectators wedged onto the narrow, two-lane Memorial Bridge, linking Portsmouth with Kittery and the navy yard, jockeying for the best view. And on the base, yard workers and visitors, some of whom had come great distances to witness the christening of every sub since the first in 1917, crammed the waterfront.

The Frank E. Booma Post American Legion band from Portsmouth played with patriotic fervor inside the ways as a covey of dignitaries arrived and climbed to the bunting-clad launch stand beneath the sharp bow of the vessel. Among them were Rear Adm. C. W. Cole, commandant of the yard, and the sponsor of the new submarine, Caroline Brownson Hart, the wife of Adm. Thomas C. Hart, president of the Navy's General Board. Cole addressed the throng, praising the work that went into the boat, after which a yard representative presented Mrs. Hart with a silver platter engraved with the submarine's design. The shipyard chaplain then offered a prayer, followed by the raising of a warning flag at 1540.

As the moment of launch neared, Bland pondered the irony of his reunion with Gainor. "We trained together for submarine duty but lost touch for eight years until we were called to Portsmouth," he recalled. "But now, here we were about to ride a submarine down the ways, by God!"

Both men were seasoned electricians who had served in all types of surface vessels, including the battleship *New Mexico*. They were among the Navy's best rates, or specialized enlisted men, chosen from throughout the fleet to man the new submarine. Bland (EM1c) and Gainor (CE) and a handful of others like them would be counted on to provide leadership and training to younger rates, such as McLees and Bryson, soon to arrive from New London. But for now the two shared in the spectacle of the launch.

The long blast of a Klaxon echoed loudly at 1543. On the launch stand, Mrs. Hart grasped the cord to a ceremonial bottle of champagne as workers began removing wedges that held the vessel in place on the skids. The submarine shivered as her great weight tugged at the loosening grip. Two bells sounded, alerting the sponsor to be ready. Then a single bell. A screech rose as the boat began to move. "Now, Mrs. Hart!" yelled the building superintendent. With both hands, she swung the champagne against the hull. "I christen thee *Squalus!*" When the bottle didn't break, she swung again quickly and it shattered, sending a cascade of foam down the bow.

Now officially named for a snub-nosed, cold-water shark, the USS *Squalus* backed away slowly from the platform as the Legion band struck up "Anchors Aweigh." Yard whistles and boats in the harbor joined the cheering multitude as the submarine, propelled by gravity, slid majestically down the ways with a large American flag undulating from her stern. Gathering speed while the band broke into the opening strains of "The Star Spangled Banner," the *Squalus* splashed heavily into the river, her cradle falling behind while she bobbed forward with a side-to-side waddle. Tugboats moved alongside to secure lines and then towed her to a fitting-out pier near her identical sister ship, the USS *Sculpin*, launched just three weeks earlier from the same ways. Work began immediately to install diesel engines, electric motors, and all the other mechanical and electrical components it would take to give both submarines life before the year was out.

With the launch, high hopes also came down the ways. The *Squalus* and the *Sculpin* were the forerunners of a new type of underseas boat named for fighting fish with enough surface speed and cruising range to accompany the U.S. fleet anywhere in the world. These "fleet submarines" could dive deeper, stay down longer, travel farther, and carry more firepower than any sub yet built. They also were air conditioned, a revolution in underseas habitability. For those gathered in Portsmouth-Kittery on September 14, the ancient quest for an ultimate naval weapon seemed at last to be realized.

So it was that the *Squalus* and the *Sculpin* of the *Sargo* class sat quietly on the Piscataqua in the fall of 1938 as prospective officers and crews began to arrive.

The area was quintessential New England, backdropped by the 5,000-foot-high White Mountains to the west. From the center of Portsmouth, cobblestone streets tumbled down Strawberry Bank to the river that separated the city from the village of Kittery and the navy yard where the nation's first government-built submarine (the *L-8*) was launched in 1917.

In Portsmouth, citizens shared in the mystique of the submarine service. The remarkable boats were something to be proud of, thus the town took to the sailors chosen for them. The crews of the *Squalus* and *Sculpin* lived together on base—the *Sculpin* rates on the top floor of an old World War I barracks, and the *Squalus* men on the bottom. Naturally, competition was inevitable. "There was a friendly rivalry between the *Sculpin* and the *Squalus* crews," said Bland. "Unfortunately, the *Sculpin* regularly beat the *Squalus* in softball. And the *Sculpin* crew always seemed to get all the girls."

The selection of crews was a deliberate process, spanning several months under Oliver Francis Naquin and Warren Dudley Wilkin, the new skippers of the *Squalus* and *Sculpin,* respectively.

Naquin, born in New Orleans in 1905 and known as the hottest jazz trumpet player in Annapolis, originally had been recruited by the famed Paul Whiteman band. But the young midshipman chose instead the stability of a naval career in consideration of his wife and family. After graduation, he served aboard the USS *New York* and later the USS *Osborne.* Wilkin, born in Kent, Ohio, in 1900, graduated from the U.S. Naval Academy in 1924, one year ahead of Naquin. As an ensign, he saw duty aboard the USS *Arkansas* and USS *Billingsley* for the next four years.

For both men, ascending the long chain of command in the regular line surface ships posed a difficult task because of the postwar scale-back of the fleet and subsequent abundance of fleet officers. But submarine duty was an alternative for them. The Navy made it a practice to send its fleet submarines to Annapolis to impress the cadets. "The contrast between the new submarines and the old ones that we trained on during summer classes was not only great but dramatic and made us all bug-eyed," said Capt. Frank Wheeler (Ret.), who attended the Academy in the early 1930s. "The smaller ships like submarines also gave you opportunity for important jobs earlier, like command."

In addition, officers who went into submarines received hazardous duty pay. "That was about 25 percent more, something that looked very good in those [Depression] days to all of us," said Wheeler, who added, "The Navy required more submariners than they did line officers at the time, so there was a subtle pressure on us."

It is for these reasons that officers such as Naquin and Wilkin found themselves drawn to submarine training at New London after several years in the surface fleet. By 1930, both men had qualified for command of the "pig-boats," as the older subs were called. They were dangerous and very cramped. The smell of leaking engine oil in the bilge, rotting food, sweaty bodies, and human waste mingled in a trapped environment. After days and weeks at sea, officers and rates alike emerged with rumpled, grease-stained clothing and bruises from being banged around by the boats, which rolled and pitched on the surface. Even to those unfamiliar with submarine sailors, there was no mistaking them in a crowd. "Diesel exhaust would be sucked below decks and we'd all reek of it," recalled Naquin of those early years. "My wife wouldn't let me in the house unless I'd head straight for the shower."

Naquin served in *R-14, S-47,* and *S-46,* where he assumed command in 1935. Likewise, Wilkin served aboard *R-11*, the *R-18*, and the USS *Narwhal*, one of the large V-class cruiser submarines. Both men distinguished themselves in technical and tactical ability, as well as the tight discipline with which they handled their men. The Navy was looking for such qualities, particularly men who acted with extreme caution, mindful of the saying, "There is room for everything aboard a submarine except a mistake."

In 1938, the Navy was confident that Naquin and Wilkin fit the profile and gave them command of the two new boats in Kittery. There, each captain and four subordinate officers assembled their crews.

Soon classes began for the rates. For weeks, under the tutelage of Bland, Gainer, and a few others, the men studied the trim and drainage systems; the hydraulic, steering, and fuel oil systems; the ballast blow systems and diving and anchor gears; and the refrigeration, air conditioning, fresh water, sanitary, and ventilation systems. They traced each—from one end of the ship to the other—in notebooks and were tested on them.

The enlisted men had trained on much smaller submarines. Some had seen a fleet boat. But few, if any, had ever been inside one. These were no pig-boats, but roomy, brightly lit vessels, paneled in satin-finish stainless steel to give them a sleek, futuristic look. Although old-timers disparaged the flush toilets, cold storage, and air conditioning, calling them "hotel accommodations," the new crews liked what they saw.

These boats were wondrous monsters, nearly twice the size of the old S- and R-boats. From topside, the *Squalus*'s deck was a narrow strip of steel, slatted with teakwood, which dried quickly and provided a firm foothold at sea. The hull ballooned outward to surround a pressurized, welded inner hull—really a ship within a ship. Between the two hulls were ballast and fuel storage tanks that girdled the craft's midsection. These could be flooded with water or blown clear with compressed air to dive, surface, or trim the ship.

On the surface near the bow, large wing-like structures were folded against the outer hull. These bow planes were deployed horizontally underwater to control dives. Rising from the deck slightly forward of midships was a steel island, known as the bridge fairwater, a rounded sheet-metal structure some 20 feet high that encircled an interior bullet- and pressure-proof conning tower, as well as the ship's ventilation duct and a 35-inch main air induction valve that provided air to the boat's diesel engines. An array of periscope shears and radio antenna jutted up above the bridge, where lookouts could scan the horizon with binoculars for signs of danger while on patrol. Midway between the fairwater and the stern was a 3-inch waterproof deck gun for surface action. Otherwise, the submarine's topside was unbroken, tapering at the stern to smaller stern planes and twin propellers.

Beyond a watertight door in the bridge fairwater was the conning tower, a large compartment filled with instruments that gave the time, the speed of the vessel, and the depth; from here, orders were transmitted throughout the ship. A large navigation wheel fronted the instruments. Here, during battle, the helmsman would navigate while others next to him operated torpedo firing panels and a torpedo data computer. A small plotting table sat near the after bulkhead, where the executive officer would read the range and bearing of targets as the skipper observed them from the periscope.

Below the conning tower was the heart of the *Squalus*—the control room—reached by a short vertical ladder. A bank of red and green lights—the boat's so-called Christmas Tree—indicated whether hull openings were sealed from the ocean. A long bank of manifold levers that emptied or filled the ship's ballast tanks lined the bulkhead nearby. Here, too, was a set of wheels where operators controlled the bow and stern planes. A tiny compartment with the boat's radio equipment was tucked into the after-end of the control room. Below the compartment was a machine shop and various pumps.

The control room was separated from the rest of the vessel by heavy steel watertight doors set into oval bulkhead openings. One had to stoop low while stepping high to pass through, continuing along a two-foot-wide central passageway the length of the boat. A plumber's delight of pipes, hand wheels, and flapper valves covered the overhead in every compartment.

Forward from the control room were the staterooms of the officers and the CPOs, plus the skipper's cabin, which was about six feet square, with a bed, a telephone to the conning tower, and a bank of instruments that tracked the boat's depth and course. A small pantry and a ship's office rounded out "officers' country." Below the staterooms in the keel rested half of the boat's 126 lead-acid storage cells, each weighing 1,650 pounds. The cells gave the compartment its name, the forward battery.

Through another watertight door was one of the largest compartments of the boat, the forward torpedo room. At the far end, under the bow, were the bright bronze doors to four torpedo tubes, arranged in two vertical tiers. Racks holding several 21-foot-long torpedoes lined the sides of the long, narrow room, with bunks for the men provided over and under the missiles.

Returning to the control room and now moving aft was the after battery room, which contained the crew's quarters, an area of folding bunks, a toilet, washroom, and showers. Further astern was the mess, with tables to seat as many as ten at a time, and a small but efficient galley, the social hub of the boat. Below deck was the other half of the boat's storage cells, plus cold- and deep-freeze storage for perishable food.

Next came the forward engine room, containing two 1,600-horsepower diesel engines, separated by the narrow passageway. Just astern, in the after engine room, was a similar arrangement of two more diesels. Unlike all other compartments, there was no bulkhead or watertight door separating the two engine rooms.

Continuing astern, the maneuvering room was really just an extension of the after engine room. The propulsion controls were located here, linked to the helmsman in the conning tower by a telegraph system of tinkling bells. Below deck were four motors for silent, battery-powered underseas propulsion.

Through the last of the watertight doors was the after torpedo room, located in the stern of the craft. Here, four more loaded torpedo tubes exited the vessel with additional missiles stored in racks leading to the firing tubes. Again, bunks were located above and below these "fish."

During critical maneuvers and in battle, an enlisted man who served as a "talker" was posted in each of the submarine's seven below-decks compartments—the control room, the forward and after batteries, the two engine rooms, and the two torpedo rooms, plus the bridge and conning tower when the boat was on the surface. Wearing headphones plugged into a ship-wide telephone line, talkers provided instantaneous communications throughout the boat at all times.

In addition to the extreme length and upgraded features of the fleet boats, they also were noted for many safety features stemming from a series of embarrassing disasters for the Navy. In 1925, the *S-51* was rammed by a steamship off Rhode Island and sank. Although the boat's oscillator continued to emit distress signals, there was no way to reach the vessel. Two years later, the *S-4* was struck by a Coast Guard vessel off Cape Cod and sank, trapping her forty-man crew at a depth of 100 feet. For three days, the survivors hammered messages to rescuers on the surface, asking, "How long will you be?" But bad weather and no means to get to the crew doomed the men. The American public was appalled, and newspapers complained that twenty U.S. subs had sunk with a loss of more than 750 men in peacetime accidents since 1904. Each disaster emphasized the Navy's inability to save trapped sailors in vessels the public considered "coffins for heroes."

Suffering under this barrage, the Navy by the early 1930s made major improvements to its new boats: watertight bulkheads between compartments; backup onboard systems; hull-stop valves in every compartment to plug leaks; marker buoys with telephones that could be deployed to the surface; Momsen breathing lungs for individual ascents from stranded vessels; and, perhaps most important, specialized escape hatches that could accommodate the Navy's new experimental rescue bell. The eight-man chamber could be lowered from a surface ship to the deck of a submerged boat and link up to the escape hatch to bring crewmen back alive. Although the Navy was confident the McCann Rescue Chamber would work, it had never actually been used in an emergency.

With the commissioning of the *Sculpin* on January 16, 1939, and the *Squalus* on March 1, 1939, trials were soon under way on the Piscataqua River. The crews practiced cohesive teamwork, and the boats themselves were checked for design flaws and equipment failures.

Navigating the three-mile stretch of the river to the Atlantic was tricky. With seven-foot tides daily, draining some 100 miles of inland waterways, the Piscataqua is the second fastest at half-tide in the United States. Such landmarks as Pull-and-be-damned Point, the Horse Races, and Bloody Point underscored the task for sailors in maneuvering and docking. "We would make turns at 15 to 18 knots at a time in the river," said Carl Bryson, who was a bridge talker on the *Squalus*. "At full ebb when the tide is going out, the current is running at 12 knots. It's not like any other place, very tricky in bringing the boat alongside the dock. It's why they have such good seamen in Portsmouth."

After passing the initial tests, the two boats began a series of practice dives in the Atlantic off the rocky coast of New Hampshire where huge mansions loomed as misty sentinels. The boats proceeded six miles out to an area off the Isles of Shoals, a string of rocky islands once used by pirates. There the confluence of the ocean's cold Labrador Current and warm Gulf Stream produced awesome fogs, often with rainbows dappling their edges as they moved toward shore. It was an area of fickle weather, where storms could arise without warning.

On the trial dives, civilian observers accompanied the crews, including inspectors from General Motors, which built the diesel engines. They studied the crews and the equipment, looking for deficiencies.

By May 22, 1939, the *Sculpin* had passed her trial runs and was certified to join the Pacific Fleet at Pearl Harbor. As the crew prepared to depart the next morning, the *Squalus* anchored in a cove of the Piscataqua after a successful eighteenth dive. Rather than return to base,

Naquin wanted the crew well rested for the next day's crucial running dive in which the boat would accelerate to flank speed and then make a crash dive in hopes of being underwater in 60 seconds, the benchmark set by the *Sculpin*. The men were confident they could do it, unaware of the tragedy ahead of them, one foretold in the Atlantic off Peru a few months earlier.

While on a shakedown cruise, the USS *Snapper* (SS-185) prepared to dive in very deep water. At the start of the descent, the 35-inch diameter main air induction valve failed to close at the top of the bridge fairwater. The diving officer, aware of the malfunction, immediately ordered all ballast tanks blown to put the *Snapper* in a hard rise back to the surface from 50 feet deep. The boat barely made it as water swamped the submarine's network of ventilation lines. By the time the *Snapper* surfaced, water was ankle-deep in some compartments. What saved the boat was the routine in the engine rooms of closing off the inboard stop valves below the induction line during a dive.

But on the *Squalus*, there was no such procedure as the sun set on May 22.

The Last Dive of the
Squalus

Under gray skies at dawn, the *Squalus* appeared as an enormous sea creature at rest in the cove off Seavey's Island. Only her teakwood deck and the black conning tower were visible along her 310-foot length. In the distance, the North Atlantic seethed with whitecaps, pushed by cold winds blowing in from the Isles of Shoals six miles out. Waves burst with a steady slap against the hull, occasionally sending spindrift over the submarine's deck, as lobstermen in small boats made for safe haven in Portsmouth in anticipation of a storm. To them, the subs were a familiar sight, so they paid little heed motoring by on the morning of the *Squalus*'s last dive.

By 0700, many in the boat's crew of fifty-nine—five officers, fifty-one enlisted men, and three civilian inspectors—climbed on deck to catch a last smoke after breakfast while drinking in the spectacular hills and precipitous coastline of New Hampshire and Maine dipping down to the narrow channel of the Piscataqua. Dressed in blue dungarees, Carol Nathan Pierce (MM2c) peered through binoculars borrowed from the quartermaster and waved to his wife who fluttered a handkerchief from the Maine shore a half-mile to the north. After two days at sea, he was eager to be home that night for supper. Turning to one of his buddies, he invited him along. "I'll bring over some beer," enthused Eugene Hoffman (MM1c).

Aft of the conn, Harold Preble also enjoyed a cigarette while trading pleasantries with those on deck. As the yard's senior naval architect, he had come aboard to observe the crew and the vessel during the trial period. For 22 years, he had ridden every new sub sent down the Piscataqua since the launch of the old *L-8*. To him, the *Squalus* was the finest. From a deck hatch the captain emerged, wearing a gray jacket to ward off the morning chill. Preble congratulated him on the progress of the boat, confiding that the *Squalus* rated a notch above the *Sculpin* in his opinion. "Take it from me, captain, the crew's in excellent spirits this morning. We ought to have a fine run today." Naquin, typically stern, nodded and conceded that, yes, "everything seems right" for the upcoming dive.

Spirits were high on the boat. She had performed flawlessly through the eighteen trial dives. Admiral Cole, the yard commander, was so impressed with the precision of the previous day's three dives that he sent congratulations that now were posted on bulletin boards throughout the vessel. There was absolutely no reason to doubt the crucial nineteenth dive, an exact rehearsal of what the *Squalus* would do before the Naval Board of Inspection in early June in order to qualify for the operational fleet. The crew's objective was to make an emergency running dive at 16 knots and be completely submerged in 60 seconds, which the Navy had deemed the safety margin in avoiding attack by enemy planes in wartime. With morale buoyed by Cole's citation, Naquin and his crew were confident they could do it. For them, it would be supremely satisfying to beat the mark set by the rival crew of the *Sculpin,* then preparing to embark from Portsmouth on her shakedown cruise to Panama.

Aboard the *Squalus,* there wasn't a hint of concern at 0730 as she left her mooring and swiftly parted the Atlantic to a point 13 miles southeast of Portsmouth near White Island, the southernmost of the desolate Isles of Shoals. Passing within a mile of the White lighthouse, Naquin directed the boat four miles further out, where a planned hour-long dive would occur. From the bridge, he passed orders to "rig for dive" as crewmen assumed their posts in the eight compartments of the *Squalus.*

In the forward torpedo room, Lt. (jg) John C. Nichols personally inspected the escape hatch in the overhead to assure it was tightly sealed. In the forward battery, Bryson put on a set of headphones as the talker for the compartment during the dive. Meanwhile, chief electrician Gainor checked a row of voltmeters in the passageway near the captain's quarters while his assistant, McLees, prepared to descend through a deck hatch into the darkened keel where half of the sub's 252 six-foot-high battery cells would power the boat's motors during submergence. McLees was to take readings on the batteries during the dive while Gainor monitored electrical flow measured by the voltmeters.

In the control room, directly beneath the conning tower, diving officer Lt. William T. Doyle, the second in command, surveyed the array of gauges, valves, and levers that would control the descent. Yeoman Charles Kuney (Y2c) was at his side as the control-room talker, wearing earphones to receive and relay messages throughout the boat. Pierce, operator of the high-pressure air manifold, was seated below him. In all, ten men were in the control room to begin the dive. Preble stood behind Doyle, bracing himself against the ladder to the conning tower. In each hand he clutched a stopwatch to time the trial.

In the after battery, ship's cook William Isaacs (SC2c), assisted by Roland Blanchard (F2c), prepared a meatball lunch in the galley as breakfast cook Robert Thompson (SC3c) slept on one of the many bunks stacked in rows in the compartment. On his way through, torpedoman Sherman Shirley (TM1c) paused momentarily to chat with Lloyd Maness (EM3c), who was to be his best man at his wedding the following Sunday. Shirley then headed back to his post in the after torpedo room. Maness, like Gainor, was to monitor voltmeters in the after battery during the dive. Two other men—John Batick (EM1c) and Arthur Booth (RM1c)—climbed down to the keel to check the cells during the dive. In a tiny cubicle containing medical lockers, pharmacist's mate Raymond O'Hara (PM1c) was preparing to examine Robert Washburn (Sea2c) who had contracted a cold.

Aft of the galley, a narrow corridor led to a heavy, watertight door with a glass eyeport. Beyond were the two engine rooms, the door closed to keep the intense heat of the powerful diesels confined to the stern. An inspector from General Motors observed the black gang (motormacs, or diesel mechanics) push the four units at full speed while awaiting instructions from Doyle. The diesels gulped huge quantities of air, funneled down to them through twin, overhead pipes, 27 inches wide. The tremendous suction in each created a roaring wind tunnel where they opened above the engines. These pipes, known as the main inductions, joined a slightly larger tube which ran up through the boat's superstructure where it yawed to the sky. Parallel to it was a smaller tube linked to a network of pipes running the length of the boat and used to ventilate every compartment during surface running. On submergence, a mushroom-shaped valve in the superstructure—the high induction valve—would slide hydraulically over the air passages of both inductions to seal them from the sea. As a safety backup prior to diving, valves in the engine rooms could be cranked shut by hand wheels located just below each of the induction openings. But the practice on the *Squalus,* like other boats, was not to do so; the valves were difficult to close quickly.

The engine rooms and the after torpedo room were the responsibility of Ens. Joseph Patterson, youngest officer on the boat, popular with the men and a talented Naval Academy runner who finished fourth in the 400-meter hurdles at the 1936 Olympics in Berlin. He, like Nichols in the forward compartments, made a careful inspection of the compartments. Satisfied that all was well, he went to the control room to inform Doyle and then returned.

At 0835, with the submarine speeding at 16 knots, Naquin ordered "stand by to dive." Doyle replied that all was ready. Then at 0840, the captain gave the final command. "All ahead emergency!"

He quickly left the bridge, climbing down the vertical ladder to the control room as the quartermaster closed the bridge hatch and spun a hand wheel to seal it from the ocean. The loud "ah-ooo-gah" of the Klaxon diving alarm sounded throughout the boat. Simultaneously, the location of the sub was radioed to Portsmouth. Unfortunately, it arrived garbled. A radioman recorded the *Squalus* at longitude 70°31′ rather than 70°36′—an error of five miles.

In the control room, Doyle ordered hydraulically controlled vent valves opened to begin flooding ballast tanks girdling the crew compartments just beneath the hull. The weight of the water would quickly drag the *Squalus* under as two sailors manning the diving planes put the boat into a steep dive. The descent required in quick succession that the diesels shut down, the main induction valve close, and battery-powered motors take over. If anything went wrong, Pierce on the air manifold could, on command, blow the water out of the ballast tanks with compressed air, forcing the boat to rise. Naquin, Preble, and Doyle studied the indicator board. One by one, the red lights of the Christmas Tree turned green, signaling that all hull openings, including the critically important induction valves, the largest openings in the boat, were closed. As a backup safety test, Pierce jettisoned a blast of high pressure air into the sub to check for leaks. The ship's barometer rose slightly, assuring the boat was airtight. "Pressure in the boat, sir!" he reported to Doyle.

The dive seemed perfect as the submarine nosed beneath the waves. "You are going to make it," raved Preble to the captain who agreed,

"This is going to be a beauty." At 30 feet, both men studied their stop-watches, clicking off the seconds as the submarine sank deeper. At 50 feet, with the boat completely submerged, they simultaneously shouted "Mark!" All watches read 62 seconds. "Extra good," noted Preble.

Suddenly Naquin sensed a fluttering of air pressure in his ears as the *Squalus* passed 65 feet and began leveling off. In an instant, yeoman Kuney on the headphones stiffened, horrified by frantic voices on the party line: "After engine room flooding!" "Forward engine room flood-ing!" Ashen, he turned to Doyle, terror fringing his voice. "The engine rooms are flooding, sir!" Clamping the earphones tight to his head, he then heard a scream on the line: "Take 'er up! The inductions are open!"

In disbelief, Naquin, Preble, and Doyle stood transfixed, staring at the green lights of the Christmas Tree, which insisted the inductions were closed. Yet, two Niagaras of saltwater poured unrestricted through the induction pipes into the engine rooms.

In one breath, both Naquin and Doyle shouted, "Blow the main ballast!"

"Blow safety tanks!"

"Blow bow buoyancy!"

In the commotion, Preble screamed, "For God's sake, close off bulk-head ventilation valves and doors."

They all knew the *Squalus* was doomed unless she got back to the sur-face immediately.

Pierce, assisted by Preble, desperately slammed every lever on the air manifold wide open, releasing compressed air with a deafening roar into the ballast tanks to force the water out and lift the submarine upward. For a brief moment, it seemed she might make it. The bare tip of her bow broke surface. But there was no stemming the thundering cascade in the engine rooms. The weight of the ocean was too much to overcome. The *Squalus* cantilevered backwards and began sliding into the inky depths. There was nothing anyone could do. Some, like Bland, believed the boat was out over the continental shelf and would be crushed by water pressure.

In the engine rooms, crewmen reaching to close the hull stop valves under the induction pipes were blasted aside by the torrent of frigid ocean water. Most retreated to the after torpedo room, their only hope if they could only get inside and close the watertight door in time. But as the angle of the *Squalus* increased, they were overwhelmed by the flood. Seventeen drowned, including Ensign Patterson, Shirley who was to be married that weekend, and Hoffman, whom Pierce had invited to dinner that evening.

The ocean surged with enormous pressure through the boat's ventilation lines, spewing furiously into the forward compartments where men fought to stop the leaks. As the talker in the forward battery, Bryson heard the scream to "take 'er up" from the engine rooms, and shouted the news to McLees, who quickly scrambled out of the battery well and into the narrow passageway between the officers' quarters. As the *Squalus* rose by the bow, Gainor, standing next to the voltmeters, glanced through the compartment doorway into the control room where he heard Preble's plea to close watertight doors. "The lights were still on with water pouring in from the overhead. It looked like it was following the round contour of the hull, forming a huge water suction hole, a dark green color. I grabbed the watertight door and was nearly swept off my feet by water hitting me in the chest. As I got the door closed, I noted water hitting the glass eyeport at the top of the door. Others were closing off the ventilation valves at the bulkhead. I felt the control room was flooded full. Knowing we were in deep water, I expected the end."

For Gainor, there was no time to dwell on such thoughts. The voltmeters were going wild. Grabbing a hand lantern, he pulled himself up the steepening incline of the deck to the hatch where he peered down in shock. Steam was pouring off the cells, whose caps bobbed on boiling acid inside. He realized immediately that the cells were shorting and that an explosion was imminent unless they were disconnected. Leaping into the narrow crawl space on the keel, he quickly located one of two large disconnect switches. When he disengaged it, a miniature lightning storm of 70,000 amps erupted, sizzling blue-white and melting insulation on the hull. Half-blinded and sure he would be electrocuted, Gainor reached for the other switch and broke the circuit just in time, blacking out the entire boat and miraculously leaving him untouched. "Got it!" he exulted.

In the forward torpedo room as the boat tilted precariously, a 1,000-pound practice torpedo broke loose, threatening to crush anyone in its path. Three men, including Nichols, jumped on it, jockeying it back in place and strapping it down. Meanwhile, torpedoman Leonard de Medeiros (TM3c) closed the watertight door to the forward battery.

Back in the control room, men tumbled about, grasping for footing as a dozen pencil-thin jets of pressurized water spewed from the ventilation pipes. Preble was knocked flat. Others were doused to the skin as they worked frantically to close off all the lines. On the awkward 50-degree incline of the deck, they held onto anything they could to stay upright. The overhead lights flickered and went out, replaced by emergency lights, which also went out 10 seconds later. Naquin, clutching the ears of one of the boat's two periscopes, ordered Maness to close the watertight door to the after battery.

There, a life-and-death struggle had begun.

Through the open control room door, Maness had heard yeoman Kuney's cry that the engine rooms were flooding just as sheets of water burst into the after battery from overhead pipes. Soaked, he hustled to his emergency station in the control room where he prepared to shut the oval, 300-pound steel door between the compartments. It would require a superhuman effort since it opened to the stern, which was sinking fast. As water swirled up toward the bulkhead coaming, Maness heard frantic cries. "Keep it open! Keep it open! We're coming!!" Six men half crawled and swam uphill out of the compartment. Basilio Galvan, a mess attendant, was first, Maness urging him to hurry. William Boulton (Sea1c) was right behind, followed quickly by Booth, Blanchard, Washburn, and O'Hara.

A seventh man, Isaacs, the ship's cook, was far behind. When the *Squalus* first lurched upward, a curtain of water splattered down on him. Instinctively, he stepped into the corridor to secure the nearby door to the engine rooms. Although it was closed, water was spilling out around the curved door frame. Spinning the door's wheel to lock it, he peered with awe through the glass eyeport. Two torrents roared furiously from the inductions above the four diesels, burying them in foaming saltwater. He could see no survivors. With the sea waist-high around him, Isaacs tried to make his way forward but slipped on the incline of the deck. Fully engulfed, he swam desperately toward the safety of the control room, colliding with a submerged mess table and grappling with underwater objects to pull himself upward. Struggling to close the door, Maness saw the cook and let the door swing open again. In seconds, Isaacs lurched through, falling to the deck out of breath. Maness, summoning all his strength, then pulled, his muscles quivering in the exertion that moved the door ever so slowly until it finally closed with a metallic click.

Behind it, no one would survive.

Unbeknownst to Maness, ship's cook Thompson who had gone to sleep in his bunk was still alive. He had floated to the top of the compartment, where he was trapped in an air bubble on the underside of a deck hatch. But as he cranked it open in an attempt to swim to the surface, the life-sustaining air leaked out ahead of him and he drowned.

The *Squalus* settled gently on the green mud of the ocean floor, 240 feet down. With the boat's stern mired in the mud, she rested upright, with a slight up angle toward the bow. Fortunately she was not on her side, which would have made rescue more difficult.

On the bottom, the survivors wondered if others were trapped in the after torpedo room. It had been less than five minutes since the dive began. "Everyone was thinking about it," recalled Danny Persico (Sea1c), in the forward torpedo room. "We tapped on air lines leading back through the hull. We all took turns. If they had heard it, they would have acknowledged. We knew then that aft of the control room, all the compartments were flooded."

In the control room, Naquin assessed the situation as hand lanterns were passed down from a shelf. With a pocket flashlight, he moved about, checking for leaks. Several feet of water had collected aft of the periscope well. The men were soaked; water had drenched everything. The captain asked Kuney, still with his headset on, if he had heard any word from aft. He replied he hadn't. Naquin took the phones and mouthpiece and listened for himself.

"Hello, engine rooms. Hello, after torpedo room . . . hello . . . hello," he repeated.

When there was no reply, he called out to the talkers in the forward compartments. Immediately, voices on the line assured him that the bow chambers were reasonably dry and secure. Naquin then instructed Eugene Cravens, the first-class gunner's mate, to fire one of the ship's forty distress rockets from the control room overhead. At 0845 it zipped to the surface and exploded 80 feet above the waves in a cloud of red smoke, but no one was there to see it.

On instruction from Naquin, Nichols released the boat's marker buoy attached to the deck of the boat near the forward escape hatch. The bright yellow float, three feet across, trailed a telephone line from the submarine to the surface. In large letters on the buoy was the message, "Submarine Sunk Here. Telephone Inside." As the buoy broke through to the surface, a valve gave way in the control room, spurting a powerful blast of oil followed by saltwater at the already drenched Isaacs, knocking him down. Men scrambled to tighten hull stops to stem the leak as others assisted the frightened cook.

In the dim light, Naquin asked the quartermaster to make a head count, confirming that four officers, twenty-eight enlisted men, and one civilian were alive. Twenty-three were in the control room; ten others in the two forward compartments. Steadying his nerves in the knowledge that twenty-six others had most certainly drowned, Naquin addressed those in the control room, packed around him so closely that he could feel their labored breaths.

"Attention, men. You all know where we are. The boat cannot surface by herself. We have released the forward marker buoy and we will continue to send up smoke rockets at regular intervals. It is only a matter of time before help comes. All hands are to be commended on their conduct. I expect no change."

A short time later, Gainor reported that saltwater was seeping into the keel of the forward battery. Fearful it would mix with battery acid to create deadly chlorine gas or that a fire could erupt from the heat of the shorted cells, Naquin told Bryson and others to gather stored blankets, food from the officers' pantry, extra clothing, and even door curtains and retreat to the torpedo room, where temperatures had dropped below freezing. Meanwhile, the door from the warmer control room was cracked long enough for others to fetch food, mattresses from bunks in the officers' quarters, additional blankets, and Momsen escape lungs. Naquin explained how to use the lungs to Preble and a few others unfamiliar with them.

In view of the crowded floor space in the control room, the captain sent five crewmen to the torpedo room. The forward battery then was sealed tight as a precaution against gas leakage. The compartment now served as a barrier between the survivors—fifteen in the torpedo room and eighteen in the control room.

Many were confident the Momsen lungs would save them. Some in the control room conceived a plan to use them in an ascent from the higher conning tower. However, Gainor said he was positive an external eyebolt from which the ascending line would be attached on the bridge was missing, thereby foiling any mass exodus. In addition, an escape from the torpedo room was very risky due to the depth, the frigid water, and the possibility of ruptured lungs if the men rose too fast by losing their grip on the line to the buoy. Still, many drew comfort from their training at New London in the escape tank. "Nobody had given much thought to dying," recalled Bryson. "We had Momsen lungs. We knew we had a chance. The escape was planned by lung. In fact, we had decided to grease down to protect from the cold of the water."

Nichols had already chosen de Medeiros, the muscular torpedoman, to lead the way—but only as a last resort. The captain realized that Preble and a few others, like Isaacs, bruised and cold from his drenching, probably wouldn't make it. He decided rather to await rescue. After all, everyone knew the *Sculpin* would be sailing through the area in two hours en route to Panama. Certainly by then the *Squalus* would be reported overdue and the search begun.

Naquin ordered the survivors to stay calm and to nap to conserve air, which he calculated might last 48 hours if used sparingly. Each compartment contained two flasks of oxygen with bleeder valves, which he would control. Carbon-dioxide absorbent powder was spread on the decks of the two compartments to avoid CO_2 poisoning. Meanwhile, a bucket was passed among the men in the control room so they wouldn't have to exert themselves going to the head.

In the dark, one sailor passed the beam of his flashlight over the door to the after battery where an oily, rainbow hue shimmered in the water-filled eyeport. Naquin ordered all lights extinguished to conserve the batteries. Later, he overhead one man discussing the fate of those in the engine rooms. "That's enough of that! There'll be no discussion of the men aft," the captain snapped.

For the survivors, it wasn't easy, lying still as temperatures dropped into the low 30s in the forward torpedo room where ice formed on the bulkheads. "The worst part was that we were so cold," recalled machinist's mate Charles Yuhas. "You'd take your hand from under a blanket for a minute and it would get numb." Crewmen whistled softly to keep up their courage. "What kept flashing through my mind," reminisced Persico, "was the fact my mother had taken out an insurance policy on me. And there was a clause that it would be null and void if I died in a submarine or diving accident."

In the control room, Naquin heard teeth chattering in the dark. Flipping on his flashlight, he located the shuddering seaman. Stripping off his own coat, the skipper wrapped the man in it. As the morning wore on, the captain decided to make an inspection of the forward compartments. Entering the torpedo room, he promised expectant faces that "we should be getting help soon. You must stay quiet. Don't talk. Try to sleep." He then huddled with Nichols. "Buzz me as soon as anyone makes contact," the captain said, referring to the rescue buoy bobbing overhead. "Tell them I think the high induction is open. Also that the after battery and both engine rooms are flooded. Say we're not certain about the after torpedo room." Before returning to the control room, Naquin whispered encouragement to the young lieutenant. "You're doing just fine," he said.

Back in Portsmouth, Admiral Cole became concerned when the *Squalus* had not reported surfacing as scheduled at 0940. The White lighthouse reported no trace of the missing submarine. By 1100, Cole was impatient for news and headed off at a brisk pace for the dock where the *Sculpin* was to cast off in 30 minutes. He took Captain Wilkin by surprise. "I want you to shove off immediately. The *Squalus* may be in trouble. We're not sure. Here's her diving point," he said, handing Wilkin the fix radioed from the *Squalus*. "I want you to pass over it and let me know what you find without delay."

As the *Sculpin* embarked, Cole returned hurriedly to his office and called New London, where the converted World War I minesweeper *Falcon* was stationed. Now serving as a naval rescue and salvage tug, the ship carried one of five experimental submarine rescue bells spread over the fleet. Since the one at New London was the closest, Cole alerted officials that the bell might be needed at a moment's notice.

Meanwhile, the *Sculpin* arrived off the Isles of Shoals to search for the *Squalus*. A half-dozen lookouts scanned the surface, not knowing they were five miles off the true bearing because of the faulty coordinates. But one officer, Lt. (jg) Ned Denby, happened to be looking in the opposite direction of the search area and noticed what he thought was the smudge of a distress rocket. Wilkin confirmed it with his binoculars, just as the smoke evaporated. The *Sculpin* swung around and headed quickly for the site as Wilkin radioed to Portsmouth, "Believe sighted smoke bomb."

Ten minutes later, at 1255, spirits soared on the stricken *Squalus* as the unmistakable cavitation of submarine propellers was clearly heard. The survivors knew it was the *Sculpin*. The boat slowed as it came upon the telephone buoy and dropped anchor, the splash heard clearly below. *Sculpin* crewmen pulled the buoy on deck and Wilkin got on the phone. "Hello *Squalus*. This is *Sculpin*. What's your trouble?"

Nichols, containing his excitement, described conditions as Naquin had directed. He then asked Wilkin to hold the line while he got the captain. Thirty seconds later, Naquin spoke calmly into the phone, "Hello, Wilkin." But just as Wilkin replied, "Hello, Oliver," the ocean heaved, stretching the telephone cable and snapping it. The phone went dead.

Helplessly, the *Sculpin* stood by as Wilkin radioed what he knew to Portsmouth. Cole didn't waste a minute. He phoned the chief of naval operations in Washington, D.C., asking him to round up the Navy's best deepsea diving experts at the Washington Navy Yard and fly them to Portsmouth at once. Cole also phoned New London, where the slow-going *Falcon* got under way for the 200-mile voyage north with the rescue bell on her fantail. Naval and Coast Guard bases up and down the coast were put on alert in case additional vessels were needed.

As the greatest underseas rescue operation in naval history got under way, news of the unfolding drama spread with lightning effect. Reporters descended on Portsmouth. Anxious wives and families gathered at the shipyard gates. Others kept a tense vigil in front of radios in homes across the nation. With the memories of the *S-4* and *S-51* disasters so fresh in mind, a doubtful public wondered if the *Squalus* crew had any real hope of rescue. In fact, few knew of the Navy's revolutionary rescue bell.

In the icy tomb of the *Squalus* on the floor of the Atlantic, Naquin maintained hope and calm while rationing air supplies. Although more than five hours had passed since the dive began, the captain was confident the rescue bell was on the way from New London. Like a large, white, inverted tumbler twice the height of a man, the device would be put to the do-or-die attempt to save a submarine crew for the first time in history.

But would the *Falcon* arrive in time?

And perhaps even more important, would the capricious New England weather, which had calmed overhead, hold long enough to make rescue possible?

The Rescue

On the morning of the *Squalus*'s last dive, Lt. Cdr. Charles B. Momsen and a group of the Navy's best deepsea experts were winding up decompression tests at the Experimental Diving Unit of the Washington Navy Yard. They had been using a breathing mixture of helium and oxygen, designed to eliminate some of the dangers of diving to great depth. Suddenly the phone rang. It was Cdr. Charles A. Lockwood in Operations at the Navy Department. The message was terse: "*Squalus* is down off the Isles of Shoals, depth between 200 and 400 feet. Have your divers and equipment ready to leave immediately."

Within two hours, the survivors' best hope—Momsen, lieutenants O. D. Yarbrough and Albert R. Behnke of the Medical Corps, and Chief Metalsmith James H. McDonald, master diver and coholder of the world's deep diving record of 500 feet—were airborne, en route to Portsmouth 500 miles to the north. Two planes followed, one with Cdr. Allen R. McCann, codesigner of the rescue bell, and the other with William Badders (CMM), the other holder of the deep-dive record. More than a dozen divers in all raced for the scene, prepared to sacrifice their lives to save those trapped on the *Squalus*.

With evening closing under a gray overcast, the

twin-motored amphibious plane containing Momsen banked into a turn and prepared to land on the Piscataqua River in Portsmouth. During the four-hour flight, the implications of the tragedy gnawed at Momsen in the silence of the passenger cabin. He and the Navy had planned for this eventuality for years and were confident their equipment would work. But would something go wrong, as it did with the *S-4* when gale-force winds stymied rescuers? "I shall never be able to record the various thoughts that flashed through my mind during the 150-mile-per-hour ride," Momsen, a husky, good-humored man in his forties, recalled later that year in an address at Harvard University. "My memory went back to the first lung experiments, thrills of 10 years ago, to the long and tedious years spent in training submarine officers and enlisted men of the submarine service to use the lung; to the first diving bell, the cranky open bell that would dump and fall and half drown us if we were not careful, of the final design produced by Commander Allen R. McCann and the comfort that it was to operate. I recalled the hundreds of thrills encountered in training and developing this device.

"Now the dreaded hour was here! Would the dreams of the experimenter come true or would some quirk of fate cross up the plans and thus destroy all of this work? How many shipmates were waiting for the answer? What were they thinking? Were they too deep?"

In many ways, the fate of the *Squalus* survivors rested in this man's hands. Had it not been for him, they wouldn't even have a chance. He had designed the Momsen lung, on which the survivors depended. He and McCann had invented the rescue bell out of the remains of the only submarine airplane hangar in the Navy, once affixed to the deck of the submarine *S1* in 1926. And it was Momsen who, with Behnke and Yarbrough, had successfully experimented with a helium-oxygen breathing air mixture that might come into play in the rescue. Momsen insisted on personally testing each invention—a method that put him at great risk but made him confident of each advance.

Out on the Atlantic above the *Squalus*, the scene was surreal. In the storm-tossed darkness, spotlights illuminated the ocean beneath two naval tugs, the *Penacook* (YT-6) and the *Wandank*, which were at anchor. Men peered over the railing of both ships, as if expecting the *Squalus* or her survivors to surface at any moment. The two tugs had spent hours dragging the area with grappling hooks, trying to relocate the sunken vessel, whose precise location had been lost when the telephone line snapped. With the use of a heavier anchor from the *Sculpin*, the *Penacook* finally latched hold of something at 1930. Amid jubilant cries from rescuers, one *Penacook* rate muttered, "God help us, and them, too, if it isn't the *Squalus* we've hooked." Nesting alongside the two tugs was a Portsmouth commercial tug, which had arrived with a medical corps doctor, three pharmacist's mates, and a shipment of fifty blankets—just in case any of the survivors made a swim for the surface. Nearby sat the ominous silhouette of the *Sculpin* where Cole was inside, organizing the rescue effort after pacing the deck nervously through most of the afternoon. He and the others could only wait. Wait for the *Falcon* with her rescue chamber from New London. Wait for the deepsea divers from Washington. And wait for Momsen, whose expertise would be crucial. The rescuers also worried about the weather, as a cold, wicked chop roiled the surface over the *Squalus*.

Skimming to a landing on the Piscataqua, Momsen's plane was met by Admiral Cole's personal barge, which promptly ferried the passengers to the navy yard for a briefing. Then the four men boarded a Coast Guard patrol boat that steamed into the Atlantic, arriving alongside the *Sculpin* at 2145 off the Isles of Shoals.

Because of fog, the second plane, containing McCann and most of the divers, was forced to land in Newport, Rhode Island, 125 miles short of Portsmouth. State and local police in Rhode Island, Massachusetts, and New Hampshire blocked intersections and flagged drivers off the road to clear the main highways as the men, jammed into three cars, roared north. The pace was so furious that one police escort couldn't keep up as the caravan sped through Boston. Still, it was 0415 on the following day before McCann and the divers reached the site. Said one, wiping his forehead, "After that trip, the terrors of deepsea diving are nothing."

Radio electrified the nation with hour-by-hour reports from Portsmouth. A banner headline across the front page of the *New York Times* proclaimed: "59 Await Rescue on Sunken Submarine." Later editions announced, "Rescue Ships Huddle Helplessly Over Spot Where *Squalus* Lies." Some newspapers speculated on possible sabotage, based on second-hand reports that one *Squalus* crewman predicted to a friend before the dive that the boat would sink.

Families of the crewmen, who came from twenty-eight states, Hawaii, and the Philippines, feared the worst. In Washington, D.C., the wife of torpedoman Alfred Priester (TM2c) prayed for his safety while quieting her two-year-old son. "All I can do is pray," she repeated over and over to reporters. "I've never been through anything like this. I pray God Al is safe. This waiting is horrible." Across town, the parents of William Isaacs, the *Squalus* cook, hung on every word from the radio. His mother clasped a picture of her son to her breast and rocked slowly in a chair. Occasionally, she paced nervously, back and forth, from her front porch to her kitchen.

The Rumanian-born wife of Robert Gibbs (TM1c), traveling by train to Portsmouth from Lexington, South Carolina, was unaware of the tragedy because she didn't speak English. Her husband's uncle met the train at Union Station in Washington, D.C. Through much hand signaling, he made her understand that Gibbs was on the sunken *Squalus*. The train began to move ahead and he had to get off, hoping passengers would console the now distraught bride. In Dover, New Hampshire, crewman Sherman Shirley's fiancée waited and prayed. "He's too good to be trapped like that," she said, fingering the wedding ring he had given her for safe-keeping. "Keep it," he had told her. "It will be safer in your possession than in mine."

At the base in Portsmouth, wives and relatives gathered at a makeshift pressroom in the yard's administration building where reporters worked elbow to elbow, monitoring events and pounding out stories. Periodically, officers rushed in to read bulletins and answer questions. Outside, the wife of Carlton Powell (MM2c) nervously walked the navy yard docks, tears in her eyes, pleading for news from workers. Also in anguish, the wife of John Chestnutt (CMM) paced nervously along the roadways of the base, clutching the hand of her young son who walked beside her.

With news that the *Sculpin* had made contact with the *Squalus*, many presumed all hands were safe. After all, there were no reports of casualties. Said Mrs. Lawrence Gainor of her husband, "He's been in scrapes before. He'll be all right." Likewise, Captain Naquin's wife, Frances, put on a brave face in a statement released to the press, voicing confidence "the whole thing will be over tomorrow." Still, rescue of the men depended on the arrival of the *Falcon*. Broadcasters kept reminding the nation of that. "Everything depends on her," said one.

All through the night, the tiny ship steamed north with the McCann Rescue Chamber firmly strapped to her fantail. It was an agonizingly slow voyage. Indeed, there was plenty of time for the *Falcon*'s own divers to overhaul their equipment and prepare mooring hawsers. Like a hare passing a tortoise, the destroyer *Semmes* (DD-189) sped by, as did the 10,000-ton cruiser *Brooklyn* (CL-40) up from the New York Navy Yard and loaded with thousands of feet of high-pressure diving hose. Finally at 0430, the *Falcon* arrived off the Isles of Shoals and by 0650 she moored over the suspected position of the *Squalus*—21 hours after the sinking.

Down below, conditions had steadily worsened. The captain had ordered all lights extinguished to save the batteries. There was nothing the men could do but lie quietly in the dark. Naquin worried about the effect of the bad air and freezing conditions on them, certain an escape by Momsen lung was becoming more remote with each passing hour. At such depth, it would be necessary for each man to ascend slowly for at least 25 minutes to avoid rupturing his lungs. Being exposed to 29° ocean water for that long, the skipper reasoned, would certainly kill some of them. By his estimation, the rescue force assembling overhead could either attach pneumatic hoses to the flooded after-section of the boat and blow the water out to refloat the *Squalus,* or the rescue bell could come for the survivors. Either way was preferable to making a swim for it. Thus, Naquin stretched the air supply, purposely allowing for higher concentrations of carbon dioxide in the boat in order to induce the crew to sleep and avoid unnecessary exertion. The captain was concerned about the weather. It could delay the rescue; there was no alternative but to ration the air to the very limit of endurance.

The survivors lay on the linoleum floor, on mattresses, or in bunks, some huddled together under blankets in an attempt to stay warm. Others sat at the edges of the compartments, their backs resting against bulkheads and their knees drawn up under their chins. Among them was Maness, the crewman who had closed the watertight door between the control room and the stern. In torment, he rocked back and forth, chewing on his hand while thinking about those trapped in the after-section, particularly his pal Sherman Shirley, who had chosen him to be his best man.

In the control room, valves occasionally hissed from the pressure buildup throughout the boat. There was little talk. The crew's labored breathing added to the condensation that hung in the air like a thick fog. Some were nauseated from lack of oxygen, soaked clothing, and fear, becoming sick and vomiting. Their shipmates calmed them, holding them in their arms. Someone produced a five-cent bar of chocolate-covered peanut butter which was shared, the captain commenting on how good it was.

In the forward torpedo room, the survivors shivered in the cold. "We were packed in like sardines," said Persico. "I thought back to the time I left a heavy cruiser for sub duty. As I was going down the gangway, a fellow I knew said, 'You know, those things are going to have a sinking.' And I kidded him back, 'Yeah, it would just be my luck I'll be aboard it.' A year later, here I was on the *Squalus.* But at age 19 you take things in stride. We just cuddled up to stay warm and waited." Nearby, de Medeiros chased thoughts of the shipmate who suggested the two trade places before the fateful dive. Arrangements were made at the anchorage, with de Medeiros moving to the forward torpedo room while his pal moved aft, where he drowned.

When the marker buoy cable to the *Sculpin* separated, Naquin had directed the boat's radiomen and signalmen to relay Morse code messages to the surface from the conning tower. They had cleared cork insulation from the steel hull and, in rotation, wielded a hammer with all their might to sound out messages they hoped could be deciphered by the *Sculpin*. Certainly, she would be listening, trying to get a fix on the *Squalus*'s position. The noise was deafening in the conning tower, but barely audible on the surface where the *Sculpin* stood by, unable to decipher the taps. The exertion of the hammer-blows in the stale air quickly exhausted the men, making one sick to his stomach. In the forward torpedo room, Lieutenant Nichols and others tapped out Morse code with hammer blows of their own. Still, there was no answer. But the survivors did hear propellers overhead, correctly guessing it was the *Penacook* drawing near to begin dragging for the *Squalus*.

At 1600, eight hours after the sinking, the signal watch finally made out a reply from the *Sculpin:* "Divers on way. Answer with four hammer taps." Energized by the contact, one signalman swung his three-pound sledge with all his might to reply with four loud bangs against the conning tower wall.

Naquin made another inspection of overhead valves that continued to hold back the sea. Canned pineapple, peaches, and tomatoes were passed out to the survivors, as well as oil-skinned raincoats from a locker. Then at 1721, the penetrating sound of an oscillator jolted the men. The coded message made it clear the *Wandank* had arrived to join the hunt for the *Squalus*. Naquin, through his signalmen, answered questions from the surface: No, the boat was not taking on water. There were thirty-three known survivors. Conditions were satisfactory but cold. The boat had an 11-degree up angle but no list.

At 2110, the *Wandank* indicated the *Falcon* would arrive about 0300 the next morning, and that a grappling line apparently had caught the *Squalus*. Naquin hoped it had, for he and his men had neither heard nor felt anything make contact with the boat.

In Portsmouth, reporters speculated on possible deaths on the *Squalus*. Four Boston reporters decided to find out. They hired a lobster boat, which took them to the site after midnight. Battling a six-foot chop for three hours left the reporters drenched and seasick. But as they came upon the *Wandank*, Harry Crockett of the Associated Press asked over a megaphone to someone standing on the *Wandank*'s deck, "How many are dead down below?" The reply indicated twenty-six unaccounted for in the flooded after section of the *Squalus*. On returning to shore, Crockett phoned in his dispatch. Within moments, wives, friends, and families of the *Squalus* crew knew for certain some would not be coming back. But which ones?

As dawn broke on the second day, fortune took a dramatic turn for the survivors. The wind abated. The sun shone brightly over gentle swells. Admiral Cole had decided during the night not to send divers down to the submarine to attach air hoses in an attempt to refloat the *Squalus*. The extreme depth would make the effort time-consuming and time was precious if the survivors were to be spared before their air ran out. After Momsen joined him on the *Sculpin,* the two plotted details of a rescue by the *Falcon*'s bell. Arriving divers also boarded the *Sculpin* to familiarize themselves with the layout of the *Squalus*.

After the *Falcon*'s arrival at 0430, the ship's captain sent a warning by oscillator to the *Squalus*—"Fire no more smoke rockets. I am mooring over you"—a message that sent spirits soaring on the submarine. The rescue vessel eased in close to the drag line from the *Penacook*. Then, four mooring lines were dropped spread-eagle from the four corners of the ship to keep her in position. Immediately, boatswain's mate Martin C. Sibitzky, who had been selected to make the initial descent, climbed onto a small diving platform rigged to a hoist, where he was outfitted in 200 pounds of rubber diving gear, including weighted shoes, 40 pounds of extra lead ballast on a belt around his waist, and a large metal helmet with thick glass view plates. The bulbous suit made Sibitzky look monstrously alien, more than a foot taller than the crewmen who worked around him. Hoses to supply him with air during the descent were attached to the top of his helmet. He also wore newly developed electric underwear, which would protect him from the cold.

At 1015, the platform and Sibitzky were uphoisted and lowered into the sea. The diver disappeared from view, guiding himself into the black depths along the cable from the *Penacook*. With him went a shackle to another line, the downhaul cable from a winch inside the rescue chamber. Three minutes into the dive Sibitzky landed with a thud on the forward deck of the *Squalus* where the anchor from the *Sculpin* had hooked her sister ship. Miraculously, it was only six feet aft of the forward escape hatch. As he made his way along the deck to the hatch, Sibitzky could hear the hammer taps of those inside.

The sounds of the diver's metal shoes clunking along the deck were exhilarating. "I was up in the escape trunk when he landed," recounted Persico. "I could hear every word that he was communicating to the surface. Every other word was a cuss word as he grappled with the line. I was so elated I wanted to holler up to him. The only thing that separated us was the thickness of the hull."

With 60-foot visibility, Sibitzky stooped to view the escape hatch and noticed the severed telephone cable. With one end coiled on the hatch, it snaked across the hull to where if fell away to the ocean floor. Immediately, the diver cut it free so that it wouldn't interfere with the rescue bell. Sibitzky looked up toward the surface, sensing the loneliness of his situation. The sun was barely visible, a dim star twinkling through an incredible gulf of blackness which stretched endlessly away from him. It took him 20 minutes to connect the loose end of the downhaul cable to a bail in the center of the escape hatch trunk, shaped like a donut to accommodate the rescue chamber. Sibitzky returned to the surface at 1124. All was in readiness to attempt the unprecedented rescue.

With anticipation mounting, Momsen, Cole, McCann, and others watched from the *Falcon* as the rescue chamber was hoisted at McCann's signal over the side. Scores of small boats circled the area at a distance, and airplanes manned by photographers, reporters, and sightseers buzzed overhead as the moment of truth neared. The light gray, pear-shaped steel apparatus—seven feet wide and ten feet high, and weighing 18,000 pounds—was divided into an upper closed compartment able to seat at least seven of the survivors at one time, and a lower open compartment separated by a horizontal bulkhead with a watertight hatch in its center. Surrounding the lower compartment was a ballast tank to control the buoyancy, and inside the compartment was a reel with 400 feet of half-inch steel wire—the downhaul cable now attached to the *Squalus*. A motorized, air-driven control shaft from the winch ran through the bulkhead into the upper compartment where two operators would control the descent. The lip of the lower chamber, open to the sea, was lined by a rubber gasket to create a watertight seal when the chamber finally made contact with the escape hatch on the *Squalus*. Attached to the top of the rescue bell were two air hoses, plus electric cables for the chamber's telephone and bright interior lights. A heavy wire used to retrieve the chamber in an emergency was shackled to the very top of the bell.

Inside were two operators, John Mihalowski (TM1c) and his assistant, Walter E. Harman (GM1c), both experienced divers. With McCann on the telephone to them, they blew the ballast in the lower chamber of the bell and began the descent. Mihalowski closely watched the winch in the lower chamber through a glass eyeport as it pulled the bell down along the downhaul cable. Meanwhile, another winch on the

Falcon played out the uphaul cable attached to the roof of the chamber. Frequently, the bell was halted so that Harman and Mihalowski could check to make sure the downhaul cable was being wound properly on the winch. At 1202, Harman reported passing 150 feet. And then 200 feet. With Harman at the controls, Mihalowski squatted over the eyeport, looking for the *Squalus* but only seeing the ripple of ocean water reflected in the chamber's lights. At last the gray form of the submarine came into view, becoming brown and then black. Mihalowski saw the deck grate and then the rescue hatch, including the center ring where the downhaul cable came to an end.

The chamber came to rest over the hatch, pulled there by the winch. Blowing air into the lower chamber, Harman forced the water out except for a few inches just above the submarine's escape hatch. The great pressure of the surrounding sea pressed down on the now dry chamber, making a watertight seal between the rescue bell and the *Squalus*. With Harman watching, Mihalowski lowered himself below where he landed on the hatch, water covering his feet to ankle depth. After attaching four bolts between the bell and the sub to ensure the chamber would stay put, he slackened the downhaul cable so he could open the hatch.

He had practiced the routine many times. But now history was being made as he prepared to free the crew of a stranded submarine for the first time.

With a heave, he lifted the hatch against the weight of the residual seawater that quickly drained into the *Squalus*. Poking his head down under the hatch, he and Harman shouted "Hello!" in unison but there was no reply. Mihalowski then realized a lower hatch had been closed by the survivors as a safety measure.

Lowering himself further down the hatch, he tapped several times and then opened the cover. Light from the rescue bell beamed down into the darkness below, illuminating the wide grins of the bedraggled survivors who were witnessing what seemed like a miracle.

Matter-of-factly, Mihalowski returned the grin. "Hello, fellows, here we are!"

Persico, who had gotten doused when the hatch was opened, was ecstatic when he saw the diver's shoes. "They were black, torn sneakers which were wet. To me, they were the prettiest sight in the world." Mihalowski passed down a pot of hot coffee, a five-gallon milkcan filled with hot pea soup, and several cans of carbon dioxide absorbent. Relieved, some of the survivors began to joke with the diver. "Why the delay?" "Where in hell are the napkins?"

The fresh air flowing into the submarine revived the men, most of whom were suffering from severe headaches, especially the captain. Without delay, the operators prepared to take a group of them back to the surface. The captain divvied up the crew into groups of seven, making sure the least fit of the survivors, including Preble, made the first trip. There were no complaints, with Naquin assuring his men, "We'll be out soon."

Preble was the first to climb up into the bell, followed by the others including Nichols, the officer Naquin designated to give a full report on conditions aboard the *Squalus*. At 1313, the chamber lifted off and made a methodical, 30-minute ascent, regulated by the downhaul cable. The operators carefully controlled the ballast, fearful of making the capsule too buoyant, and thereby possibly snapping the downhaul cable and causing the bell to crash through the keel of the *Falcon*, sinking both her and the rescue chamber.

On the *Falcon*, Momsen waited anxiously. "We tried to appear calm and maybe others were," he recalled. "But to me this was the most exciting moment of my life. Eleven years of preparation, combating skepticism and constructing imaginary disasters, all telescoped into one moment. Who could remain calm?"

The bell came into view as a greenish splotch and in moments was hauled alongside the *Falcon* where the hatch was opened. With *Falcon* crewmen standing on top of the bell, a haggard face appeared. It was Nichols, blinking into the intense sun. Helping hands eased him up to the deck of the *Falcon* where a blanket was thrown around his shoulders. Movie cameras recorded the historic event as a sense of incredible triumph swept the flotilla. One by one, the other six survivors emerged into the light of day. The fresh air was so intoxicating that one weakened man fell backwards in a faint and was carried to the deck. As the rescue chamber prepared to return for a new cargo, the survivors were given more hot coffee and first aid, including warm towels placed around their abdomens. They also were placed for a short time in the *Falcon*'s decompression tank as a precaution against bends. News of the Navy's amazing rescue flashed around the world. The names of the seven were posted at the navy yard where relatives rejoiced, giving others new hope.

On the way back down for another group of survivors, Badders, the operator on the second descent, decided to change the rescue plans. "I got to thinking that I had operated this chamber probably more than anyone else in the Navy, and I knew it could handle more than seven passengers and two operators," he recalled years later. "I decided I was going to bring more men up. The weather was fair when we started the rescue, but I knew how quickly squalls could spring up, and the havoc they would wreak on this operation. Also, there was the danger of a bulkhead giving way in the submarine and flooding the area where the men were."

With Badders at the controls, the rescue chamber brought up nine survivors at 1600. "I hadn't said a word to anybody topside about this, I just came up—with no difficulty—with nine men," said Badders. "Lt. Cdr. Swede Momsen was on the deck when I came up. He said, 'You brought out too many men on this trip, but do it again,' which I did."

At 1850, the third bell rescued nine more, including Jud Bland. Later, McLees who made the first trip up, nuzzled up to him, reminding him that Bland had sold an old car to him on the installment plan. But the car was wrecked. "When I saw you come up in that bell," he laughed, "I thought, 'Oh my God, I'm going to have to pay for that car.'"

With Nichols's help, Admiral Cole prepared a list of all the survivors, unaware that William D. Boulton (Sea1c) had been omitted. The names were radiocd to Portsmouth where they were released to the public. Boulton's wife Rita in New York City collapsed twice, first when she was told her husband was missing, then a few hours later when the Navy announced he had been rescued. Jeanette Priester, wife of *Squalus* torpedoman Alfred Charles Priester, broke down at her home in Washington, D.C., when his name wasn't among the survivors. "Al is gone. I know it. He is gone and my baby and I are alone," she wailed. Across town, William Isaacs's parents got the news he had survived. His father passed out and was put to bed. Weeping tears of joy, his mother told reporters, "They've taken my boy to the hospital. I don't know how badly he is hurt, but I do thank God for answering my prayers and bringing him out of that dreadful thing alive."

At the navy yard in Portsmouth, Mrs. Eugene Hoffman broke into uncontrollable sobs. Having maintained an around-the-clock vigil in the pressroom, she had just been informed her husband would not be coming back. Likewise, Mrs. John Chestnutt, who had paced the yard with her young son, broke down when news arrived. "It can't be so!" she shrieked. "Last night I could see John's body floating around in that water out there. I prayed and prayed that it wasn't so." Robert Gibbs's wife, just arrived in Portsmouth after her long train ride, simply stared into space when her husband's death was confirmed.

Nearby, Mary Jane Pierce, the young bride of Carol Nathan Pierce, rejoiced. "When he left me to go on this trip, I told him I wasn't worried—that he was too ornery to die. Please don't misunderstand," she told reporters. "That's just a kidding expression we use around my home town of Kansas City." Mrs. Evelyn Powell, the attractive wife of Carlton Powell, beamed through her tears when he was listed among the rescued. "I had almost given up hope. This is the most wonderful thing in the world," she sobbed in the pressroom.

At sea, the survivors of the first two bells gathered on the Coast Guard cutter *Harriet Lane*, which headed for the navy hospital in Portsmouth. All sixteen appeared to be in relatively good condition, though exhausted. When they arrived at dockside after an hour-long voyage, a guard of marines stood by as 150 spectators watched in silence. The men stepped ashore to awaiting ambulances, although two were carried on stretchers. The wife of one rushed to his side, sobbing, "Oh, you poor kid." Two other women broke through the crowd and kissed one haggard-looking sailor as tears poured down their cheeks.

In the Atlantic, the McCann Rescue Chamber prepared to descend a fourth time to the deck of the *Squalus* for the last group—Naquin and seven others. At 1945, Lieutenant Doyle, Bryson, Persico, and others boarded quickly, Naquin following as the last to leave the ship. The two operators—Mihalowski and James H. McDonald—flooded the lower compartment and then blew the main ballast to give the bell upward buoyancy, which broke its seal with the *Squalus*. At 2014, the bell began its crawl up the downhaul cable. But at the 160-foot level, the chamber inexplicably slowed. "Something's wrong," McDonald reported to the surface. Reversing the motorized winch, the bell moved a few feet down and then stalled, stuck fast. All attempts to budge it failed.

On the *Falcon*, Momsen and McCann exchanged grave expressions, realizing the chamber would have to be pulled up from the *Falcon*. However, the downhaul cable to the *Squalus* held the bell in place. The nine men would have to be lowered to the ocean bottom long enough for a diver to descend to the *Squalus* to cut the cable. "Flood main ballast," McCann ordered over the phone to McDonald. The bell started down with the survivors staring helplessly at the depth gauge. Amid assurances of their safety from the two operators, Naquin and his men said nothing. Clearly, they all were worried as the bell came to a halt, suspended off to the side of the *Squalus* and listing from the sideways tug of the downhaul cable.

On the *Falcon*, Walter H. Squire (CT) prepared to make the dangerous dive. The depth and darkness posed an incredible risk; Squire would have to concentrate amid the mind-numbing sea pressure. Down the grappling line from the *Penacook* he slid until he landed heavily on the submarine three minutes later. He could see the dull light of the rescue chamber nearby, and walked slowly under the beam of a head lamp to the escape hatch where, with difficulty, he managed to break the cable with wire cutters. The rescue chamber swung free like a pendulum, bouncing heavily off the side of the *Squalus*.

McDonald turned to the rattled survivors. "You fellows have really got something to talk about now. A collision between a rescue bell and a submarine at more than 200 feet! It isn't everybody that can tell a story like that."

The crewmen returned his smile but were worried nonetheless. "I was real scared," recounted Persico. "We all were. I remember Bryson mumbling, 'I should have followed my old man's advice when he said to use a mule's ass for a compass and you won't get lost.'" But lost they seemed now, at the end of the *Falcon*'s uphaul cable. McCann ordered the ship's winch to begin bringing up the chamber—slowly. The uphaul proceeded normally until a dozen men on the *Falcon* cried out, "Hold it!" The weight of the rescue chamber on the cable began snapping the steel strands, making them pop like firecrackers until just a single strand remained. Quickly, the chamber was lowered back to the bottom to prevent the cable from breaking altogether, thereby ripping out the air, light, and telephone hoses and thus suffocating the men inside. The bell landed with a thud on the green clay beside the *Squalus*.

Despite the gravity of the situation, the two operators seemed unconcerned, chatting with the survivors on a variety of subjects to take their minds off their predicament. "Here we are nice and steady on the bottom and we've got plenty of good air and lots of light and everything," enthused Mihalowski. As they waited, the survivors laughed about Cravens's crack to McDonald when the first bell arrived. "Say, Mac," he said, "tell them topside to send us down a quart and I don't care whether it's a quart of soup, ice cream, coffee, or whisky." To which another survivor had replied, "Make mine a blonde."

Mihalowski divided some bars of chocolate and passed them around to the survivors. "You know what I want when I get up out of here? I want a steak," said Bryson. McDonald repeated the request to the surface over the phone line as laughter broke out in the rescue bell. "Be sure and have it well done," McDonald instructed over the *Falcon* loudspeaker. Another survivor quickly added, "I'll have mine rare." McDonald kept the conversation going, smacking his lips in exaggeration. "You fellows just think of that juicy steak waiting up there for you. Any particular cut of steak you want?"

Cravens broke into a grin, chuckling, "Just cripple a big, fat steer and let him run past me. I'll get the part I want as he goes by."

Up above, the rescue divers marveled at the merriment piped over the loudspeaker. Rescue chamber operator Orson Crandall commented, "That's the kind of stuff that makes this navy go."

Meanwhile, Cole, Momsen, and McCann discussed what to do. At 2149, diver Jesse E. Duncan (TM1c) was sent over the side with a new cable to attach to the top of the bell. On the way down, his suit caught on the frayed wire. He worked himself free and landed on top of the chamber six minutes into the dive. There his lines became entangled with those to the bell. Duncan struggled frantically to free himself. In the exertion, he nearly slipped off the bell, which would have caused him to plunge head-first onto the ocean floor. That would have killed him instantly, the enormous sea pressure forcing his entire body into his helmet. Now almost incoherent, Duncan was hoisted back to the surface, and another diver was sent over the side. He, too, landed on the roof of the rescue bell but became fouled in the various lines. For 33 minutes, Edward Clayton squirmed to get free and then attempted to attach the new uphaul cable. But again, he got entangled in the lines. The subsequent exertion to free himself caused him to nearly black out. Immediately, Momsen ordered him back to the surface, and called off further attempts to attach the new cable.

There now remained only one possibility of rescuing the rescue bell. By carefully controlling the ballast, the operators could give the chamber just enough buoyancy that it would rise slowly, allowing the frayed cable to be pulled up by hand on the *Falcon*. As McCann relayed orders to blow ballast at 15-second intervals, six men on the *Falcon* gripped the uphaul line and eased it aboard. Ever so slowly, the bell moved higher until it surfaced at 0038 on Thursday May 25, 39 hours after the *Squalus* sinking.

The men, relieved and laughing, were greeted with handshakes from their rescuers plus plenty of hot towels and warm food. Naquin, the last out of the rescue bell, looked up at the beaming face of Momsen. "Welcome aboard, Oliver!" "I am damn glad to be aboard," replied the captain. The survivors later fell into a deep sleep in the *Falcon*'s recompression chamber and were transported the following morning by the *Harriet Lane* to Portsmouth.

The rescue chamber made one more trip to the *Squalus* in the remote chance survivors still were alive in the after torpedo room. For Lt. Halford R. Greenlee, industrial manager of the Portsmouth yard who stood by Cole throughout the rescue operations, it was his only hope that his son-in-law, Ensign Patterson, the *Squalus*'s assistant engineering officer and track star, might still be alive.

A diver was sent back down to the *Squalus,* carrying with him a new downhaul cable. Making his way along the deck, he finally reached the after torpedo room escape hatch and attached the cable. Badders and Mihalowski were chosen to make the descent in the bell, aware that it could be the most perilous of all: If the after torpedo room were dry, would poisonous CO_2 trapped inside swiftly overcome Badders and Mihalowski? Or, if the room was flooded, would the seawater inside surge into the rescue chamber, drowning the two operators? The chamber made a normal descent, with Badders attaching the four bolts to hold the bell to the submarine. He then prepared to open the hatch.

"Well, Skee, stand by for anything," Badders said to Mihalowski. "Here she goes."

Turning the hand wheel on the hatch cover, Badders loosened it. It began to tremble from compressed air in the interior. A blast of air rushed into the bell before the hatch was entirely unsealed, followed by a geyser of water that quickly buried Badders to waist deep. Mihalowski reacted instantaneously, venting more compressed air into the bell from the surface to push the seawater back into the *Squalus.* It saved Badders's life.

The two operators were certain now that the entire torpedo room was flooded. Yet, orders came down from the *Falcon* for Badders to lift the hatch cover and look inside—just to be sure. As the hatch was undogged, Badders stared down at the sight of a completely water-filled hold, thus confirming the death toll. There was nothing left to do now but return despondently to the surface.

In Portsmouth, a large crowd greeted the last group of survivors. Naquin, who reminded many of the stereotypical Hollywood sub captain with his tall, erect stature, waved but wouldn't repeat the gesture at the urging of photographers. He insisted his men go ashore first. Then he stepped onto the gang plank and started toward his wife. The mother of two young children, she had been very tense, verging on collapse. Now, she worried that photographers would spoil what she felt should be a private moment. Motioning to the cameramen, she mouthed to him as he approached, "Don't kiss me, don't kiss me." But he did so anyway. The captain waved off the ambulance ride, preferring instead to travel with his wife by sedan to the hospital.

There, the survivors, dressed in pajamas and bathrobes, faced reporters. Maness told of his heroics in closing the control room door which saved the 33 survivors. But in the end, all insisted each man had acted in accordance with his training. "There were no heroes," said Nat Pierce. "A guy is trained to do something. And he does it or he dies." Lieutenant Nichols said, "It was a living hell, but nobody made any dramatic speeches." Naquin, dressed in a bathrobe like the others, unshaven and his hair disheveled, quietly discussed the rescue. "My officers and men performed 100 per cent. There was never any doubt in my mind at all that we would come up, especially after we heard from the *Sculpin* that the *Falcon* was under way. The *Sculpin* was over us first and did some grand work." He added that, in his opinion, he and all the others owed their lives to Maness.

To honor twenty-six men entombed in the *Squalus,* the *Brooklyn* and *Semmes* sent up a twenty-one-gun salute which roared over the waters hiding the boat on May 30, Memorial Day. Simultaneously, the thirty-three survivors gathered at a tiny hillside cemetery in Kittery to pay homage. The navy yard chaplain led them in prayer as a shaft of sunlight broke through gray clouds, illuminating the spring greenery. A marine detachment fired three traditional volleys that echoed down the Piscataqua. A plaintive bugle played "Taps."

Out on the Atlantic, Ruth De Sautel, 20, laid a wreath on the ocean above the *Squalus* in memory of Sherman Shirley of Little Rock, Arkansas.

It was the day they were to have been married.

Birth of the "Ghost Ship"

Within days of deliverance off the Isles of Shoals, successive submarine tragedies claimed 329 lives. In the Bungo Channel of southeast Japan, eighty-one perished aboard the Japanese *I-63*. Sixty-three died on the French boat *Phenix* in a practice dive off Indochina. And, on June 1—only six days after the *Squalus* rescue—the new British sub HMS *Thetis* went down during a practice dive in Liverpool Bay. Although the boat was 160 feet deep by the bow, its after hatch was only a few feet below surface. Nonetheless, ninety-nine men had no means of escape and suffocated. Scorn was heaped on the British navy for being unable to reach the trapped men. Many felt the admiralty could have saved the men had it only copied the McCann Rescue Chamber. One *Falcon* diver agreed. "They could have had them. It's never been a secret."

Now, with the *Squalus* as a shining example of what could be done to save trapped submariners, new respect was found for the U.S. Navy. Newspapers trumpeted the amazing rescue. "A splendid page in the annals of the U.S. Navy," said the *Illustrated London News*. "The American Navy has accomplished a feat of seamanship which deserves universal acclaim," enthused *Boerson Zeitung* in submarine-conscious Nazi

Germany. Similarly, the *Deutsche Allgemeine Zeitung* noted, "The achievements of the rescue crew in those tense hours will be counted among the most impressive peacetime accomplishments of the United States Navy."

In the glow of their rescue, the survivors and Momsen's divers were hailed as national heroes. For their unprecedented feat, rescue-bell operators Mihalowski, McDonald, Badders, and Orson L. Crandall (CB) were awarded Congressional Medals of Honor in elaborate ceremonies in Washington. At Little Boar's Head near Portsmouth, famed conductor Arthur Fiedler and the Boston Pops Orchestra staged a benefit concert. Merchants in the Kittery-Portsmouth area donated to the cause and forgave debts owed by the families of the deceased. Meanwhile, each of the survivors expressed determination to go back into submarines just as soon as possible. "Well," said ship's cook Isaacs to one reporter, "the safety record still looks impressive to me. It took something like a hundred thousand dives in our navy before we had our accident, and that's a good enough record for me."

But Naquin, who took command of the *Squalus* to accelerate his career, wondered whether he ever again would command a ship. Nothing could wreck a naval career more quickly than a ship you commanded, especially a new one, being sunk. The captain, like his crew, was certain a mechanical malfunction of the induction valve had doomed the *Squalus*. Over and over, he rehearsed the fatal dive in his mind, each time coming away with no sense of guilt. "I know that I reacted correctly. We all did," he later said. But would the Navy's court of inquiry agree? Or would human error be cited? Or was sabotage to blame as auto mogul Henry Ford conjectured, saying it was a plot by munitions makers to get America into the war in Europe?

Hearings got under way in Portsmouth on June 19 under Rear Adm. W. T. Tarrant. For a week, each of the thirty-three survivors appeared before investigators after filing a written report of the accident. Alfred G. Prien (MM2c) testified he closed the induction valve lever as soon as the engine rooms reported the diesel engines had shut down. He said the control board lights were all green, indicating the induction had closed. Doyle and Preble also testified that, yes, the Christmas Tree was definitely green. Pierce told of how he bled air into the boat to assure the induction was closed; a rise of the ship barometer proved the hull was airtight as the dive began. Why the high induction opened seconds later was inexplicable.

Naquin was on the stand for an entire day, describing in detail what happened on May 23. The induction must have been closed, he said, because the *Squalus* had passed the 50-foot mark before it began to flood. The captain accompanied the court to the *Sculpin* where he demonstrated the sequence he followed during his boat's last dive. One hearing examiner focused on why the inboard induction valves were not closed prior to the dive. A survivor told of the laborious process of winding them shut with hand wheels, making it impossible to get them closed in time during a quick dive. The practice on the boat was to leave them open, relying on the high induction to seal off the ship. The court suspended the hearings to await the salvage of the boat, after which it intended to inspect the induction before issuing its findings.

For the Navy, the rescue was a much needed morale boost, particularly in view of the earlier *S-4* and *S-51* disasters, which earned the service so much wrath. The sinking of the *Squalus* did nothing to diminish the Navy's enthusiasm for its fleet submarines. Within days of the rescue, bids were opened for three new submarines, nearly identical to SS-192. Simultaneously, the *Sealion* (SS-195) was launched at the Electric Boat Company in New London, and the War Department decided to try and refloat its $4.3-million investment lying on the floor of the Atlantic.

Efforts to raise the *Squalus* got under way immediately. Permanent descent lines for the salvage divers were dropped from the *Falcon* to the submarine. Officers in Portsmouth requisitioned all the pressure hoses, tools, spare parts, and other devices needed to bring the boat back to the surface unscathed. But the task of doing so from such depth was daunting. Aboard the *Brooklyn* at anchor near the *Falcon* and *Sculpin*, Capt. Richard S. Edwards, senior aide for the salvage unit, explained:

"We hope to drag the *Squalus* under water, using pontoons, until she grounds herself stern first in about 160 feet of water some two miles nearer Portsmouth. Four pontoons will be suspended over the stern, attached to chains under the hull, and two pontoons will be placed over the bow. These pontoons will be blown with compressed air, and fuel and ballast tanks inside the *Squalus* will be blown. The submarine will then be lifted partially off the bottom as the pontoons seek the surface.

"It is not going to be an easy job, or a simple one. We know that it would be dangerous to bring the *Squalus* up in a single lift at this depth. One end always surfaces first when a large submarine is being lifted from the bottom and if that happened in 240 feet, she might take such an angle that nearly all the air in the main ballast tanks would be spilled out and permit her to sink again, despite the pontoons."

Edwards described how a series of tows would be used until the *Squalus* was in 100 feet of water. At that point, fifty hard-hat divers could work comfortably and the submarine would be brought to the surface and towed into Portsmouth by the *Wandank*. "That is the plan on paper," he noted. "Remember our divers must work in cold water in a pressure that will crush a log into pulp. Above all, we must guard against permitting the submarine to rise too rapidly. It calls for plenty of hard work, not to mention our full share of luck."

With the *Squalus* survivors as hose and line handlers on the *Falcon*, the plan was to have divers descend to the ocean floor alongside the boat, then fasten the chain slings around the hull. Doing that at the bow was no problem since it protruded off the ocean floor. But the stern was mired 18 feet into the Atlantic mud. It was clear the divers would have to tunnel under the hull. Momsen had hoped to use normal compressed air for the descents. But the first divers experienced delusions and dizzy spells. Forrest E. Smith (B1c) blacked out from nitrogen narcosis, a numbing of the mind caused by nitrogen in his bloodstream. At the surface, nitrogen—which makes up 80 percent of the atmosphere— is present in the human bloodstream at only very low concentrations. However, under extreme pressure such as the divers faced, the gas is squeezed to the point it freely enters the bloodstream along with life-sustaining oxygen. Once inside the body, the gas can cause hallucinations.

After Smith was pulled up from the bottom, Crandall was sent over the side. He too suffered from narcosis, calling out football signals from the hull of the submarine. A third diver mistook his air hose and life line for an obstructing cable and attempted to cut them with his knife. Both men were quickly yanked up to shallower depths to avert injury or death.

To Momsen, there was no alternative but try a new approach. "It was clearly indicated that we had little chance of success unless we used helium," he later wrote. The experimental air developed at the Washington Navy Yard replaced nitrogen with helium. Simulated test dives proved the helium eliminated narcosis, even when divers descended to depths twice that of the *Squalus*. In fact, it made all the difference. The divers sent down to the *Squalus* suffered none of the mental aberrations of before. The only drawback was communication to the surface: Helium affected the vocal cords, making each diver sound like Donald Duck over the *Falcon* loudspeaker.

Day after day, Momsen's team descended in rotations to the stern of the craft where, using a tunneling lance made of seven sections of pipe shaped to the contour of the hull, they blew pressurized water and air under the boat until the pipe emerged on the other side of the submarine, nearly a month after salvage work began. Three thin steel cables, like plumber's snakes, were pushed through the pipe to create slings that would be used to pull three battleship chains under the stern between the hull and propeller shafts. Similarly, two chain slings were fastened under the bow near the diving planes. Finally, the five chains—each link weighing 75 pounds—encircled the submarine, and passed upward through a series of gigantic, submerged pontoons. More than a dozen—each made of steel and sheathed in protective wood, 14 feet in diameter and 32 feet long, with compartments that could be flooded or blown with air to control buoyancy—would be needed to lift the boat. The pontoons were clustered at various levels on the chains that led to the *Falcon*.

With the *Sculpin* used as a schooling boat on the surface, the divers worked in 20-minute shifts, attaching scores of air hoses to the pontoons and control valves on the deck of the *Squalus*. The work was difficult and exacting, carried out in the daytime when sunlight barely illuminated the ocean bottom. The divers' courage and stamina were tested.

Chief Torpedoman W. H. Squire, one of the largest divers in the crew, overexerted during the tunneling. He lost consciousness while inflating his suit and passed through the normal 90-foot decompression without stopping. He bobbed to the surface with his suit blown to twice its size. The diver's arms and legs were stretched straight out, and compressed air roared out of his helmet.

McDonald, who operated the fateful fourth rescue bell, dived overboard, fully clothed. Reaching Squire, he climbed atop the diver's inflated suit where he shut off the air control value and then, with a knife, ripped through the canvas to deflate it. Simultaneously, a winch on the *Falcon* pulled the diving platform up underneath the unconscious diver. McDonald yanked the unconscious diver onto the platform and then rode with him as it was hoisted aboard ship. There, Squire's helmet was yanked off, catching his nose and causing it to bleed. There was no time to delay as McDonald and others carried the prone body to the recompression chamber where two doctors and a pharmacist's mate were waiting. "If they had not done that as quickly as they did," said Bland who watched from the deck, "it would have been just a short time until his lungs would have expanded from the helium and probably killed him. McDonald was smart enough to know that when he jumped over the side."

McDonald joined the three attendants inside the chamber as it recompressed to 190 feet deep. "When Squire regained consciousness," said Bland who could see the scene through the chamber's eyeports, "he was incoherent and became wild. It took all four men to restrain him. They had to humor him as if he was still on the dive." At one point, Squire saw a telephone cord hanging down inside the chamber. Thinking it was a life-line to the surface, he threw the four men off of him and tried to climb up the cord. Exhausted, he finally fell back, still incoherent. Slowly, the four men coaxed the diver back to the "surface," where his breathing eased and he realized he was in the recompression chamber. Looking at the faces staring in at him through the eyeports, he waved feebly and grinned, knowing the chamber and McDonald's quick action had saved his life.

Through hundreds of other dives, few additional mishaps occurred. One diver had to go through recompression as a safeguard when he complained of stomach cramps caused by residual helium bubbles trapped in his bloodstream. Occasionally the divers got fouled in their lines, or had difficulty maneuvering the pontoons and attaching the many pneumatic hoses that would be needed to lift the boat. And there was always the disruption of summer squalls during which the *Squalus* survivors would have to disconnect the air hoses from the *Falcon* and attach buoys to the ends before throwing them overboard to keep them from snapping.

The salvagers made slow but methodical progress. Sighed Momsen, "You know, I think it must be the gnomes down there that are holding up the works. They don't like to have us infringing in their domain." To which Captain Edwards replied, "We've got to be more respectful of the gnomes." The salvage unit picked up on Momsen's vignette, the divers referring to "ga-nomies" each time difficulties were encountered.

Finally, on the morning of July 13, all was in readiness to raise the *Squalus*. The Navy had arranged for heavy media coverage, with photographers, motion-picture cameramen, and reporters stationed on vessels a safe distance from the *Falcon*. The weather was perfect, the ocean a glassy expanse as the *Sculpin* eased in alongside the *Falcon* so the air compressors of both vessels could be linked together to power the coming lift. From the air manifold on the bridge of the *Falcon*, more than two miles of air hose seemed like a pile of black spaghetti, falling overboard into the ocean.

From 0930 until 1450, the preliminary blow began to the pontoons and ballast tanks of the *Squalus*, producing a large circle of effervescent water foaming around the *Falcon*. Below, the submarine's water-filled stern rose 80 feet off the ocean floor, buoyed by the stern pontoons, just as planned. However the boat's cantilevering caused her nose to descend into the mud, becoming mired. The forward pontoons and fuel tanks of the sub were blown clear to try to bring the bow to the same level as the stern so that the tow could begin. For more than an hour, as winds picked up and the ocean became choppy, the blow continued without success; the mud would not relinquish its hold on the *Squalus*. The divers decided to blow the main ballast tank. "If that doesn't break her nose out of the mud, nothing will," said one.

White water began to boil furiously on the surface in a widening circle as air from the *Falcon* poured down into the largest tank of the submarine. Divers, reporters, and survivors stared, mesmerized, wondering what would happen next. "There was a tremendous roaring of air coming up. The water was just boiling from the air. Then the pontoons started coming up. It was frightening," recalled McLees. "The water was boiling and bubbling and we just knew something was going wrong."

Admiral Cole on the bridge of the *Falcon* cupped his hands over his mouth in shock as geysers of water shot 30 feet into the air from pontoons popping to the surface unexpectedly. The hissing sound of compressed air split the atmosphere. Clouds of spray spewed above the commotion. And then, the black bow of the *Squalus* lunged vertically from the surf, out of control, like a great, wounded creature of the deep. At a 60-degree angle, she hung there, 30 feet above the surface, water cascading from her forward torpedo tubes and "192" clearly visible on her bow. She seemed alive, trying to shake cables tethering her to pontoons that bobbed wildly about her. Then she slid backwards and disappeared. "The boat came up so fast and then went back down so fast, we didn't know what to think. We were stunned," McLees said.

The carefully rigged cradle to the *Squalus* now was in shambles as the submarine plunged back to the ocean bottom. Hoses aboard the *Falcon* uncoiled in a frenzy. Pontoons on the surface shook violently from the compressed air inside them. Crewmen with axes chopped the air lines on the *Falcon* as divers in small surf boats risked their lives to chase the pontoons and climb aboard to close the valves to keep them from sinking. All the while they bucked in the sea, one flipping on the top of another, propelled by the air venting from them. Miraculously, none of the divers was injured, although one pontoon was lost.

That night, as a storm raged overhead, despondence gripped the men aboard the *Falcon*. Forty-five days of hard work had come to naught. In Portsmouth, when the news arrived, *Squalus* survivor Lieutenant Nichols, tears in his eyes, told Booth, the boat's radioman, "The bow got away from them." For the next few days, the *Falcon* crew sorted out the ship's 13,600 feet of tangled air hose. During the cleanup, a wire rope from the *Falcon* to the *Squalus* slipped off a roller and slashed out across deck. Momsen and others ducked just in time. But Lloyd E. Anderson (GM1c) was struck in the abdomen and had to be rushed to shore for emergency treatment.

As the days stretched into weeks, the salvage unit finally rerigged the pontoons and air hoses to the *Squalus,* this time with a sixth battleship chain slung around the bow. On August 12, reporters and photographers again were ferried to the site where conditions were ideal. The lift proceeded perfectly to the cheers of the salvage crew. The boat hung from the pontoons on an even keel 80 feet above the Atlantic floor and 160 feet below the surface.

The *Wandank* got under way, towing the sub—stern first—to the intended grounding area two miles closer to shore. The ship used a path mapped out earlier by the *Sculpin* which charted the ocean floor all the way back to Portsmouth. Naquin and the *Squalus*'s quartermaster took bearings every two minutes from the *Falcon,* which trailed overhead, her many air hoses still attached to the *Squalus.* Unexpectedly, the submarine grounded a bit short of its destination due to an unmarked pinnacle 10 feet higher than the intended grounding depth.

The following day, a summer storm stymied divers from going down to prepare the *Squalus* for the third lift. President Roosevelt, on a vacation cruise aboard the cruiser *Tuscaloosa* (CA-37), set anchor near the *Falcon.* The president was anxious to visit the 400 men of the salvage crew but was unable to do so because of the rough surf. Instead, Cole and a small party of officers made the trip over to the cruiser. Later, as the *Tuscaloosa* pulled away, Roosevelt radioed congratulations to the men: "Am greatly pleased with the efficient and arduous services performed by the officers and men of your unit. Well done!"

On August 15, divers returned to the *Squalus* and made a startling discovery. A hatch over the after battery was undogged and open. Had someone tried to escape? Most believed it had somehow sprung open when the *Squalus* fell back to the sea floor following the first lift.

In the days to come, the salvagers prepared the submarine for the third lift to the 100-foot level. At one point, the *Squalus* survivors dreamily watched from the *Falcon* as the *Sargo* (SS-188) stood in to make a test dive nearby. Harold Preble monitored the dive from the sub's control room, becoming the first of the survivors to return to submarine service. Gunner's mate Cravens, pausing with his shipmates to view the dive, muttered how much he wished he were aboard the *Sargo.* The men of the *Squalus* were a dispirited lot. The U.S. Comptroller General had ruled they were not entitled to extra pay for submarine duty, retroactive to the moment the submarine came to rest on the sea bottom. Despite vigorous protests from the Navy Department, which argued how hard the survivors were working to salvage their boat, the ruling stood. Isaacs, speaking for the other survivors, was downcast. "We've been docked our extra pay right back to the time we were on the bottom. We certainly were aboard our vessel then."

On August 17, the third lift occurred without problems and the *Wandank* towed the *Squalus* until she again grounded five miles closer to shore. Divers went over the side, this time to attach the necessary equipment to finally bring the boat to the surface. As September arrived, gales blew with fury out of the Gulf of Maine, producing giant combers that smashed against the *Falcon*. For days, the divers battled the elements. Clouds of silt stirred up by the storms obliterated their view as they walked the deck of the *Squalus* and the ocean floor. The submarine rocked side to side from the power of the ocean. Two divers, working near the keel, narrowly escaped death when the vessel moved, crushing the area they had just been in.

Two other divers were sent down in an attempt to enter the submarine from the after escape hatch. If they could somehow get to the watertight door between the after torpedo room and the engine room and close it, then the engine room water level could be reduced by pumping compressed air into the compartment. The men landed in a cloud of silt near the hatch cover that had been broken earlier by a collision between a pontoon and the boat. One of the divers dropped his legs into the escape trunk and proceeded to climb down into the vessel but was stopped by an obstruction. He climbed back out. Both divers lowered a light into the hatch so they could see what the problem was. To their horror, the face of one of the victims stared back at them. The plan to enter the ship was abandoned.

At last, on September 13—113 days and 628 hard-hat dives after the salvage began—the last lift was set. After weeks of relentless surf, the day broke with warm sunshine and a flat ocean surface. At 0800, the blowing of the pontoons and the *Squalus* began. Naquin was excited, preparing his men to board the vessel after it was on the surface. "He was real hot for all of us to ride the *Squalus* back in," said McLees.

But all didn't go as planned. Several times the conning tower emerged from the waves but keeled over and sank. By blowing and venting the many pontoons, the boat finally came to the surface and stayed there on a slight list. But only the conning tower and tip of the bow remained above water, foiling Naquin's plan. Too much water remained in the submarine to bring her any higher.

At 1511, Admiral Cole gave the order to begin the final tow. With flags at half-staff in memory of those inside the *Squalus*, the *Wandank* and her tiny flotilla headed for port in a solemn procession. As the sun began to set, the *Squalus* and her pontoons slowly moved up the Piscataqua River as thousands of people lined the hills and beaches overlooking the channel. The submarine, her central tower with "192" visible to all, slid past silently.

By nightfall, the *Wandank* nudged the boat carefully past the rocks of Pull-and-be-damned Point and brought her to a gentle grounding next to a coal refueling pier at the navy yard. There, a gargantuan tripod crane lowered a cable to the conning tower where it was attached to the boat. Then the crane exerted upward pull as the process of pumping out the water began. It took the rest of that night, the following day, and into the next night before the vessel could be floated into a drydock, which was drained to expose the entire vessel. The forward part of the conning tower was smashed inward. Wire strands littered the deck, and her hull appeared splotched and rusty in places. But otherwise she seemed undamaged.

More water had to be siphoned from the boat before the medical corps could go in to retrieve the bodies. "They had no choice but to put a big firehose down into the boat to take the water out," recounted Bland. "Who do you think had to do that job? The survivors! No one balked but we saw so many people standing around on the dock we thought they could have found someone else to go down there. We had been fearful all along that they would have us take the bodies off."

A group of eight survivors entered through the forward torpedo room, dragging the firehose behind them as they moved through the forward battery, the control room, and then into the after battery. "There weren't but two or three bodies in there," continued Bland. "Nevertheless, we saw them. It was revolting to the point I never made any effort to stretch myself to see them."

The men immediately returned to the dock as the pumping resumed. The bodies of the men in the after battery were taken from the vessel by medical corpsmen. Later in the day, pharmacist's mates from the hospital located the rest of the deceased. One was in the well of the after battery and two were in the after engine room. In the after torpedo room, the rest were found, including the compartment talker who was still wearing his telephone headset. Autopsies concluded the shock from the pressure of the water pounding in on the men, plus the frigid temperature, induced merciful comas before they died from drowning. Could they have saved themselves? "I think the men in the torpedo room didn't have the guts to close the door on the two in the engine room," speculated Pierce. "They left the door open too damned long and they all drowned."

One body was missing. He later was identified as Thompson, the ship's cook, who had undogged the submarine's after battery hatch in an ill-fated attempt to escape the morning of the tragedy. His body apparently was thrown from the open hatch during the first lift; many believed the corpse was driven into the mud by the boat as she settled to the floor again.

On September 15, the court of inquiry reconvened to tour the submarine in hopes of determining what caused the sinking. Donning oilskins, a group of eleven—four investigators, five newspaper reporters, Captain Naquin, and Lieutenant Doyle—entered the vessel through the after torpedo hatch. Cables and paraphernalia were heaped about from the jostling the boat had taken. The group passed waterlogged mattresses, clothing, blankets, door curtains, and tablecloths. A greasy film coated almost everything. In the galley, Isaacs's pots and pans and the range on which he had been cooking the noontime meal were corroded by saltwater. A frozen cube of butter floated in a pool of water. Single file, the observers passed through the control room, where the induction valve lever was found in the closed position, and on to the forward battery where they saw a message scrolled in pencil by Preble on a stateroom door: "11 degrees up, 0925. Taking food, etc., to for'd torpr. room. All fine as can be expected. Capt. Naquin, Robie and Nichols for'd." The party returned to the control room, where they closely examined the induction control. With power restored, the court had Doyle try to close the high induction. The valve didn't budge. Workmen then applied oil to the hydraulic system. Doyle again pushed the lever to engage the valve and this time it closed tightly, as it should have during the fatal dive.

Why it didn't on May 23 could not be resolved.

While the court adjourned to prepare its findings, the *Squalus* survivors fanned out across the country, accompanying the bodies of their shipmates to their hometowns for burial. The Navy tried to carefully pair each body with a close survivor to help comfort relatives. For instance, Pierce traveled to Jackson, Michigan, to deliver the flag-draped coffin bearing his good friend Eugene Hoffman. The man's widow, previously broken-hearted over her inability to bear Hoffman a child, grieved deeply over his death. "She met me at the train and started crying when she saw me, someone she knew. It was real tough. But I was so glad that I had the privilege of taking him back and that it meant so much to her," said Pierce. Another widow, Bette Ward of Drumright, Oklahoma, mourned as the body of her husband, Marion L. Ward (RM3c), was returned to her. Two months later she gave birth to his $7\frac{1}{2}$-pound baby son.

The court of inquiry cleared Naquin and his men of any wrongdoing, and praised the captain's leadership during the ordeal. The court attributed the sinking to a mechanical malfunction of the main induction valve. It recommended several modifications to all fleet boats to avert future incidents. An additional bulkhead and watertight door were to be installed in every boat to separate the forward and after engine rooms. Also, the hand-cranked valves in the engine rooms were to be replaced by quick-closing, spring-driven inboard shut-off valves. Actuating mechanisms of the new valves would be located far enough from the hull openings that a rush of seawater would not prevent anyone from closing them.

Many of the *Squalus* rates later expressed the belief that the court exonerated the crew after it became aware of incidents on the *Snapper* off South America and the *Skipjack* (SS-184), where the main induction took in a small amount of water on a test dive. The *Skipjack* crew, made wary by the incident, kept the hull valves well oiled in the engine rooms so they could be spun shut quickly. "The *Skipjack* people were more knowledgeable about the problem, were more fearful of what could happen or were just smarter than we were. They shut those valves on a dive," said Bryson years later. Doyle admitted it was "a damned dumb thing" not to have closed the inboard hull valves before the *Squalus*'s last dive. He said he was unaware of the *Snapper* incident, but "I wish I would have known."

Charles Edison, the secretary of the Navy, accepted the court's overall findings. However, he faulted Naquin for not training his men to always close inboard inductions prior to a dive. He concluded "the training, supervision and indoctrination, necessary to ensure the timely closure of these important hull stop valves, while diving, was lacking in emphasis." For Naquin, it was a bitter footnote, particularly since so many other boats operated no differently than his.

The survivors initially were barred from submarine duty; plans were made to transfer all of them to surface ships. Outraged, Naquin went to Washington to appeal the decision to Edison. The secretary reversed course, allowing all but the captain and his executive to rejoin the undersea navy.

In coming weeks, Portsmouth workers swarmed over the *Squalus*, removing all of her internal components, irreparably damaged by saltwater. On November 15, 1939, the noise of air drills and hammers ceased while the boat was moored next to the *Sculpin*. Naquin, lieutenants Doyle, Robertson, and Nichols, and twenty-eight other survivors mustered on deck for the last time. The boat's commissioning pennant fluttered in the cold wind as the skipper prepared to address the crew. Naquin was about to be detached and sent to San Diego, while the rest of the crew was to be assigned temporarily to the sub school in New London. A marine color guard marched down the slope to the dock where they stood at attention for the arrival of Admiral Cole and three aides. "Attention!" Naquin ordered. The survivors, dressed in winter blues, formed two lines at the deck rails, standing rigidly, their heads turned slightly toward the captain who stood before the conning tower. He unfolded a sheet of paper and began to read in a strong voice, "The Chief of Naval Operations expresses his appreciation to the commanding officer, the officers, and men of the USS *Squalus* for their wholehearted and voluntary participation in the salvage operations."

The survivors cracked a smile at Naquin, who tucked the short speech into his pocket and took an order passed to him. In the brief silence, the survivors stirred, turning their faces directly to the captain as he began to read the decommissioning order that would take the *Squalus* out of the fleet. He went through it quickly, turning the boat over to the captain of the yard. The order released each crewman to duty elsewhere. A solitary bugle sounded "Retreat" as the commissioning pennant that had once held so much promise was lowered permanently.

Soon after, the *Sculpin* under Wilkin cast off for the Pacific to join the fleet at Pearl Harbor. The $1.4-million refit of the SS-192 resumed, a process that would take another year.

With the reconditioning of the *Squalus* coming to an end in May 1940, the Navy decided to give the boat a new name to diminish her sad legacy. Inspiration came from President Roosevelt's reference to a Pulitzer Prize–winning photograph of the *Squalus* shooting up through the surface in the disastrous first lift of the boat. Roosevelt, an avid deepsea fisherman, said the picture reminded him of a tethered sailfish battling for its life.

Thus was born the USS *Sailfish*. And at the helm would be a tough new commander. In him, the Navy placed the task of shaking the boat's early reputation as a "ghost ship," a vessel doomed to repeat her fate.

PART TWO

The Last Dive of the *Sculpin*

You say I'm punchy? You'd be too,
  If you'd been with me in '42,
So just sit still 'till my tale is told
  Of a submarine on war patrol.

"THE FIRST WAR PATROL," FOUND
ON A LOCKER TOP ABOVE TORPEDO
SKIDS OF USS *CACHALOT* (V-8)

War Games in Paradise

Danny Persico often pondered the irony of his years in the submarine service. "When I was on the bottom in the *Squalus,* the American Navy did everything possible to save me. During the war, when we were being depth charged, the Japanese navy was doing everything possible to destroy me." He and others, of course, couldn't have predicted the horrors to befall them. But even in 1939, conflict in Europe and Asia foretold an ominous future for the *Squalus* survivors and the men of the *Sailfish* and *Sculpin.*

On the day the *Wandank* churned up the Piscataqua River with the battered *Squalus* in tow, Nazi infantry had overrun Poland. By June of the following year, France, Denmark, Norway, Belgium, Luxembourg, and Holland had fallen, while Italy, allying itself with Berlin, conquered Greece and invaded British Somaliland to keep the pressure on. By late 1940, England was fighting for its very life, seemingly alone, as the United States maintained a stubborn neutralist position. For Japan, it was an unprecedented opportunity to expand its war with China and perhaps seize the oil-rich East Indies.

Taken together, the events of 1939–40 made it abundantly clear the U.S. Navy would need every ship it could muster—including the *Sailfish.* Her eight-

77

month refit proceeded in earnest as managers at shipyards in Portsmouth and elsewhere began to recruit metalworkers, welders, pipe-fitters, machinists, and electricians for the rapidly expanding submarine construction program.

Still, during the winter of 1940 in Portsmouth, war seemed unthinkable. The biggest news in town was the Navy's decision to rename the boat the *Sailfish*. Dockworkers and enlisted men didn't miss a beat, dubbing her the *"Squailfish"* to the unending annoyance of the top brass. Yet, it was a moniker that was to follow her all the rest of her days.

In view of the vessel's past, the Navy sought an iron-handed skipper, and it found him in Lt. Cdr. Morton Claire Mumma Jr. At age 36, Mumma was a soft-spoken, no-nonsense, by-the-book leader, known unofficially as "Summary Courtsmartial Mumma" for the frequency with which he once handed out punishment for shipboard infractions. "Mort Mumma was a tough skipper," said Lt. Joseph R. Tucker, who served as the *Sailfish's* communications officer. "He demanded nothing but top performance out of his officers. He frequently gave us all hell for no apparent reason, but he did it because he thought it would improve the performance of the ship."

That hard-driving determination made Mumma one of the fleet's most respected skippers, a man with a fine sense of humor and well liked among his peers, but very precise and rather humorless aboard the *Sailfish*. Commanding a submarine, especially one with SS-192's history, demanded precision and maximum caution—just what the Navy was seeking in those prewar years when so few warships were available because of the international disarmament treaties of the 1920s and 1930s.

Mumma, born in Manila in 1904, the son of an Army colonel, followed his father into military service. He entered Annapolis in 1921 where, as a plebe, he gained quick recognition as the captain of the Academy's rifle team. After graduation in 1925, he served successively in the *Colorado* (BB-45), the *Marcus* (DD-321), the *Dale* (DD-290), and the *Dallas* (DD-199). Like Naquin and Wilkin, he was eager for command of his own ship and thus enrolled in submarine school in 1927. He later served in the submarines *0-6* (SS-67), *S-9* (SS-114), and *S-23* (SS-128), and finally commanded the *S-43* (SS-154).

The new skipper of the *Sailfish* assembled a crew with few ties to the old *Squalus*. He passed over most of the survivors, choosing only a handful, including Eugene Cravens, Gerald McLees, Leonard de Medeiros, and Lloyd Maness (who later transferred off the boat prior to the war). The others were disappointed as they reported for duty on other boats.

"A lot of us applied to go back aboard the *Sailfish*, but Mort Mumma said he didn't want any cliques on the boat," said Carl Bryson. The skipper was not only bent on putting together a new crew, he was determined to eliminate any references to the *Squalus*. He tolerated no dark jokes among the rates or any discussion of the earlier history of the boat. "Mumma wanted to avoid thoughts of 'ill-fated.' All mention in the media about the *Squalus* was always prefixed by that word. It was an old, old seafaring superstition," said *Sailfish* electrician Lester Bayles (CEM/AA).

So determined was he to leave the *Squalus* legacy behind that Mumma blistered whenever anyone dared refer to the submarine as the *Squailfish*. He quartered no on-board foolishness and trained his men to the point of exhaustion. "Morton C. did favors for no one," according to the boat's quartermaster, Claude E. Braun (CQM-PA), who came to admire the captain's dedication. "He was a stickler—an absolute disciplinarian."

Who could really blame him, taking command of one of the most notorious submarines in naval history? Mumma knew command of this vessel would be formidable because of the sinking and the whispered mutterings that the boat was sure to sink again.

On May 15, 1940, the submarine was recommissioned and training began for the new crew. Coming and going on the Piscataqua, the *Sailfish* was a curiosity, viewed with awe by those who would never forget the events of the previous year. In September, trial dives began in the Atlantic with *Squalus* civilian survivor Preble aboard. The boat performed flawlessly. On January 16, 1941, she embarked for San Diego escorted by two destroyers. After a brief stopover, she headed west to Hawaii, mooring alongside the *Sculpin* at the submarine base in Pearl Harbor in March 1941.

Hawaii, to many crewmen, was unimaginably beautiful. The men of the two boats bunked together at the base in a gray, three-story barracks with screened-in porches framed by towering coconut palms. Trade winds blowing in over the inland Koolaupoko mountain range of Oahu set the palms in motion above the clear waters of a large swimming pool fronting the barracks where the crews engaged in water-polo. "It was like paradise," said McLees. "The weather, the pool, the palm trees—that was something I had never experienced. I remember when I was in boot camp, the names of forty men who were being transferred to Pearl Harbor were posted on the bulletin board. I don't think there was a one of us who even knew where Pearl Harbor was. We never even heard of it."

George Rocek, a native of Cicero, Illinois, and an engineman on the *Sculpin,* remembers how excited he was when Diamond Head came into view as the submarine put in at Pearl Harbor in 1940. "I got a pair of binoculars, expecting to see hula girls in grass skirts like you'd see in the magazines," said Rocek. "I was so surprised. There wasn't a one to be seen."

The submarine force at Pearl was headed by Rear Adm. Thomas Withers Jr., a kindly veteran of World War I submarines. He established a rigorous program of practice torpedo drills and trial dives for the thirty-three fleet subs under his command. He realized a whole generation of submariners had come of age who were woefully unprepared for combat. He insisted the boats dive to their maximum test depth—250 feet for the fleet boats. He took his skippers up in aircraft to demonstrate just how clearly an enemy pilot could see a submarine at the normal depth of 100 feet. Withers was aware of the need to steel his crews to combat conditions, so he made training as realistic as possible. At sea, during weeks of constant exercises, the *Sailfish* and *Sculpin* were depth-charged by friendly ships to acquaint the crews with the bone-rattling, mind-testing feel of war (although the charges exploded a safe distance away). Pilots also dropped "firecracker" bombs on any submarine they happened to spot; one boat surfaced with an unexploded bomb resting on her deck.

Amid these stressful tactics, the admiral secretly shared with his captains some confidence-building information. The Navy had a top-secret weapon—the Mark VI magnetic exploder for its improved Mark XIV torpedo. The mechanism was designed to detonate by just passing close to any metal-hulled warship. If Japan pursued a naval conflict, Withers said, it would rue the day. The Mark VI gave the force a decided edge.

Nevertheless, naval strategy at that time called for submarines not to expose their periscopes, but rather to depend on passive submerged listening and sonar "pinging" to track target ships—despite estimates that one of every eight such attacks would end in fatal damage to the submarine. This strategy produced skippers who were overcautious rather than aggressive on the eve of war.

Significant differences existed between Mumma on the *Sailfish* and the new skipper of the *Sculpin.* Whereas Mumma was a tough taskmaster, aloof from his crew, Lt. Cdr. Lucius Chappell oversaw a more relaxed operation. A native Georgian, Chappell, 36, graduated from the Naval Academy in 1927 and served in a number of destroyers and the battleship USS *Idaho* (BB-42). After submarine training in 1933, he served aboard the *S-28* and *Snapper*, where he was executive officer. On May 6, 1941, he assumed command of the *Sculpin*.

Both he and his subordinate officers established a laid-back, friendly command. "Officers and crew alike responded confidently to [Chappell's] cool, relaxed leadership. His smile was a trademark," reflected then Lt. (jg) Corwin Mendenhall, who served as torpedo-gunnery officer on the boat. "I never once saw him exhibit any temper or nervousness, nor did I ever hear him raise his voice. He seemed perfectly at ease under all circumstances." The men of the *Sculpin* were an amicable lot under Chappell. "It was a tribute to all the officers," said Rocek. "We had high morale on the boat. We had good chiefs. Good Lord, we used to have a lot of fun on the boat."

On the *Sailfish*, life was more arduous, marked by tension due to a continuing feud between the chief of the boat and the yeoman. Frequently, the bickering had to be settled by executive officer Hiram Cassedy. Mumma, meanwhile, constantly demanded more of everyone to keep the boat in top shape.

All the while at Pearl, Mumma was taking heat from the division commander. "Oh, did he hate Morton C.," recalled Braun. "Morton C. could handle the ship. But criticism would come over the radio constantly, criticizing Morton C. for the turn he made, the time lapse, the drift, the transfer the ship made. Nothing was right. But you never knew it bothered Mumma. You had to be an idiot not to see how the division commander was riding him."

Mumma continued to be haunted by the boat's past. In addition to banning any references to the *Squalus*, he blacklisted her former skipper at Pearl. Knowing that Oliver Naquin was then attached to the battleship *California*, Mumma gave orders that under no circumstances was he to be allowed aboard the *Sailfish*. "One afternoon, when I had the duty," said Tucker, "the topside watch informed me that there was an officer on the dock who would like to talk to me. I went on the dock and it was Lieutenant Commander Naquin. We had a half-hour conversation in which he asked me about the boat, who was aboard, and how things were going. I brought him up to date and apologized for not being able to invite him aboard. But he was most gracious and understood."

The *Sailfish* and *Sculpin*, like the other subs in Pearl, spent most of the time on training runs in waters around Hawaii as the military formulated a war plan should Japan attack. Most believed the first blow would be struck against the Philippines; an attack on Pearl Harbor was inconceivable. "There was no sense of war. We had no idea of it. I don't remember anyone even mentioning it," said McLees. "To us, it was just exercises, just training."

Indeed, the boats were rarely at the base. "In Pearl Harbor, we had alerts about every two or three weeks brought on by the intelligence community," said Tucker. "I remember on one occasion, our instructions for subs at sea were to rendezvous off of Lanai Island, preserve radio silence, and form a column and run around the island and await further orders. Well, they forgot about us and it was several days before someone back in Pearl Harbor finally got around to remembering us. It was incidents like this which developed a climate of 'So what?' when we had another alert."

The incessant training took its toll. "We were operating like crazy," according to Bayles. "Squads east, squads west. In between, we'd fire a fish, pick it up, haul it back aboard, lower it down into the ship through the forward torpedo room loading hatch. Then we would overhaul the practice fish and fire it again. We were doing this continuously, 24 hours a day, five days a week."

Aboard the *Sailfish*, frequent dives inevitably raised the specter of the open main induction that had sunk the *Squalus*. "I remember one guy aboard named [Willard] Blatti [TM1c]," said Braun. "Whenever we dived, he used to holler up, 'Be sure and check the main vent. Look for a two-by-four and get it out.' Even Morton C. would have to laugh, though he would turn away so no one could see." Cross-training led to a near disaster during a practice dive. Mumma had invited a group of marine officers aboard as observers. Crewmen Aaron Reese (Sea1c) and Philip Dolan (Sea1c) were to operate the diving planes. "Phil and I both were pretty new at this. We gave 'em a ride all right. We went down like this," Reese recalled, dipping his hand at a near vertical angle. "Mumma was screaming, 'Blow everything! Blow everything!' When we finally popped up to the surface, Mumma stood there with one hand on Dolan's shoulder and one hand on mine and said, shaking, 'You boys know how to drive an automobile?' 'Yes sir!' 'Well, this is just like driving an automobile, except instead of going right and left, we go up and down, real easy like.'"

By the fall of 1941, the *Sailfish* was scheduled to return to San Francisco, where radar was to be installed on the boat. However, sailing orders were canceled half an hour before she was to depart. What most aboard didn't know was that war was imminent.

Indeed, naval intelligence was quite aware of most of Japan's plan. U.S. cryptoanalysts had cracked Japanese secret codes. The resulting

ULTRA and MAGIC information revealed that Tokyo planned a naval and army blitzkrieg to quickly capture all of the Far East, including the Philippines and perhaps Australia. But just where the initial strike would come could not be determined.

With no time to waste, the *Sailfish* and the *Sculpin* in two divisions of twelve fleet boats departed in utmost secrecy for Manila in late October 1941. For the first time, each of the boats was armed with the ultra-secret magnetic exploders and had orders to shoot if obstructed by Japanese vessels. Still, none of the rates knew where they were going. "We had little betting pools going on the boat," said Rocek. "Are we going to Guam? Are we going to Australia? Are we going to the Philippine Islands? Are we going to China? Nobody knew but it was a good topic of discussion all that time. I think it was basically the skipper who told the officers not to tell the crew, to keep them guessing because it would keep morale up. And it did."

On the *Sailfish*, the captain made it clear the men were going to war. "I remember Mumma sitting in the control room on the way out and talking. Listening to him, you would think he couldn't wait to go to war so he could go out there and show his stuff," said McLees. That seemed to be the officers' view as well. "We all had supreme confidence in our crew, our officers, and our boat," recalled Tucker. "We felt that we would beat the hell out of the Japanese."

Yet crewmen like Reese could hardly comprehend the news. "The skipper said, 'Well, we're going to war. The sooner the better.' But the reaction of the men was, 'Go to war? What the hell is he talking about?'"

Days of Infamy

The *Sculpin* and the *Sailfish*, in league with six other
fleet submarines, made the 5,000-mile passage to the
Philippines with every expectation of a skirmish with
Japan. Although they were armed for war on the 14-
day voyage, war didn't come—yet.

On November 8, the column of boats negotiated
the minefields off the island fortress of Corregidor, a
four-mile-long rock, honeycombed with tunnels and
controlling the entrance to Manila Bay. The squadron
then sailed another 30 miles northeast across the
mountain-rimmed bay to the capital city, where they
anchored in a nest within sight of Manila's prosperous
business district. Adm. Thomas C. Hart, the crusty
64-year-old commander-in-chief of the U.S. Asiatic
Fleet, immediately paid a visit to the famous boat his
wife had christened. Both Mumma and Tucker
impressed on him the need for an engine overhaul.
"We had been running all over the Pacific and all of
our engines were way beyond the number of hours
used when they should have been overhauled,"
Tucker explained. "So Admiral Hart told the skipper
to sit right where he was and overhaul all four main
engines before we did anything else. And that's the
only thing that kept us going for the next 15 months."

The crews were briefed on local customs, and

swarmed ashore on 48-hour leave. For them, the contrast to Honolulu was amazing. At Pearl, the military buildup had overwhelmed the city, causing such friction that there were frequent fights and intercession by shore patrols. But Manila, a sprawling metropolis, absorbed the rates easily. "It was the best liberty that I ever had," said the *Sculpin*'s Rocek. "Everything was wide open. Anything you wanted, you could acquire. Liberty was cheap. Your money went two for one."

Although life seemed carefree, there were clues to the impending war. Each time the *Sailfish* and *Sculpin* returned to Manila after training runs off Luzon, both were outfitted with enough stores for 90-day patrols—a sure indication the brass expected something. Also a steady parade of barges loaded with scrap iron bound for Japan from Manila had come to an end. And radio KZRF in Manila continuously broadcast sobering news from China and Europe, overshadowed by saber-rattling between Washington and Tokyo.

Hart, a veteran of World War I submarines, knew he was woefully mismatched in any face-off with the Japanese fleet, the largest armada ever assembled in the Pacific to that time. The newly arrived fleet boats were a help but hardly sufficient. Until the admiral's arrival in 1940, the Asiatic station had been a refuge for those officers past their prime and winding down their naval careers. Hart immediately shook up the command and, in a highly unpopular move, ordered the evacuation of all naval dependents from the islands. He wanted the undivided attention of his men so they could concentrate on war training exercises. Also, there would be no need for a risky emergency evacuation should Japan launch a surprise attack.

Exactly how the United States could defend the Philippines was unclear. Three times in 1941 Allied plans had changed but eventually Gen. Douglas MacArthur, commander of American and Filipino ground forces, persuaded the War Department that his 100 long-range B-17 Flying Fortress bombers and 100 fighter planes could adequately hold the islands until the U.S. battle fleet from Pearl arrived to vanquish the Japanese. But Hart was skeptical. Decoded MAGIC intelligence pointed to a surprise Japanese attack, probably on Manila. As a result, the admiral began dispersing his fleet to British and Dutch harbors in the Indian Ocean.

In fact, a Japanese imperial conference on November 5 approved unprecedented military action—simultaneous assaults on Pearl Harbor, Manila, and Singapore, all aimed at neutralizing Britain and the United States, securing the oil reserves of the Dutch East Indies, and resuming the conquest of China. If the United States could be dealt a decisive blow—destruction of its Pacific fleet—then perhaps Roosevelt could be forced to the peace table. But Adm. Isoroku Yamamoto, commander of the Japanese navy, feared that failure to do so quickly could lead to a war of attrition, with the colossal industrial might of the United States eventually overwhelming Japan.

In Manila, submarine training drills quickened in November. The boats put out to sea on Mondays and returned on Fridays. Under way, the men of the *Sailfish* and *Sculpin* fired practice torpedoes and engaged in countless emergency drills. In port, the *Sailfish*, as usual, drew attention as the former *Squalus*. "General MacArthur decided to take a visit over to Corregidor and inspect the area that would become his headquarters in the event of war," said Tucker. "We were assigned the job. Of course, the general was completely aloof, never went below decks and spent the entire trip on the cigarette deck [aft of the conning tower] surrounded by his staff. I don't think he even talked to the captain."

On November 27, Hart received an ominous dispatch from the chief of naval operations: CONSIDER THIS A WAR WARNING. NEGOTIATIONS WITH JAPAN LOOKING TOWARD STABILIZATION OF CONDITIONS IN THE PACIFIC HAVE CEASED AND AN AGGRESSIVE MOVE BY JAPAN IS EXPECTED WITHIN THE NEXT FEW DAYS. . . . EXECUTE AN APPROPRIATE DEFENSIVE DEPLOYMENT.

Immediately, the admiral sent his submarines on coastal scouting patrols while tightening security at Manila and Cavite with its huge stockpile of torpedoes. Under Operation Zed, the *Sailfish* and *Sculpin* embarked from Manila to circle Luzon, with torpedoes primed for war. Hart's plan, once hostilities began, was to send his surface ships south to rendezvous with British, Dutch, Australian, and New Zealand vessels in hopes of blunting Japan's southward drive. The submarines, the only naval weapons remaining in the Philippines, would be divided into three fighting units. Eight boats were to be sent afar to patrol Japanese bases; another eleven were to maintain station around Luzon on the lookout for enemy forces; and the remaining ten boats would be held in reserve for use against the Japanese fleet once it was located. Two other boats, including *Sealion*, were at Cavite, the U.S. naval station, for overhaul and thus unavailable.

On November 29, the day of the traditional Army-Navy football game, when the services stand down, many thought Japan would spring a surprise. But nothing happened.

On Sunday morning, December 7 (December 6, Hawaii time), the *Sailfish* and *Sculpin* returned to Manila to take on supplies. Capt. John Wilkes, commander of the Manila subs, was so fearful of attack by saboteurs or carrier-based bombers that he spread out the subs, anchoring them singly with armed seamen posted on deck. All small craft in the harbor were ordered to stay clear or risk being fired upon. Tension was so high that Bayles on the *Sailfish* strapped a .45-caliber handgun to his side in the duty section of the boat. The officers and most of the crew took brief liberty to participate in a standing softball game with other boat crews; the losers paid for a keg of beer afterwards. That evening, many of the officers went to the Army-Navy club to socialize, and crewmen straggled back to the boat, crashing in their bunks after hard drinking and partying ashore.

At exactly 0315 on December 8, the world as they knew it came to an end. A message was flashed to the submarines from Hart's headquarters. *Sailfish* and the *Sculpin* signalmen jotted down the startling news: FROM COMMANDER ASIATIC FLEET . . . TO ASIATIC FLEET . . . URGENT . . . BREAK . . . JAPAN HAS COMMENCED HOSTILITIES . . . GOVERN YOURSELF ACCORDINGLY.

Aboard the *Sailfish*, the order was passed down the conning tower hatch to Bayles who went to awaken Cassedy, the fiery duty officer. "Cassedy got up and read the message. He half jumped out of his bunk and yelled, 'Hold reveille!'" recounted Bayles. "I went into all the sleeping compartments and turned on the lights and said, 'Wake up! The war has started!' I remember someone in the after battery yelling back, 'Bullshit!'"

A Japanese force of two battleships, three carriers, forty-five destroyers, and 100 transports bearing 43,000 Army troops and supported by 500 land-based aircraft, was en route from Taiwan to take Manila. As Mumma hurried to the *Sailfish* from the Army-Navy Club, a second message was received from Hart at 0330: CONDUCT UNRESTRICTED AIR, SURFACE AND UNDERSEAS WARFARE AGAINST THE EMPIRE OF JAPAN!

No bombs had fallen, so the crews could only wonder what had happened, completely unaware of the waves of Japanese warplanes that were decimating Pearl Harbor and the Pacific Fleet, including the battleship *California* (BB-44) to which Naquin was attached.

With the *Sailfish* crew assembled topside at daybreak, Mumma addressed them forcefully to prepare them for the boat's long-awaited first war patrol. "This is what we have been trained for," he began. "This is what our tradition has been for. We have never been tested. Our effort in World War I was negligible. We didn't have the equipment to compare with the German U-boats. But now we are proficient, and now we are going to do a good job." The captain then vowed to strike hard at the Japanese. "You are going to sail with the coldest-blooded man who ever captained a ship. I am going to carry you across the line. If anybody is scared, now is the time to get off."

"Those were his exact words," recalled Aaron Reese. "I will never forget them."

At daybreak, with still no evidence of a Japanese attack or any word of what was happening elsewhere, the submarines in Manila prepared to depart. The *Sailfish* and the *Sculpin*, each manned by six officers and fifty-eight crewmen, sidled up to two oilers to top off fuel tanks and then to the sub tender *Holland* (AS-3) to take on ammunition and extra water. They exchanged practice torpedoes for live ones and installed the secret magnetic exploders already aboard. At 1000, the first air-raid siren—a false alarm—sounded over Manila as the sub captains mustered in Wilkes's quarters for operational orders. He impressed upon each of them the danger and urged extreme caution. His assistant, division commander Stuart "Sunshine" Murray, was more emphatic: "Don't try to go out there and win the Congressional Medal of Honor in one day. The submarines are all we have left. Your crews are more valuable than anything else. Bring them back." Wilkes reminded the skippers to be sparing in their use of torpedoes because of a shortage but promised "amazing results" due to the magnetic exploders.

Mumma and Chappell returned to their boats and cast off, as enemy fighter planes and bombers descended over Clark Field, 50 miles to the north, where MacArthur's air force was caught on the ground and destroyed.

In the harbor, the *Sculpin*, under cover of darkness on December 8, escorted the aircraft tender *Langley* (AV-3), the tanker *Pecos* (AO-6), and the destroyer tender *Black Hawk* (AD-9) toward Borneo. In an orderly procession, more boats exited Manila Bay through the night and into the next day, each with a different mission. On December 9 reserve subs, including *Sailfish*, raced down the bay to Corregidor. At 2100, the boat picked her way through the minefield and moved up the western coast of Luzon off loosely defended Lingayen Gulf, a likely landing point for Japanese infantry.

For two days, the boat scoured the area—submerged in the daytime, on the surface at night—as Mumma prowled the boat nervously. "Captain Mumma was a very intense individual. He had to know what was going on in his ship all the time," recounted Tucker. "This attitude was fine in peacetime, but when the war began, he could not relax. He walked from bow to stern almost constantly the first four or five days we were under way. So when we made our first attack, he was completely exhausted."

Contact with the enemy's advance ships came on the fifth day (December 13) at 0230. Tucker, who was the officer of the deck at the time, confirmed three specks on the dark horizon (away from the moon). Because of the sub's silhouette in the moonlight, the warships spotted the *Sailfish* and turned toward her, dropping depth charges as they came. "We dove and began listening on sound," said Bayles of the hydrophones extended into the ocean below the sub. "According to the soundman, there were three sets of propellers. We knew then that three destroyers were operating together. Our soundman was very experienced."

Mumma used sound bearings to set up an attack. At 0250, with the boat at periscope depth, he fired two torpedoes. "I was in the conning tower after the first exploded," recalled signalman Claude Braun. "Mumma was on the periscope at the time. But there were no breaking-up noises of any vessel going down. He says to me, 'Braun, see if you can see anything.' So I stepped into the periscope and he said, 'Leave it right there. We haven't moved that much. You will see one or two [destroyers] up there.'

"'I see a shape up there, sir, but I don't see any fire or explosion. Nothing.' I looked right at Mumma and his face turned white.

"Then the second torpedo hit at a longer range without exploding. When the second one was a dud and the guy on the hydrophone said he had a hit, Mumma said, 'You got a hit?!' And nothing happened, no explosion. His knuckles stood out as he gripped the periscope ears. And that's when he put the ears up, lowered the scope, and said, 'Take her down!'"

The submarine descended silently below 200 feet as the captain pondered what to do, shocked at the thought that at least one of the "foolproof" Mark VI exploders had not detonated, although the other might have sunk or at least damaged one of the warships. Overhead, the destroyers zeroed in.

"The soundman reported pinging by the enemy," said Bayles. "When the old man heard it was pinging, he was still in the conning tower. He had a transmitter and a loudspeaker directly connected to the forward torpedo room where the soundman was stationed. So when the word came on his loudspeaker that 'the [Japanese] are pinging us!' and he knew that [Raymond] Doritty [RM1c] was on sound and was a first-class radioman, the old man said, 'Ask Doritty what kind of whiskey he's been drinking.' Doritty replied, 'If you don't think it's pinging, listen to it yourself.' So Mumma did, at which time he voiced concern that we might have sunk an American destroyer. Ray said, 'No, these aren't American destroyers. American destroyers use a different frequency. This has to be [Japanese].'" According to Bayles, the revelation was a rude shock to Mumma. American destroyers operating with U.S. subs earlier had positively convinced submarine skippers that with sonar they could sink any submarine. "So, now the old man was convinced he was a dead duck."

The destroyers obliged by lacing the ocean with twenty depth charges.

An ashen Mumma turned to his exec. "Mr. Cassedy, I'm going into my cabin." Braun, witnessing the scene, was stunned. "I knew something had happened with Mort. It was a horrible thing to see, knowing this man."

As it turned out, the depth charges exploded a safe distance away, causing minor damage as the *Sailfish* slithered away in the commotion. But the skirmish was enough to convince Mumma that he was not cut out for submarine warfare. His unnerving was a precursor to what soon would be revealed as a service-wide "skipper problem"—older boat captains coached in conservative tactics who were unwilling to aggressively attack enemy ships out of fear they would be doomed by unreliable torpedoes and enemy countermeasures.

On December 14, as scores of Japanese transports closed on Lingayen Gulf, Mumma, still in his cabin, told his exec in private that he wanted to return to Manila. Cassedy wrote up the request, encoded it, and bypassed Tucker, the communications officer, to take it directly to the radioman for broadcast. "The radioman reported back to me that the message had been sent and gave me the coded copy," said Tucker. "I, of course, thought, 'What message?' I didn't know anything about it. So I went back to my small room and decoded it. It had been very poorly phrased, I thought, but it implied that the skipper had broken down, which no one on the sub had any indication of, and desired to return *Sailfish* to Manila."

Other submarines at sea intercepted the news with disbelief. Reuben Whitaker, executive officer of the *Sturgeon* (SS-187) on patrol off Taiwan, recalled the message: ATTACKED ONE SHIP . . . VIOLENT COUNTERATTACK . . . COMMANDING OFFICER BREAKING DOWN . . . URGENTLY REQUEST AUTHORITY TO RETURN TO TENDER.

On the run back to Manila, Braun spoke briefly with Mumma. "I told him, 'Captain, I know we are going to Manila, and I suspect you are going to leave.' He said, 'Yes, I am.' I wished him the best. He cried."

The *Sailfish* anchored off Corregidor, then submerged during the day because of heavy bombardment of Manila, the naval base at Cavite, and Corregidor. That night, December 16, the boat slipped unnoticed across the bay to Manila where she anchored alongside the camouflaged tender *Canopus* (AS-9). The crew mustered on the deck. "It was the eeriest damn night," recalled Reese. "A searchlight every once in awhile would flash around. Dark as hell. Then we hear Mumma's voice out of the dark."

According to Bayles, "With a teary voice, Mumma said he was sorry, that he was leaving, and that Lieutenant Commander [Richard George] Voge was coming aboard, was a good man, and was a classmate of Mumma's. All he wanted us to do was give him the same loyal service as we had given to Mumma." Voge had been skipper of the *Sealion*, which had been sunk by a Japanese bomber alongside the dock in Cavite, now in flames with its crucial stockpile of 233 torpedoes in ruins. The Navy tried to put the best face it could on the Mumma incident at a time when it was reeling from defeat on all fronts, and awarded him the Navy Cross for the attack and presumed sinking of the destroyer. "Looking back on it," said Tucker years later, "I have a lot of respect for Captain Mumma for doing what he did. He realized he didn't have it as a wartime sub skipper and said so. There were a lot of other skippers in Subs Asiatic Fleet who had less guts than he, who ran away from everything they saw for several months until the brass caught up with them and relieved them."

The new skipper of the *Sailfish*, Voge, seemed much like Mumma. As one of the most experienced sub skippers in the fleet, the 37-year-old captain had served as skipper of the *S 18* and *S-33*. Prior to that, he had seen duty in *S-29*, USS *Pittsburgh* (CA-72), *Pecos*, and USS *Trenton* (CL-11), and served a brief stint as engineering instructor at the Naval Academy. To the men aboard the *Sailfish*, Voge was all business. "He was very competent but rather cold. He looked like he was perpetually mad," said Reese. But, as Braun put it, "conditions on the boat seemed more relaxed. It was very apparent to the men."

Hart held Voge and *Sailfish* at Manila for five days as preparations were made for her second war patrol. Then on December 21, she embarked for the coast of Taiwan. Five days later, as Japanese troops rumbled across the northwest plains of Luzon toward Manila, Admiral Hart and two staff officers abandoned the city, bound for the Dutch naval base at Surabaya, Java, on the USS *Shark* (SS-174). On New Year's Day, Wilkes withdrew all remaining submarines south toward

Surabaya. Mort Mumma was among the last to be evacuated, boarding the USS *Seawolf* (SS-197), which sailed from Corregidor to Darwin on the north coast of Australia.

To the far north, the *Sculpin* patrolled the Philippine Sea. Each day was spent submerged, cruising at three knots in stifling heat. A breakdown of the sub's air conditioning compounded the situation. At night, she surfaced and raced back and forth in her patrol quadrant, recharging batteries and looking vainly for enemy ships. Radio reports from other submarines revealed repeated failures of torpedoes despite perfect set-ups. They seemed to run under enemy vessels without exploding, or prematurely exploded for unknown reasons. On the *Sculpin*, the officers concluded the Mark XIV torpedoes were running too deep and adjusted the "fish" to run on the surface.

Nightly, lookouts were amazed by the strange phosphorescence of the ocean near the equator. The combination of tropical heat and abundant micro-organisms caused the sea to glow as the submarine moved across the surface, making the crew fearful of being spotted. Occasionally, large displays of luminescence flashed on and off like a lightbulb, with smaller displays created by schools of fish passing close to the submarine. It wasn't until late in December that the *Sculpin* finally encountered enemy shipping moving in and out of Lamon Bay off Luzon. However, bad weather made it impossible for Chappell to attack.

Faced with the futility of an encounter in the patrol area, Chappell headed south toward Australia on January 9. The next day, off Mindanao, the southernmost large island of the Philippines, the boat intercepted a 3,000-ton Japanese cargo ship accompanied by a second ship. During a night surface attack, Chappell fired four torpedoes from a distance of 800 yards. Two exploded against the side of the ship, producing flames 200 feet high. The skipper and his lookouts watched as pinpoint beams from flashlights raced helter-skelter across the deck. Machine-gun fire erupted as the doomed ship listed, the shells forcing the *Sculpin* to dive. Below, crewmen listened for the first time to a ship in its death throes—the horrifying screech of metal collapsing and tearing, signaling the breakup of the freighter on its way to the bottom of the 30,000-foot-deep Philippine Trench.

On January 16, the submarine crossed the equator into the Southern Hemisphere for the first time. The next day the men surveyed the dense jungles and towering peaks of mysterious Borneo through the periscope. At sunset, the *Sculpin* surfaced off Balik-Papan to pick up a Dutch lieutenant pilot who guided the submarine inland on a jungle river in pitch blackness. "The jungle, towering on each bank of the river, gave the feeling of being in a black hole," recalled Corwin Mendenhall, the boat's junior ensign. The boat put in alongside a dock where rotting manila mooring lines were used to secure the vessel for refueling. Chappell went ashore for a meeting with the Dutch port captain, who informed him of the destruction of the U.S. Fleet at Pearl Harbor, the siege of MacArthur's 200,000 troops in the Philippines, and the retreat of the Allies in Malaysia.

Quickly, the skipper returned to the boat where a string of lightbulbs had been strung over the deck to illuminate the refueling operations and the transfer of torpedoes from deck storage to the forward torpedo room. At dawn, the *Sculpin* set sail again, heading further south to Surabaya, Java, where she arrived on January 22.

Java was the main prize in the Japanese drive. Rich mineral supplies and tremendous reserves of petroleum ensured the strategic importance of the Dutch island. The harbor at Surabaya, a modern metropolis of 300,000 on the northern plains, contained a major Dutch submarine repair facility where a quick refit of the *Sculpin* began. The bearded, unwashed officers and crew were divided into two staggered groups and sent inland by train for a few days' rest at a camp operated by the Dutch Submarine Force in the mountains at Malang 100 miles away. Rocek and seven other crewmen spent one day on horseback, riding through the countryside past lavish Dutch homes and encountering an elaborate Javanese wedding.

While the crew tried to forget the war, MAGIC intelligence tracked a Japanese fleet steaming toward Java from the Philippines. The *Sculpin* crew returned to the boat at once on January 30, departing in haste for the boat's second war patrol. Chappell was ordered to rendezvous with the *Sailfish* south of the Philippines in hopes of intercepting the fleet. Wilkes put every available boat on line to sink the warships, sending eleven subs with the urgent call to "ATTACK. ATTACK. ATTACK. ATTACK." But again, the force either failed to make contact or inflicted negligible damage because of defective torpedoes.

The *Sailfish* was able to successfully attack only one ship, a cruiser, in a daylight periscope approach off Mindanao. Voge launched four torpedoes at the warship, which was guarded by two destroyers. One exploded, damaging the cruiser's propellers. The submarine had no chance to follow up since the destroyers immediately came after her. Voge took the boat to 260 feet for three hours, after which a periscope scan revealed no enemy ships in sight. The boat later surfaced and headed for a three-day refit at Tjilatjap, a poorly equipped port on the arid, dusty south coast of Java. She arrived on February 14 to a harbor crammed with British, Dutch, Australian, New Zealand, and American craft, all clamoring for spare parts, fuel, and food in the only bomb-free port left in Java.

As the Japanese relentlessly closed in, the outlook was grim. In three months of action, Wilkes's twenty-eight subs had sunk a mere six ships, all freighters, at a cost of three boats—the *Shark, Sealion,* and *S-36.* Japanese torpedo bombers sank the British battleships *Repulse* and *Prince of Wales* off Singapore. English troops failed to thwart enemy troop landings on the Malay peninsula. Hong Kong was under siege. The Philippines were overrun. Wake Island, the Marianas, Solomon, Marshall, and Gilbert islands in the Central Pacific had fallen. Ships loaded with refugees dotted the Indian Ocean, leaving Java for safety in western Australia. Bombing runs on Darwin, the sweltering northern Australian port, left the new U.S. submarine logistics center in ruins. And, as the *Sailfish* prepared to cast off from Tjilatjap on her third war patrol on February 19, ninety-six enemy transports supported by forty warships moved on Java from the north and south.

The magnitude of defeat for the Allies was unimaginable to the beleaguered *Sailfish* crew, which was completely in the dark. "We had never been told what had transpired at Pearl Harbor. The Japanese knew, our politicians and diplomats knew, everybody at Pearl Harbor knew, but we poor bastards out there doing the fighting were not so privileged," said Tucker.

On February 28 at 0030 in the Java Sea, the *Sailfish* made contact with a cruiser and two destroyers and prepared to attack. While closing in, Voge and his lookouts suddenly realized the cruiser might be the *Houston* and broke off the foray. Just as suddenly, the ship turned a searchlight in the direction of the submarine, forcing her to dive and pull clear. In fact, it was the *Houston.* She and the remnants of the combined Allied Asiatic fleet—five cruisers and five destroyers—were steaming west from the disaster at the Battle of the Java Sea in which two Allied cruisers and three destroyers were lost. The *Houston* and several other warships barely escaped. Now they were sailing west into a Japanese trap in the Sunda Strait separating Java from Sumatra, where all ten ships would be lost.

The 100-foot Submarine Escape Training Tower as it appeared in 1943 at the national submarine school in Groton, Conn. *(U.S. Navy photo)*

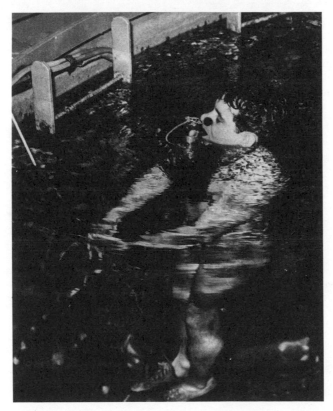

A student surfaces in the Submarine Escape Training Tower with a clip on his nose while breathing through a Momsen lung. The breathing device, strapped around the chest, supplied oxygen during the 100-foot ascent.

A stern view of the USS *Squalus* on the day of her launch in 1938; note the cradle built under the submarine. The cradle carried the boat down a rail track and into the Piscataqua River at the far, open end of the ways at the Portsmouth Naval Shipyard. *(U.S. Navy photo)*

The *Squalus* at the fitting-out pier in Portsmouth Naval Shipyard on January 7, 1939. The number S11 was a hull designation number for shipyard purposes. Later, 192 replaced the number. *(U.S. Navy photo)*

Diver Martin Sibitzky about to begin his dive to the deck of the sunken *Squalus* on the morning of May 24, 1939. *(courtesy of George Rocek)*

The USS *Sculpin* sends an air hose to the USS *Falcon* to boost air pressure during the salvage of the *Sculpin*'s twin sister ship, the *Squalus*. On August 12, 1939, divers used the *Sculpin* during the rescue and salvage operations. It was the *Sculpin* that discovered the whereabouts of the *Squalus* and her trapped crew. *(U.S. Navy photo)*

Squalus rises out of control during the first lift attempt of the salvage operations. This picture gave President Roosevelt the idea of renaming her the *Sailfish*. (*USNI Collection*)

Battered conning tower of *Squalus* after she was towed back to Portsmouth. (*U.S. Navy photo*)

Some of the *Squalus* survivors and other crewmen at a reunion in late 1939. Those whose names are followed by an asterisk were not aboard for the ill-fated voyage. *Bottom row, left to right,* S. L. Savage,* Roland Blanchard, Allen Carl Bryson, Gavin J. Coyne, Basilio Galvan, Lawrence J. Gainor, and Donato Persico; *second row,* William D. Boulton, Harold C. Preble (a naval architect and the only civilian survivor), Lt. (jg) R. N. Robertson, Lt. Oliver F. Naquin (holding the silver sailboat given to him by the survivors), Lt. William T. Doyle Jr., Lt. J. C. Nichols, and Theodore Jacobs; *third row,* Raymond P. O'Hara, Charles A. Powell, Gerald McLees, Carlton B. Powell, S. C. Farwell,* Lloyd B. Maness, Arthur L. Booth, and Roy H. Campbell; *top row,* Charles Yuhas, Judson Bland, Warren W. Smith, Eugene Cravens, William Isaacs, Robert L. Washburn, Willard W. Blatti,* and Alfred G. Prien. *(courtesy of Carl Bryson)*

The *Sculpin*, circa 1940. *(U.S. Navy photo)*

Left: Lt. Cdr. Lucius H. Chappell, skipper of the *Sculpin* for the boat's first eight war patrols. *(U.S. Navy photo) Right:* Lt. Cdr. Morton Mumma, first captain of the *Sailfish. (National Archives)*

Boats tied up alongside USS *Proteus,* one of a small fleet of sub tenders in the Pacific during World War II. *(U.S. Navy photo)*

George Rocek, *Sculpin* engineman, on his return home from the warfront in 1943. Rocek was a survivor of the *Sculpin*'s last dive, was taken prisoner by the Japanese, then survived the sinking of a Japanese carrier and 19 months in prison camp. It was the *Sailfish* that sank the carrier where he was held captive with twenty other shipmates. *(courtesy of George Rocek)*

Sculpin crewmen in 1943. *Kneeling, left to right,* Carlos Tulao, Lt. Corwin Mendenhall, Weldon E. Moore, and Lt. John H. Turner; *standing,* John J. Pepersack, Alvin W. Coulter, Keith E. Waidelich, John B. Swift, John J. Hollenbach, Ralph S. Austin, Frank J. Dyboski, and Chesley A. DeArmond. *(courtesy of George Rocek)*

Admiral Nimitz presenting the Presidential Unit Citation to Capt. Robert Ward for the tenth war patrol of the *Sailfish*, July 1944, Pearl Harbor. During the patrol, the boat sank nearly 30,000 tons of enemy shipping, including the Japanese carrier *Chuyo*, on which twenty-one *Sculpin* POWs were imprisoned; only one (George Rocek) survived the sinking. *(courtesy of Larry Macek)*

The happy *Sailfish* crew on their return to Pearl Harbor after the tenth war patrol in 1944. *Kneeling, left to right,* Clemon E. Newkirk, Albert A. Kasuga, Robert Bradley, Lester Warburton, and John M. Good; *standing,* Lt. Joseph Sahaj, Thomas L. Ulhman, Henry K. Robertson, and Maurice D. Barnes. *(courtesy of Larry Macek)*

The footbridge spanning the Watarase River and linking the POW camp (against hillside in background) with the town of Ashio, where twenty *Sculpin* survivors were forced to labor in the Ashio copper mine. *(courtesy of Arthur McIntyre)*

The POW camp at Ashio, with barracks to left and right. *(courtesy of Arthur McIntyre)*

George Brown *(left)* before capture and *(far right)* after his liberation and arrival in Guam to discuss his ordeal with Admiral Lockwood and his staff. Brown was incarcerated at the Japanese secret prison of Ofuna for a year and a half and not listed as a POW. Later he was attached to a labor camp in central Japan where prisoners built a hydroelectric project. Forty-three Americans died there; Brown brought their ashes back to their relatives in the United States. *(courtesy of George Brown)*

The last dive of the *Sailfish*, October 27, 1945, in the Piscataqua River at the Portsmouth Naval Shipyard. The people of Kittery, Maine, and Portsmouth led a successful fight to keep the former *Squalus* from being scrapped in Philadelphia. The boat's conning tower is today preserved at the shipyard as a memorial to the rescue of the *Squalus* survivors and as a World War II submarine shrine. *(courtesy of Larry Macek)*

Lowering the colors at the decommissioning of the *Sailfish* on Navy Day, October 27, 1945, in Portsmouth, N.H. *(U.S. Navy photo)*

George Rocek (*left*) talks with Capt. Bob Ward at the first *Squalus/Sailfish/ Sculpin* reunion in Mobile, Ala., in 1979. Ward, who died less than a year later, was captain of the *Sailfish* when the boat sank the carrier *Chuyo,* where Rocek was held prisoner with twenty other POWs. *(courtesy of George Rocek)*

Adm. Oliver Naquin (*right*) talks with Rear Adm. Corwin Mendenhall (*Sculpin* veteran) at the national reunion of crews of *Squalus/Sailfish/Sculpin,* Baltimore, 1989. *(courtesy of Carl Bryson)*

Left to right: Squalus survivor Jud Bland, *Sculpin* survivor George Rocek, and *Squalus* survivors Leonard de Medeiros and Danny Persico at reunion in 1993 in Pasadena, Calif. *(courtesy of George Rocek)*

Lombok Nightmare

Conditions had deteriorated steadily aboard the *Sailfish* and the *Sculpin* as February 1942 came to an end. The boats had been on war patrol for three consecutive months, hampered, like the rest of the underseas force, by torpedo duds and aggressive antisubmarine attacks by Japanese destroyers.

The men were exhausted. Voge noted in his log how bad the situation had become on the *Sailfish*: "This patrol was started after a period of only five days in port following a patrol of 56 days duration. As a consequence, personnel were pretty well worn out from the start, and, with lowered resistance, practically all hands developed bad colds and coughs." Chappell on the *Sculpin* described even worse conditions: "The physical and, to a greater extent, the psychological well-being of the men is deteriorating at an accelerated rate. Manifestations are sleeplessness, chronic headaches, general lassitude, loss of appetite, marked decrease in mental alertness, emotional instability, and increasing nervousness. . . . Any radical change in the ship's course or speed, particularly at night, would cause a noticeable tension to develop. . . . The slightest physical ailment would affect the men out of all proportion and it was therefore necessary to make rather free use of sedatives."

Cruising in 86° equatorial waters exacerbated the situation. Because of the constant threat of enemy patrol planes and ships, the boats could only patrol on the surface by night for six to eight hours while the huge diesels recharged batteries. Each dawn, the red-hot engines were shut down, as was the air conditioning. The boats submerged to periscope depth (60 feet) for the rest of the day. Thus the heat generated by the diesels was trapped with the men inside the vessels. Temperatures in the engine rooms pegged out at 132°. Heat generated by the batteries lining the keel hit 120°. The coolest compartment on the ship was the forward torpedo room. "At the end of an all-day submerged run, the temperature there was 95°. It was very uncomfortable from the time we dove at daylight until around noon when the boat finally started to cool off," said *Sailfish* chief electrician Bayles.

"The guys were running around naked, some of them. [Walton] 'Round Belly' Young [EM1c], I remember, was naked. He was wearing a pair of sandals and a towel around his neck which he used to wipe his brow. But most of the guys wore skivvies, cut-off dungarees. Doc Miller, the pharmacist's mate, demanded that everyone at least wear underpants when they went to chow. He insisted that sitting at the mess bench naked was unsanitary."

Most submariners were able to tough it out under the most arduous circumstances, a testament to their earlier psychological screening and intensive training in New London. The only thing they had not experienced before the war was depth bombing, but now the crews of both boats had experienced that as well and took it in stride. Yeoman Reese on the *Sailfish* recalled how, later in the war, a recruit who had never been through a depth charging reported for duty. He was a 19-year-old electrician with red hair and freckles. "We had gotten a hit on a [Japanese] ship and rigged for depth charge at 300 feet," said Reese. "In the silence, he says to me, 'Boy, I bet they're depth charging us up there now, aren't they?' I said, 'When they do, you'll know it.' Ten seconds later, KAWOOM! I think it took three days for that kid to get his freckles back and he transferred off the boat when we got back in."

Added to the periodic horror of combat was the exhaustion of back-to-back operations. Yet, the demands of combat in the early months and the determination to find some way to stop the Japanese required Voge and the other submarine commanders to push onward.

On the *Sailfish* and *Sculpin,* cockroaches were brought aboard unknowingly in the foodstuffs in Java. In the torrid heat, conditions were ideal for breeding and soon the insects swarmed over the mess halls of both boats. On the *Sailfish*, they became part of a nightmarish encounter with Japanese forces.

The boat had taken up station on March 2 at the north entrance of Lombok Strait, a 12-mile-wide, 20-mile-long channel between Bali and Lombok Island, separating the Indian Ocean to the south from the Java Sea to the north. It was deep and ripped by violent cross-currents and eddies, a kind of submarine highway between war and peace. For those heading south, it meant passage into the wide Indian Ocean and a peaceful voyage to Australia for R&R. But for those going north from the subcontinent, it held an air of mystery and dread, guarded in the southern approach by two lofty mountains on each shore, gloomy, cloud-shrouded sentinels standing watch over curling mists on the strait that hid Japanese destroyers and patrol boats, all listening for the screws of submarines passing through. The boats could run with the current in one direction submerged, but it was too swift going the other way, forcing them to "run the gauntlet" on the surface.

With the battle for Java in full force, the *Sailfish* had been ordered to interdict any enemy warships headed through the strait to support the Japanese invasion. On the morning of March 2, Voge sighted a destroyer and tracked it for 24 minutes before firing two torpedoes. One missed but the other hit the ship in its engine room without exploding, although it did cause the destroyer to temporarily lose propulsion.

At first, Voge thought both missed and ordered the boat to dive. But then he realized the destroyer had lost power and decided to stay at periscope depth and go after her. Bayles, on the battle phones in the maneuvering room, awaited the dive but nothing happened. "This goes on for what seems like an interminable amount of time when all of a sudden, 'Kaboom!' . . . the loudest explosion I've ever heard from a depth charge," said Bayles.

Unbeknownst to Voge, two enemy aircraft had spotted the submerged silhouette of the *Sailfish* and dropped four bombs, one of which exploded alongside the boat. The detonation left ears ringing. The boat shook wildly, the power of the blast compressing the hull to expose momentarily the boat's steel ribs. The lights went out, leaving the crew in utter darkness, some losing their balance, as the submarine plunged toward the bottom. All instruments were switched off, including the refrigeration, ventilation fans, anything making noise, so the boat could make a silent getaway on the idle turns of a single, battery-driven propeller.

"We get the order to rig for depth charge and silent running, which we did," recounted Bayles. "But this was just the beginning of our ordeal."

The submarine sought safety at 230 feet, where she stayed until nightfall. At 1920, she surfaced and soon sighted another ship on a southward course in the path of the moon. The *Sailfish* submerged to periscope depth and began an approach.

As the range steadily decreased, Voge discerned the black form of an aircraft carrier, mistaking it for the vaunted *Kaga*, one of the warships involved in the attack on Pearl Harbor. Four destroyers screened the carrier, one at the bow, two on either side, and one lagging it. The formation moved at a slow eight knots. Not wanting to risk detection by moving in too close, the captain decided instead on a long-range torpedo attack. Voge reasoned that the *Sculpin* could succeed because of the size and deep draft of the target and the fact that it was moving so slowly.

For the crewmen, the opportunity presented mixed emotions. They were anxious, like the captain, to fire torpedoes into the convoy to sink the carrier. But they knew what it meant for them: a severe, possibly fatal counterattack by the destroyers. Having survived close calls in the first three months, they knew what was coming and were apprehensive.

The captain swung the *Sailfish* around 180 degrees to bring the stern tubes to bear. In quick succession, four fish were fired from 4,000 yards. Steadfastly, Voge held the boat in position, watching mesmerized through the periscope at this chance to be the first submarine of the war to sink a carrier.

It took more than four minutes for the torpedoes to cross the gulf between the *Sailfish* and the flattop. The destroyers heard them coming but it was too late. Four minutes and nine seconds after the first fish left its tube, an explosion ravaged the carrier, Voge describing flames shooting 150 feet up the side of the target. The second and third torpedoes missed. But five minutes and nineteen seconds into the attack, the fourth broadsided the ship at a range of 4,500 yards, causing a second explosion clearly audible inside the *Sailfish*. The carrier, which turned out to be a much smaller aircraft ferry, the 6,500-ton *Kamogawa Maru*, was doomed.

The escorts now had nothing to protect so they set out to nail the submarine. They raced back and forth above the boat, sending out electronic beams that brushed her hull with a slight whisper, and echoed back as an audible "ping, ping, ping" to sound detectors, revealing the sub's approximate location. Depth charges rained down on the vessel—at least forty in the first hour and a half. Silverware and crockery in the boat's galley crashed and clattered with each explosion. Lightbulbs shattered, littering the deck with glass. Rivets and the outer hull creaked ominously, threatening to rip open and instantly drown the crew. Emergency lights revealed air filled with tiny flecks of cork, shaken loose from insulation inside the hull. Vibrations the length of the vessel created clouds of dust in all compartments as the boat drifted, 300 feet down. The men were frozen in place, not risking detection by making the slightest noise between depth charges. Conversations were held in a whisper. Only the hissing of hydraulic equipment disrupted the silence.

At 2400, a faint throbbing outside the hull could be heard in the stony quiet. It grew in intensity to a "thum, thum, thum"—a destroyer making a depth-charge run, drawing a bead on the submarine. The hypnotic rhythm of the ship's propellers rose to a screaming pitch, filling the compartments with foreboding. The warship passed directly overhead as the *Sailfish*'s crew, with hearts in their throats, turned an ear to the protective hull above them. The swishing screws faded. The splash of eight depth charges could be heard. The men braced as explosive canisters fell toward them.

Then a "click" of a detonator going off, followed by a tremendous concussion—a gigantic sledgehammer smashing against the hull of the boat. It drove her downward. Seven other bombs exploded in quick succession, whipping her from side to side. Men, some exclaiming "Oh, God!" were thrown a foot into the air as deck grates in the compartments jumped with each blast. Ventilation pipes vibrated to the point they seemed they would break and fall from the overhead. The steel frame of the submarine groaned and bent but held.

Almost miraculously, the depth charges failed to destroy the *Sailfish*. The Japanese had underestimated her depth, setting the explosives too shallow.

The boat maintained depth for the next three hours, finding a cold-water temperature gradient that deflected the destroyers' sonar beams. Stagnant air and headaches caused by the explosions sapped the crewmen. They fumbled sluggishly amid the heat and sweat. At 0305 on March 3, five hours after the attack on the carrier, the *Sailfish* surfaced with no warships in sight. But after only two hours of full-power operation—recharging the batteries, starting up the air conditioning, the power steering, and refrigeration—the destroyers made contact once again, forcing the *Sailfish* to dive.

The depth bombing resumed at once.

With the boat running silently, officers moved through the vessel, whispering encouragement and status reports while making inspections. The silence was nerve-wracking. Even the squeak of sandals caused crewman to bristle, fearful the destroyers would hear the noise. Increasing humidity and insipid air brought on great fatigue. Many wrapped themselves almost obscenely around water pipes or anything cold to relieve the heat. Carbon dioxide absorbent and blasts of pure oxygen from canisters fixed to the overhead did little to ease the discomfort.

"This went on for a solid week," said Bayles. "Every night we would go up and get in an hour or two of battery charge, and the destroyers would come after us. At 0300, they would leave and we would surface and get another hour or two of battery charge. Then down we'd go again at 0430 with the dawn light. The engines would heat up and then we'd dive and run at periscope depth all day.

"The general overall heat made it difficult to sleep. I had nightmares. I thought I was going to crack up.

"In my dream, I saw the indicator of the ship's ventilation valve. I saw it move from shut to open and knew the boat would be flooded. Everyone was asleep in their bunks. I tried to get out of my bunk to run to the control room to tell them the valve had opened while we were submerged. But I couldn't get out. It was a nightmare but it was so vivid.

"I could feel my skin crawl. Feeling your skin crawl was, to me, a sign of impending insanity, having read that some place. It was hard not to believe my nightmare was really happening.

"Finally, nearing the end of this week of unbearable heat which left us all debilitated and the tension from the destroyers chasing us down every night and only being on the surface three hours a day to the usual six, seven or eight, this guy comes to me and says, 'That Jim Crowell is a filthy so-and-so. You ought to see his bunk. It is just full of cockroaches.' I said, 'Cockroaches!' So I went over to my bunk and screwed in the lightbulb and there's my bunk just full of cockroaches, beautiful cockroaches.

"I was so glad to see those cockroaches," he said, realizing the insects crawling across his skin had affected his dreams. "Though I dreaded the thought of them crawling all over me, I was glad to see them because they convinced me I wasn't going crazy."

With his men at the breaking point, Voge got off a message to sub headquarters, now on the southwest coast of Australia, requesting permission to break off the patrol. The request was granted in the nightly

FOX schedule broadcast to submarines at sea and containing directives to all of them so none had to break radio silence.

The *Sailfish* settled into an easterly course north of the Dutch East Indies, then turned south through the Sapi Strait to the safety of the Indian Ocean and the eight-day run to Australia. Finally the men were able to relax while laughing off intercepted radio broadcasts from Tokyo claiming the U.S. Fleet had been destroyed at Pearl Harbor and that the *Sailfish*, the most famous submarine in the world as the former *Squalus*, had met her doom under the Japanese fleet.

On March 19, the boat passed through protective minefields to Fremantle on the southwestern coast of Australia. The port sits at the mouth of the Swan River, 12 miles downriver from the city of Perth, one of the most isolated cities in the world. The submarine idled in on her own power, tying up alongside the submarine tender *Holland*, which had escaped Manila unscathed. Although passengers and crew aboard the *Holland* cheered the *Sailfish*'s arrival, the mood was decidedly downcast.

The harbor was crowded with refugee ships from Java and Malaysia, and the U.S. Navy was smarting over its many defeats. It was, as one American officer put it, "an atmosphere of depression." Yet, the people of Perth greeted the arrival of the submarines as a godsend. Anxiety gripped the continent, since most of Australia's army was in the Middle East fighting the Germans. Shops in Perth were boarded up and sandbagged in anticipation of an attack by the Japanese. Predictions of an imminent invasion were born on the news that the combined Asiatic fleet, including the Australian cruisers *Perth* and *Exeter*, had been annihilated in the Java Sea.

At the same time, U.S. codebreakers had tracked a fleet of six Japanese carriers and two battleships to Kendari in the Celebes Islands, 800 miles northwest of Darwin. Preemptive strikes by enemy planes left the Australian port in flames. Cattle and sheep ranchers began driving their herds south into the deep Outback in preparation for an anticipated invasion. The only chance of stalling the assault, it seemed to most, was to send refitted Fremantle subs—including the *Sculpin*—north to intercept the fleet. The *Sailfish*'s sister ship had had only seven days to prepare, coming off a torturous war patrol in which she sank a destroyer and damaged a cruiser but sustained severe counterattacks. One such depth charging threw the submarine into an out-of-control dive because of jammed diving planes. The boat finally leveled off at 340 feet after frantic action by the captain and crew. As a result of the patrol, the navy awarded Chappell the Navy Cross for heroism.

In Fremantle and Perth, word spread quickly that the old *Squalus* had somehow survived. Voge, like Chappell, was awarded the Navy Cross for the sinking of the carrier, earning him great respect throughout the fleet and Australia. President Roosevelt, in a nationally broadcast radio address in the United States, hailed the achievement, while reminding the nation that the old *Squalus,* now the *Sailfish,* had redeemed herself.

The arrival of the *Sailfish* in Fremantle confirmed what the crew had difficulty believing—the attack on Pearl Harbor. "Tokyo Rose put out only bum news. But, I must admit," said Lt. Joseph Tucker, "she did tell us that our battleships were on the bottom of Pearl Harbor. Of course we didn't believe her!" Yet it was true, and now the three *Squalus* survivors aboard—McLees, de Medeiros, and Cravens—could only wonder if their old skipper, Oliver Naquin, was among those lost on the *California.*

There was little time to relax in Fremantle. The *Sailfish* quickly prepared to embark on a rescue mission to Corregidor where MacArthur's army held out. Brig. Gen. Dwight D. Eisenhower, who had served under MacArthur and was now assistant chief of staff in the Operations Division of the War Department, was moved by the plight of those trapped on the island. Although he realized they were probably doomed, he still concluded, "We must do everything for them that is humanly possible." The only way to get through the Japanese blockade was by submarine, and the *Sailfish* was one of three designated to make the run.

The boat was fumigated to eliminate the cockroaches. All torpedoes were off-loaded except for eight left in the firing tubes, leaving room for 1,856 rounds of three-inch antiaircraft ammunition and medical supplies that were stuffed into every nook and cranny aboard.

On April 22, the *Sailfish* embarked on the hazardous voyage with every intention of bringing back a group of Army nurses who were to be evacuated. But the crewmen, like Eisenhower, realized the situation was hopeless, even if the *Sailfish* got through. "The mood was very bad," said Braun, the quartermaster. "Depressed, yes. We knew the fall of Corregidor was inevitable."

The *Spearfish* (SS-190) had preceded the *Sailfish,* arriving off Corregidor on May 3. Because of a Japanese minesweeper and a destroyer operating close to the island, the submarine moved in cautiously and silently at 180 feet deep. She surfaced after dark, and at 2025 a small patrol craft from the island rendezvoused with the submarine. The *Spearfish* took on twenty-seven passengers—twelve officers, the first group of twelve female army nurses, the wife of a naval officer, and two stowaways. The submarine then headed to sea, diving under the destroyer-cruiser screen off the island and remaining submerged for the next 22 hours in a nerve-wracking getaway to Australia.

On May 4, with the *Sailfish* within a few days of arrival, the last message broadcast from Corregidor was deciphered by the *Spearfish:* ONE HUNDRED AND SEVENTY-THREE OFFICERS AND TWENTY-THREE HUNDRED AND SEVENTEEN MEN OF THE NAVY REAFFIRM THEIR LOYALTY AND DEVOTION TO COUNTRY, FAMILIES AND FRIENDS.

Just short of their goal on May 6, the men of the *Sailfish* were ordered to return to Fremantle. The defenders of Corregidor had surrendered.

Sanctuary

Somberly, the crew of the *Sailfish* turned south along the Borneo coast, making the lonely return trek across the Indian Ocean as Australia's winter closed in. After five months at war, there was little to cheer about. Japan's well-rehearsed war machine had met nearly all objectives and now threatened the subcontinent. In Perth and Fremantle, residents expected a strike by carrier-based enemy bombers at any time. But the attack never came. "It was fortunate for us since western Australia was the only convenient place left for our submarines," said Bayles. "It was important we had a place where we could rest, relax, pull alongside the tender to get refitted and get ready for the next patrol. That the Japanese overlooked that little area, thank goodness."

Rear Adm. Charles Andrew Lockwood had taken the reins at Perth. At age 52, he was energetic, brisk, and tenacious, known to fly in the face of naval rulebooks. He was the submariners' submariner—"Uncle Charlie" to them. He also was no stranger to the men of the *Sailfish* and the *Sculpin,* for it was he who got the *Squalus* distress call at the War Department in 1939, putting into motion the heroic rescue.

In Perth, the admiral was appalled at conditions on returning boats. "All hands look tired and thin," he wrote in his diary, noting in particular how drawn Chappell seemed when the *Sculpin* arrived on April 27. The men looked like refugees, having lost weight from the intense heat aboard. Several sported what Lockwood termed "beautiful apostolic beards." He worried about the stress of nonstop patrols and the inability of the men to get enough sleep on the noisy sub tenders. Resolving to do something about it, he borrowed an idea from Adm. Chester Nimitz, the new commander of the Pacific Fleet at Pearl Harbor who had leased the posh Royal Hawaiian Hotel as R&R facilities for aviators and submariners. Lockwood did the same in Perth, renting four hotels—two in town, two at the beach—for the sub crews arriving from war patrols. The residents of Perth also pitched in. Every courtesy was extended the men who were likened to saviors of the continent.

To the crews, the city of 400,000 was unique, endearing, and beautiful, a place where black swans graced the central river and laughing kookaburra birds soared over terracotta roofs. Here, at the western portal to the vast deserts that isolate Perth, the Americans spent carefree hours hunting, playing tennis, sightseeing, and partying while spending money with abandon. "We never cared about money. You never knew if you would come back from a patrol run anyway," said the *Sculpin*'s Rocek who made three liberties in Perth. "Whatever money you had, you spent. At that time, most of us believed that, if you made four successful patrol runs, you were pressing your luck. You would never make a fifth. Your chances were nil. So we felt, 'Hey, go for broke. Live it up. Enjoy yourself while you can.'" That they did, being drawn to an abundance of unattached women in a city where young local males were serving the British overseas. "There were girls everywhere. We had no problem with girls, nice girls," the *Sailfish*'s Braun reminisced. "All the taxis were driven by girls, very beautiful girls." So infatuated were the submariners that many proposed marriage, including three on the *Sculpin*.

Despite the pleasures of Perth, the dread of beginning a new war patrol was ever-present. Lockwood did what he could to lift spirits. He was there to see each submarine off, and he made a point of leaping aboard on the return before the lines were even secured. He engaged the crewmen in conversation and, with a cup of coffee in hand, settled into the skipper's cabin to discuss the just-completed patrol with each captain. He arranged for bands to herald all arrivals and departures. In keeping with the American Old West ambiance of western Australia, the bands played the Gene Autry tunes "Empty Saddles in the Bunkhouse" when the boats departed and "Back in the Saddle Again" when they returned. All of this was Lockwood's way of showing appreciation and keeping up morale.

Still, the task of sinking enemy ships was indomitable. Only nineteen fleet submarines were available to patrol the vast Southwest Pacific and only one-third actually could be on patrol at a time. All others were either undergoing refit, or making the long voyage to and from the war zone. Furthermore, Fremantle was at the extreme end of a long, slow resupply line from the United States. Thus limited torpedoes and spare parts were available, forcing most boats to set out with insufficient supplies of each.

It was a schizophrenic period for submariners. The horror of combat alternated with the joy of Aussie life every six to eight weeks. One month, the men were barely escaping a devastating depth charge attack, and the next they were placing bets at an Outback racetrack. One week they were sinking an oil tanker and fleeing enemy destroyers, and the next they were sitting on a dock in the Fremantle sunshine with apples stuffed in their pockets, chewing on stalks of celery while reading letters from home. One day, they were cursing submarine service while trapped at great depth in stifling heat, waiting out an enemy overhead. Days later, they were doing the "Hokey Pokey" in Perth. And they all knew it could end quickly in some nameless patch of the ocean. Indeed, the troubles with the Mark XIV torpedoes ensured that every patrol was hazardous to the extreme.

Lockwood was convinced the weapon was flawed; he had read too many reports not to believe the skippers. He was particularly drawn to the *Sculpin*'s Kendari patrol in which Chappell had hoped to intercept the Japanese fleet believed massing for the attack on Australia. Although the armada turned west and left the scene, the boat intercepted a 5,000-ton merchant ship on March 31 and fired three torpedoes at close range. "It seemed impossible that they could miss, yet no explosions were heard, no hits were observed and the target was heard to continue to run without pause," the skipper, who was furious, wrote in his patrol log. "If the truth be told, the Commanding Officer was so completely demoralized and disheartened by repeated misses that he had little stomach for further action until an analysis could be made, the finger put on the deficiency or deficiencies responsible, and corrective action taken."

Intent on rooting out the cause, Lockwood convened a meeting of sub captains, including Chappell, in Albany, an old whaling station and sub base around the southwest corner of Australia, two days' sailing time from Perth. The admiral arranged for the *Skipjack* to test the torpedoes by firing them at a fishing net suspended vertically from the ocean bottom outside Albany's harbor. The tests proved the torpedoes were running too deep and corrections were made. It was an immediate boost to morale. Yet erratic guidance, premature explosions, and duds continued to haunt the force. In fact, it would be another year before all the ills were worked out.

Through the Aussie winter, the subs operated out of Albany where nothing stood between them and the South Pole but the Antarctic Ocean. When the *Sculpin* arrived in May, wintry cold had settled over the town of 5,000 overlooking Princess Royal Harbor, a small bay protected on three sides by barren limestone cliffs and low hills. "It reminded me of a town in the Old West," said Rocek. "A boardwalk ran in front of the stores which had overhangs. It was quaint and neat. You would feel that you were in another time."

As in Perth, the townspeople laid out the welcome mat. "The crews from all submarines and the USS *Holland* were loved by all Albany people," said Clarrie Smith who was a 14-year-old school boy at the time. "I would obtain the home addresses of those from *Sailfish* and *Sculpin* and write letters to their mums or wives. It certainly beat the censor and let the families know the location of their son's or husband's ship and his health."

The crews were invited into homes all over town, and the sailors reciprocated by giving tours of the boats. The *Sailfish*, in particular, drew gawks because of her checkered history as the infamous *Squalus*. The big spending strangers enthralled the town. "Never had I seen so much money in my life," said Smith, who earned tips by preparing sandwiches during poker games at hotels where the sub vets stayed. "The bigger their win, the bigger my tip. After the first week, all the pubs were cleaned out of anything that came out of a bottle. I remember how before the submarines arrived, I would walk down the streets past the hotels and notice the stocks of Scotch, brandy, rum, and vodka all covered in dust. No one could afford it. It was beer, beer, and more beer."

In the piano lounge at the Freemason Hotel, officers and crewmen wiled away the hours, singing a gusty version of the popular Aussie tune, "Bless 'Em All": "Sink 'em all, sink 'em all, Tojo and Hitler and all; Sink all their cruisers and carriers too; Sink all their tin cans and their stinking crews."

Meanwhile, the *Sailfish* and *Sculpin* underwent major modifications. The conning tower superstructures were cut down to reduce their visibility to enemy ships. And newly developed SD radar was installed, which would allow the boats to detect incoming enemy aircraft and thus avoid attack. By June, both boats were ready and embarked for the South China Sea, where neither was particularly effective. In the course of two months, they damaged four small cargo ships and a tanker but no sinkings could be confirmed.

In early August, both returned to Albany where townspeople celebrated encouraging news. The Battle of the Coral Sea north of Australia had resulted in a stalemate, forcing Japan to abandon thoughts of invading Australia. And on August 7, as the *Sculpin* moored alongside the *Sailfish* in Princess Royal Harbor, U.S. Marines landed on Guadalcanal in the Solomon Islands east of New Guinea to begin one of the bloodiest battles of the war. In Albany, the crews of the two boats were swept up in the enthusiasm of what seemed a turning point in the war. But within two weeks, both boats were ready to head back to war.

The *Sculpin* got under way first, sailing for Fremantle, with the *Sailfish* to follow. Plans changed abruptly en route. "The beachhead at Guadalcanal was in jeopardy," explained Tucker. "Our surface forces had been clobbered and we were fresh out of carriers. At one time, every sub in the [South] Pacific was directed to head toward the Solomons." Thus, the *Sailfish* and *Sculpin* reversed course to make a 3,000-mile voyage around the southern coast of the continent.

They arrived in Brisbane after an 11-day journey. As brief "voyage repairs" got under way, the crews spread out in the gritty seaport known as the New Orleans of Australia. At the same time, there was a change in command aboard the *Sailfish*. Voge was ordered back to Pearl Harbor to become submarine combat operations officer for the fleet. The new skipper was 37-year-old Lt. Cdr. John Raymond "Dinty" Moore, a Tennessee native who had distinguished himself as commander of the *S-44* by sinking two merchant ships and an enemy cruiser, earning him the Navy Cross.

The *Sailfish* and the *Sculpin,* with Chappell still at the helm, cast off within a week of each other, heading for the Solomons in what would become a harrowing ordeal for both boats.

On September 28, off the Bismarck Archipelago, the *Sculpin* torpedoed a cargo ship. For three hours, two destroyers counterattacked, one coaching the other as they tracked the submarine. Bombs straddled the boat, causing her to briefly lose power and spring numerous leaks. The crew worked furiously to stop the flooding while maintaining silent running. Lt. (jg) Corwin Mendenhall discovered a powerful stream of water shooting from the officers' head into the forward battery compartment. Desperately, he used his hands to hold back the flow while yelling for help from crewmen who arrived with plugs and turnbuckles to stem the high-pressure leak. It took a bucket-brigade more than an hour to collect the water taken in, thus preventing it from flooding battery cells on the keel, which would have produced deadly chlorine gas. The black gang did the same in the engine rooms, where numerous leaks threatened to short-circuit the electric motors, then turning at two-thirds speed to keep the boat from sinking to crush depth.

The men were taxed to the limit doing what was necessary to save the *Sculpin*. The attack had loosened rubber bearings in tubes housing the propeller shafts, causing them to emit a high-pitched scream at great depth. Nevertheless, the boat slipped away, with Chappell determined to strike back.

On October 7, the boat sank a 4,731-ton transport off New Ireland. A week later, she dodged a destroyer to sink a smaller cargo ship. And on October 18, she inflicted damage on the light cruiser *Yura* before being driven off by gunfire. The boat then headed back to Brisbane for repairs.

In the *Sailfish's* patrol to the north off Guadalcanal, the boat was unable to attack a fast-moving Japanese cruiser screened by eight destroyers that passed over the boat. Two days later, the submarine attacked a minelayer. When all three torpedoes missed, the boat dove. The enemy countered by dropping eleven depth charges over the *Sailfish*, causing extensive minor damage. Bad weather and overwhelming odds due to heavy concentrations of enemy warships thwarted the rest of the patrol, forcing the boat to return to Brisbane. She arrived on November 1, five days behind the *Sculpin*.

By then, both boats were in sad shape. They had been at sea for nearly three years, long past the time they should have returned to the States for repairs. Ralph W. Christie, captain of the sub squadron in Brisbane, viewed both as in "poor condition and in urgent need of major overhaul back in the U.S." That view was shared by Voge before he left the *Sailfish:* "The ship is beginning to show the strain of spending seventy-four percent of the time under way and steaming 26,400 miles in the past six months."

By mid-November, the two were ready to make the long journey home through enemy territory. On November 18, the *Sculpin* embarked for Truk Islands, Japan's Central Pacific fortress. Six days later, the *Sailfish* followed. For both boats, the journey would prove to be a near disaster.

12

Going Home

In mid-December, the *Sculpin* arrived off Truk, a foreboding group of fifty volcanic peaks bristling like ragged teeth raised above the horizon. Chappell moved in carefully, skirting dangerous coral reefs. Numerous inlets allowed enemy ships to come and go, the Japanese frequently changing routes to foil submarines laying in wait. But on the night of December 18, the *Sculpin* finally sighted an aircraft carrier led by three destroyers. At 0040, with the boat closing rapidly on the surface, she was detected. Two escorts pealed off in pursuit. The submarine turned away, trying to outrun the destroyers. For a moment, it seemed to Chappell she might make it.

But suddenly a searchlight fully illuminated the boat. Both destroyers opened fire from 6,000 yards. Shells fell in great geysers around the boat as she dove. The destroyers pinpointed her on sonar and raced over, lobbing depth charges intended to finish her.

The *Sculpin* slid downward in an elevator plunge to 300 feet. Anxious crewmen stopped in their tracks. Clattering diesels were stilled, as were all ventilation fans, the air conditioning, and any other mechanical devices. There was only the nearly noiseless hum of the boat's electric motor in the keel, powering the getaway. The crewmen stood in stony silence, listening intently for the thresher-like sounds of the oncoming destroyers. The men moved about only when necessary, and then very deliberately. The officers issued few commands, passed in a hush over the boat's telephone line to the talkers, who repeated them in a whisper to the men.

The commotion of one destroyer dropping depth charges and the two others dashing about played into Chappell's favor, masking the *Sculpin*'s movements below. The enemy lost contact as the submarine proceeded away "at creeping speed," the captain later reported. He kept the boat deep for the next three hours, moving up gradually to periscope depth where no vessels at all were detected. At 0400, the submarine burst to the surface, the crewmen throwing open the deck hatches. Simultaneously, the powerful diesels came to life, sucking cool night air through the boat in a huge torrent that practically lifted the men off the deck.

After a few hours, the boat submerged for the day and then resurfaced at sunset to resume prowling the southwest shipping lanes to and from Truk for the next several nights, sinking an oil tanker as it rendezvoused with a destroyer. A few days later, Chappell and the lookouts watched as a Japanese hospital ship passed, all lit up like a floating jewel so submarines would not attack.

On New Year's Eve, as the boat prepared to begin the open ocean run back to Pearl, the joy of homecoming was duly noted in the *Sculpin* logbook: "G'bye Australia and all you diggers, Too hard there to rill your jiggers. We'll navigate by sight and sound, We can't get lost when we're homeward bound."

Meanwhile, 800 miles to the south, the *Sailfish* passed New Britain in the Solomons as the Japanese retreated. "The Japanese were having their own little Dunkirk at Lae and Salamaua where Australian and U.S. forces were forcing the Japanese into the sea," said Tucker. "*Sailfish* was put specifically on the Rabaul-Lae-Salamaua route to intercept these ships." On Christmas Eve at midnight, the boat sank a Japanese submarine, silhouetted in bright moonlight and completely unaware of the *Sailfish*'s presence. A few days later, two other attacks on a convoy and a destroyer misfired. For the next week, the boat journeyed north uneventfully until January 8, when radar picked up a fast-closing airplane. The boat made an emergency dive but heavy seas pounded the vessel, slowing her descent. As she passed the 90-foot mark, a 500-pound bomb exploded, staggering the submarine. The concussion shattered lightbulbs and knocked paint chips loose from the overhead. But once again, the *Sailfish* escaped. She later surfaced and, like the *Sculpin*, headed for Pearl.

After a year at war, the crewmen of both boats needed extended R&R. On the *Sculpin*, Chappell feared the Navy might transfer his men to newly constructed submarines, thus putting them right back on the firing line, before they could take extended leave. Most of the crew, he noted in his patrol report, had been together from the first day of the war and "are approaching physical and nervous exhaustion." They needed time to relax, to return on leave to their families in the United States. He estimated that out of 397 days at war, fully 300 were spent at sea, much of the time submerged.

The two sister boats traveled the surface by day and night. Four lookouts manned the bridge, binoculars draped around their necks while supporting themselves against the pitch and roll of the boat by wrapping their legs around the railing. They held the glasses to their eyes, making a steady sweep to take in the sky, the horizon, and the sea in four quadrants all around the boat, each quadrant slightly overlapping the other. They had to be on guard for airplanes of any sort; more than once an unmarked sub had been bombed accidentally by friendly forces. The vigil went on day and night, with nothing to be seen but mile after mile of endless ocean. And in the twilight, thousands of stars pinpointed the sky all the way down to the horizon.

For the men below, such breathtaking sights were seldom seen. Most preferred to stay inside through the entire patrol. Except for the captain, every officer and crewman stood one eight-hour watch daily. The shifts were useful in managing the cramped space. Sharing bunks was the only way to provide enough sleeping quarters for the crews. As one man woke up to begin his shift, another was coming off and climbed into the just vacated bunk—thus the term "hot bunking."

Another nuance was the practice of "reversa," the deliberate reversal of normal daily routines after arriving in enemy waters. During daylight hours, the boats stayed submerged, allowing most of the crews to sleep. At night, as the vessels rose from the depths to begin searching for targets, they came alive with lookouts posted and men at stations, ready to attack or prepare for counterattack at a moment's notice. This nightly routine affected many old habits. Thus, breakfast on the *Sculpin* would be served in the evening, around 1800, and dinner would be at dawn of the next day. After many weeks of this, crewmen began to lose any sense of time. "You never went topside. Just the lookouts," said engineman Rocek. "So, sooner or later you would wonder what the hell day it was. Was it morning or was it night? And when you woke up, you would wonder if you just ate or are you going to eat."

Although reversa was practiced on the *Sailfish*, there was a difference:

"We had two meals a day, both submerged, breakfast after diving in the morning and dinner before surfacing in the evening. In that way bad weather didn't affect our meals," explained Lieutenant Tucker.

There was plenty of time for relaxation on patrol, as much as five hours of free time daily. Inevitably, poker games for high stakes got under way in the after battery compartment. There, the mess hall was the social center of each boat. Submarine crews in effect ate their way through a war patrol. There was little room at the beginning of a voyage because of huge stores of food. But toward the end, space opened up all over the boat. The forward torpedo room became a second social hub because of newfound space, a place where 16mm movies could be shown. Submarines often sidled up to one another at sea to exchange as many as fifteen reels. The crews regularly tuned in Tokyo Rose—for laughs. What astonished them most about radio from Tokyo and Manila was the enemy's preference for American military music, particularly the oft-played "Stars and Stripes Forever."

Both the *Sculpin* and the *Sailfish* had libraries in their mess halls, where dog-eared magazines and well-read novels accumulated. Each of the rates was assigned a locker the size of a medicine cabinet near his bunk. To break the monotony on patrol, practical jokes abounded, and the victims always extracted good-natured revenge.

After seven days of surface running, the *Sculpin* arrived off Oahu on January 8, a week ahead of her sister ship. The boat was met by the USS *Litchfield* (DD-336), which escorted her past bristling coastal defenses. On her way up the twisting channel leading to Pearl Harbor, the boat motored solemnly past the overturned hull of the battleship *Oklahoma* and sunken wreckage of the *Arizona*, then proceeded past the towering navy yard cranes, turned in the channel, and headed for the submarine base dead ahead. A welcoming band played the "Star Spangled Banner" as the submarine heaved to. Scores of dignitaries received the boat, repeating the gala receptions accorded her in Australia. Later, rates who had been promoted to chiefs at the end of the run were ceremonially dunked at dockside by fellow crewmen.

After a three-day layover, the *Sculpin* embarked for San Francisco, followed nine days later by the *Sailfish*. On January 18, the *Sculpin* rendezvoused with a blimp detailed to protect her from being mistaken for an enemy submarine. Chappell and the lookouts watched as the orange magnificence of the Golden Gate Bridge came into view. The boat passed slowly under the span as motorists beeped their horns and waved enthusiastically. The submarine rounded Fisherman's Wharf, passing between it and the federal penitentiary of Alcatraz before putting in at the Bethlehem Steel Company's shipbuilding yard in the city. Just over a week later, the *Sailfish* arrived, mooring at the Mare Island naval shipyard directly across the bay from the *Sculpin.*

It would take a few months to complete the overhauls. In the meantime, the crews of both boats headed east on passenger trains in a country brimming with vitality. Gone was the hopelessness of the 1930s. In its place was a strong sense of purpose and a booming economy. The United States had become what President Roosevelt termed "the great arsenal of Democracy," producing munitions at a truly phenomenal rate. In Southern California, one B-24 bomber came off assembly lines every 23 minutes. In Detroit, a trainload of new tanks emerged from the Ford Motor Company every day. And in Philadelphia, a new troop ship slid down the ways every eight hours. Factories large and small produced whatever was needed. Merry-go-round manufacturers made gun mounts. Toymakers built bomb fuses. A third of the nation's women poured into the factories, joined by their teenaged children. Everyone got into the act. The blind sifted floor sweepings for reusable rivets. The deaf manned production lines in plants where noise levels were intolerable. And little people inspected the insides of airplane wings.

It was all remarkable to George Rocek, eastbound on a troop train for his home in Cicero, Illinois, where his family didn't know he was coming. He watched from his passenger window as train after train passed in the opposite direction, bound for the West Coast with an endless stream of artillery, tanks, and weapons of every make.

Arriving in Cicero, he caught a cab home. His father, who operated a tailoring shop adjacent to the family home, was at work when his son—tall, bearded, and smiling—stepped through the door. "I said, 'Hi!' But he didn't know who the hell I was. And I said, 'Pa, it's me! George!' The tears came to his eyes. He grabbed me and hugged me. And then he just broke down," recalled Rocek, his voice cracking at the memory.

Into the wee hours, he and his family talked about the war and their younger days. "Every summer, . . . all the families would go out to the forest reserve about 20 miles away and have a lamb and a pig roast. We did this every two weeks on Sunday. Everybody brought side dishes. There were ball games, singing, hiking, playing cards and dancing. You wouldn't get home until eight or nine o'clock at night. Then in the winter, they would hire a hall and do the same thing once a month. . . . Those days put an anchor, a concrete foundation in you. Later in the war, I would think about it often and say to myself, 'Gosh, what a wonderful time for a youngster to go through.' It shows you how those people really enjoyed life then."

In the final days of his leave, he posed for a series of newspaper photographs with his younger brother. When the day arrived for Rocek to return to the awaiting *Sculpin*, it was a tearful farewell. "I wasn't fearful about going back. But my mother cried. My dad, though, was solid."

By April, the crews of the *Sailfish* and the *Sculpin* had regrouped as the overhauls were coming to an end, marred by tragedy for the *Sailfish*. Two motormacs, returning from liberty in Sacramento, were killed when their car ran under a truck in heavy fog. Tucker was called on to identify the bodies.

The two boats had undergone significant modernization during the overhaul. Two vapor compression stills were installed to provide an abundance of fresh water while on patrol. The three-inch stainless steel deck canons were moved from aft to forward of the conning tower. And twin 20mm antiaircraft guns were mounted on the bridges of each vessel. But what truly revolutionized them was the addition of SJ radar. Both boats could now track enemy vessels by day and night, precisely locating them under any conditions. Submarine commanders salivated at using the boats' great speed and maneuverability on the surface under cover of darkness to deliver radar-directed torpedo salvos on target. The SJ units promised to greatly enhance the force's war records.

There was difficulty putting the *Sculpin* back together, delaying her departure. The *Sailfish*, on the other hand, was ready on schedule. After two days of sea trials, she cast off for Pearl Harbor on April 22 with Moore, the boat's third skipper, still at the helm.

A week later, the *Sculpin* prepared to follow, confident of another successful patrol under Chappell's leadership. Earlier, an interview with the skipper made newspapers across the country. The *Chicago Herald-American* led page 1 with the headline, "Sub Sinks 13 Jap Ships." Although the *Sculpin*'s name was purposely left out, Chappell told of the boat's first six patrols in a story cleared by U.S. censors. It made a national hero out of the captain, and added to his stature among his men. Yeoman Reese evoked the feeling of many. "We'd go to hell and back with him. That's how we felt about Lucius Chappell."

As noon on May 1 arrived, wives, children, friends, and relatives waited anxiously on the dock to bid farewell to the *Sculpin*. A few sobbed openly. Hoses, electrical cords, and mooring lines were cast free. Slowly, the boat backed away from the dock with a long, forlorn blast of her whistle. Then she pulled clear, her battle flag whipping in the afternoon breeze. The renovated diesels powered the boat forward as the crowd cheered. She made the turn around Fisherman's Wharf and headed due west under the Golden Gate Bridge, where motorists again stepped from their cars to shout encouragement as the submarine passed under.

The boat arrived at Pearl Harbor on May 9, 10 days behind her sister ship. Both went into drydock for inspections while Chappell and Moore huddled with naval intelligence to receive their orders.

By the spring of 1943, enough submarines were available to form a blockade around Japan. All the while, new submarines were riding down the ways at the rate of three a month from shipyards in Portsmouth, New London, Philadelphia, Manitowoc (Wis.), and Mare Island. But for boats on patrol, losses were mounting, partially due to a U.S. blunder. The Allies had learned early on that Japanese depth charges were set to go off too shallow; a sub simply had to dive to 300 feet to escape. Incredibly, Congressman Andrew Jackson May, 68-year-old member of the House Military Affairs Committee, made this known in a press interview in the fall of 1942 to rebut enemy claims of massive submarine losses by the United States. Japan learned of Jackson's statement through a Honolulu newspaper and, by year's end, had readjusted depth charges to explode much deeper. Furious, Lockwood wrote a confidant, "I hear Congressman May said the [Japanese] depth charges are not set deep enough. He would be pleased to know [they] set them deeper now." Now, the weapons not only exploded deeper but they packed twice the power of earlier depth charges and were cited for the loss of six submarines between the time the *Sailfish* and *Sculpin* arrived for overhaul in the States and their departures three months later: The *Argonaut* (SS-166), the *Amberjack* (SS-219), the *Grampus* (SS-207), the *Triton* (SS-201), the *Pickerel* (SS-177), and the *Grenadier* (SS-210) had vanished with nearly 500 men.

Now, both the *Sailfish* and *Sculpin* risked the same fate, embarking on perilous missions to the coast of Japan itself.

13

Empire Waters

The *Sailfish* left Pearl Harbor on May 17. With many new crewmen aboard, Moore ran them through a daily combat problem, radar tracking drills, and battle surface exercises. The skipper wanted them well rehearsed for action. But he kept them loose as well, building morale by moving about the boat, chatting with his men. "He approached you on a fatherly basis," recalled Braun, still the boat's quartermaster. "He was a great storyteller."

The boat proceeded to the Kurile Islands, passing from the Pacific into the Sea of Okhotsk with its frigid Arctic waters north of Japan. Two U.S. destroyers and an oiler lay off the Kuriles in the Pacific as the *Sailfish* and another submarine already in the area searched for the Japanese fishing fleet. If either made contact, it would radio the destroyers, which would dash in for a hit-and-run attack. But heavy seas, freezing rain, and considerable fog beset the *Sailfish* all the way up to the ice line. The fog sweeping the superstructure made conditions on the bridge miserable. In the compartments, clammy dew pervaded the ship. "The difference between the temperature in the sub and the water outside was so great that all the water in the air inside condensed and formed large globules which dropped off the overhead and kept the boat wet all

117

the time," said Lieutenant Tucker, now the boat's executive officer. "When we slept we wore rainclothes with a tarp over us."

The quest for the fishing feet proved futile, so the *Sailfish* headed south. On June 3, she took up station on the east coast of Honshu, the heart of Japan. By day, she prowled submerged, passing under many small fishing boats and twice snagging fishing nets. "Each time we headed out to sea until we could take the risk of surfacing and cutting the fishing net clear," said Tucker.

The boat lingered off Todo Saki, the easternmost cape of Honshu, waiting to sink ore ships arriving at the nearby Kaimishi Iron Works. However, the submarine continued to be vexed, first by a breakdown in her torpedo firing computer and then other nuisances. At one point, the boat ran into a mine cable while submerged. The men held their breaths as it scraped across the hull without blowing up. Later the boat snagged a heavy cord to a large yellow balloon and began dragging it. "Fortunately, Captain Moore did not believe in diving deep but staying at periscope depth," said Braun. "We were constantly being depth charged. Boom. Boom. Boom. Constantly. We couldn't understand it since we hadn't surfaced. At night there was nothing. But during the day when we were submerged, we were depth charged. And we never could pick up why in the periscope." The answer was discovered one night when a crewman who was cleaning the periscope found what looked like a fishing line. "The officer of the deck says, 'Hell, no one's been fishing,'" said Braun. "So we pulled the damned thing in and it was two hundred yards of cord with this yellow balloon on it. For two days, we had been pulling it. But Moore, since he was running shallow, was always 200 yards ahead of the balloon. And that's why the depth charges never hit."

As the *Sailfish* continued her patrol, the *Sculpin* arrived in her quadrant to the south off Tokyo, having left Pearl seven days after the *Sailfish*. A few days went by, producing no results. Then, in the span of two weeks, action embroiled both boats.

The *Sculpin* seriously damaged the light carrier *Hiyo*. But then three other attacks were foiled by erratic torpedoes. Chappell was so furious he disconnected the magnetic warheads. On June 19 at 1328, the boat came upon an armed sampan believed to be operating as a surreptitious radio ship. The vessel was about to enter a fog bank so Chappell waited, preserving the element of surprise. At 1640, the *Sculpin* battle surfaced astern of the target. Lt. Joseph R. Defrees, the battery officer, darted with his men across the deck to man the boat's deck gun. As the sampan opened fire, bracing the submarine with machine-gun fire, the

Sculpin returned fire. The sub quickly overwhelmed the smaller ship, leaving it smoldering and sinking. Chappell directed a boarding party to see what could be found.

Lt. George Brown, the engineering officer, and three rates, each carrying .45-caliber handguns and with knives tucked under their belts, jumped to the bloodied deck of the sampan. As they began their search, two enemy sailors hiding in the forecastle opened fire. Guards on the *Sculpin* shot back, killing them. In the commotion, Defrees leaped from the sub to assist Brown. But he misjudged the distance and plunged into the ocean alongside sampan survivors who hid behind the hull as *Sculpin* deckhands took shots at them. Defrees screamed, "Don't shoot me! Don't shoot me!" In the cease-fire that ensued, Defrees swam to the stern and was hoisted back aboard. Meanwhile, the boarding party abandoned ship because of a fire in the sampan's hull. The submarine pulled away, leaving the *Miyashoma Maru* in flames.

Unlike the *Sculpin*, the *Sailfish* had fewer targets to shoot at, primarily because of a reluctance to go in close to shore due to minefields. Nevertheless, she was able to sink a large merchant ship on June 15. Ten days later she torpedoed another cargo ship. As Moore returned to periscope depth to confirm the sinking, a plane bombed the boat. "The blast knocked me flat on my back in the conning tower," said Tucker. The explosion fractured the periscope lenses, shattered glass throughout the boat, and knocked a ventilation fan loose in the radio shack, clobbering Raymond Doritty (CRM-PA) in the head. "There wasn't a man aboard that would have given a plugged nickel for his chance for life after that first one hit," he later recounted. As the *Sailfish* dove, enemy patrol boats sped to the scene and dropped more than seventy depth charges. Once again, the submarine narrowly escaped. Because of the broken periscope, Moore terminated the patrol and headed for Midway Island, arriving on July 3, one day ahead of the *Sculpin*.

Chappell had expected a rebuke for tampering with the torpedoes. He noted in a confidential memo to higher-ups that "it seemed the only possible course of action." By then, Charles Lockwood, now commanding all Pacific submarines from Pearl, and Nimitz had made up their minds to junk the magnetic exploders.

As for Moore on the *Sailfish*, he was dunned for what was deemed a less-than-aggressive patrol. The captain, according to Tucker, refused to defend himself. He was relieved and sent back to Pearl as Lockwood's engineering and maintenance officer. Tucker also left the boat. The new skipper was Lt. Cdr. William Robert Lefavour, 33, who had made only one prior war patrol as prospective commanding officer on the

USS *Sawfish* (SS-276). When Tucker realized Lefavour knew little about submarine warfare, he appealed to Moore to get him off the boat. Moore advised him of the consequences to his career from such a move. But Tucker had no confidence in Lefavour's ability and thus Moore got him transferred to Pearl, later becoming an instructor at the sub school in New London. After their refits, the *Sculpin* and the *Sailfish* steamed from Midway for the coast of China on July 25.

Although the Navy anticipated an aggressive patrol from Lefavour, his boat patrolled aimlessly. Only two targets were tracked, and neither was attacked. The crew began to resent the skipper for his unwillingness to go in close to enemy harbors where targets could be picked off. By mid-September, the *Sailfish* returned to Pearl empty-handed. Not a single torpedo had been fired. Division commander Frederick B. Warder was harshly critical and relieved Lefavour.

On the *Sculpin*, Chappell was still at the helm, one of the few commanders to stick with one boat from the beginning of the war. He was anxious to make this last run, to try his luck with torpedoes free of the magnetic warheads. The patrol started off well when on August 9 the boat sank a cargo ship off Formosa. But in three successive attacks over the next month, the torpedoes failed. On the last attack, Chappell watched incredulously from the periscope as a torpedo hit the side of the target, causing a splash but no detonation. Demoralized, the crew returned to Pearl.

An official assessment of the patrol praised Chappell's aggressiveness: "Although touchdowns only are counted, had the torpedoes exploded when they hit the target, no doubt the kill for this patrol would have been much larger." Lockwood decided to again test the torpedoes. Several were fired from different angles into a submerged cliff. Charles Momsen, the famed rescuer of the *Squalus* survivors, found one dud in 50 feet of water, "the warhead split open with big chunks of TNT lying around," he later said. Tests proved the firing pin was too fragile. Immediately, Lockwood radioed all submarines at sea to launch torpedoes only at oblique angles. From that point on all major exploder problems disappeared.

As for Chappell, the Navy decided he had been on patrol long enough and detached him from command.

While minor overhauls of the *Sailfish* and the *Sculpin* got under way in Pearl, the Navy cast about for new skippers for both boats. It turned to Lt. Cdr. Robert E. M. Ward to resuscitate the dispirited *Sailfish*. He and the former *Squalus* seemed an ideal match. Both were survivors. In January 1942, Ward was the junior officer on the *S-26* when she accidentally was rammed by a Navy patrol boat in the Gulf of Panama. Ward and two others were thrown from the bridge, the only three to get off alive. He later served as executive officer on *Gurnard* (SS-254) before taking command of the troubled *Sailfish* at age 30.

At the same time, Lt. Cdr. Fred Connaway, 32, was picked to helm the *Sculpin*. Connaway had been commanding officer of the *S-48* for two years. Stepping into shoes vacated by the legendary Chappell, however, posed a great challenge. Even more daunting was the fact that much of the boat's crew transferred out, including many who had served under Chappell from the start. Connaway would have to mold a new fighting unit. And all the while he would be under the watchful eye of a submarine division commander who decided to come along on the boat's horrifying return trip to Truk.

Contact

Edwin Keller was a frustrated young man as he surveyed the *Sailfish* and the *Sculpin*, laying end to end in a Pearl Harbor drydock in the fall of 1943. Going to war on a submarine had been his dream. And it seemed he had achieved his ambition when orders arrived for him to join the *Sailfish* earlier that spring. Keller, 19, had just graduated from submarine school where stories were still being told about the *Squalus*. Suddenly, he found himself aboard the very same ship, now a combat veteran making her way back to Hawaii from Mare Island. He couldn't have been more pleased, fitting in nicely as a seaman second class. Tall and lanky, with a booming voice, he was imminently likable to his fellow rates, who dubbed him "Whispering Ed."

So it was a rude jolt when he arrived in Pearl to find he had been assigned to the base—as a mess cook! Summer turned to fall. Submarines came and went. Yet, there he was, still stuck behind a griddle. Heroes went to sea, he grumbled. Grunts stayed on the base.

Now, in early November, with the *Sailfish* nearing the end of a refit, he decided to give the boat another try. But again it was no use; there were no openings as the submarine prepared for a return trip to Japan.

Noting Keller's great disappointment, a *Sailfish* officer went to the *Sculpin* to lobby for him and discovered the boat needed an electrician striker. "He came back and told me to pack my seabag. 'You sail tomorrow morning!' I felt so great the hair stood up on the back of my neck."

On the afternoon of November 5, the *Sculpin*'s diesels roared to life in a cloud of blue exhaust smoke. Simultaneously, a whistle hailed the boat's imminent departure. A crowd of dignitaries, including Admiral Lockwood, stood on the pier to see her off. With the hull vibrating from the throb of the engines, the gray, unmarked vessel moved away slowly to the strain of "Aloha" and "Sink 'Em All" played by a Navy band. The boat throttled ahead into the harbor, passing the overturned hull of the USS *Arizona*. Those on deck saluted as the ignominious reminder of Japan's surprise attack slipped by. The crew then went below, banging shut the hatches as the *Sculpin* headed into the Pacific. Her ninth war patrol was under way.

Keller, of course, was ecstatic to be aboard. But he, like others, was mystified by the fact two commanders were in the boat—Connaway and a squadron commander, Capt. John P. Cromwell, who had come aboard at the last moment. The men couldn't figure it out, reasoning that maybe Cromwell was along to oversee the skipper who was making his first patrol on a fleet sub.

But that was not the case. Lockwood had designated Cromwell to be the commodore of a three-submarine wolfpack being deployed off Truk. The *Sculpin* was to be his flagship. With new submarines joining the fleet every month, there were enough available to allow Lockwood to experiment. He was intrigued by submarine wolfpacks employed so successfully by the Nazis against Allied convoys in the Atlantic. Whereas the Germans controlled attacks from shore, the vastness of the Pacific made that impractical. Thus, the admiral conceived shifting control to a squadron commander who would ride into battle aboard one of the submarines. When one boat located a convoy, she would alert the others, bringing all three into action. It was chancy but seemed worth the risk. However, the first such unit—*Cero* (SS-225), *Shad* (SS-235), and *Grayback* (SS-208) in the East China Sea in October—turned in miserable results because of communications problems. The commodore, Momsen on *Cero*, considered the tactic a failure. Lockwood preferred to try again with Cromwell on *Sculpin*.

Truk was chosen due to the concentration of enemy vessels in and around the atoll. Furthermore, the United States was preparing to invade the Gilbert Islands, a string of mini-atolls strung across the equator 2,600 miles east of the Philippines. It would be the first major penetration of Japan's outer ring of heavily armed island defenses. Japan had long expected the Americans to launch a major offensive, but it didn't know where. Nimitz suspected the enemy would hold its main fleet at Truk, waiting to see whether the United States would strike at the Solomons, the Gilberts, the Marshalls, or eastern New Guinea. Once that was known, the enemy fleet would storm forth to vanquish the Americans.

Cromwell's immediate aim as the commodore for the *Sculpin*, the *Searaven* (SS-196), and the *Apogon* (SS-308) was to intercept and sink a group of cruisers and aircraft carriers en route from Japan to strengthen Truk. The three subs would be deployed approximately 200 miles apart on the northern approaches to Truk. When one made contact, the others would rush to assist.

Just before the *Sculpin* sailed, Lockwood had confided to Cromwell all aspects of Operation Galvanic, the invasion of the Gilberts. The admiral impressed on him the need for utmost secrecy. "I cautioned him not to impart this information to anyone, in order to lessen the danger of exposure of the plan of campaign, in case the submarine was sunk and prisoners taken," Lockwood later noted.

Cromwell knew a lot more than the plan for Galvanic. He had helped planned the U.S. submarine offensive and understood Lockwood's future strategy. He also knew all about ULTRA, the greatest secret of the war. Although submarine commanders received daily ULTRA intelligence on enemy ship movements, they could only guess as to how it had been obtained. They purposely were kept in the dark for fear they might be captured and tortured. Cromwell, on the other hand, was among a select few in on the secret.

In the *Sculpin*, the crew knew very little about the upcoming patrol. They weren't even aware the boat would operate in conjunction with two other boats. All they knew was that they were heading for Truk. "We knew the greatest hunting was near Truk," said Keller. "You had visions of coming back having sunk a carrier or a battleship. Submarine men went to sea with the idea they would sink half the Japanese fleet. Thus morale was very high. We knew we were going to deep water, the hunting was very good, and we knew we could always get away from the Japanese."

After refueling at Johnston Atoll southwest of Pearl, the *Sculpin* voyaged 3,500 miles further southwest, arriving at Truk on November 16. For two days, the boat searched in vain for the enemy. But on November 19 at 0030, radar made contact with a distant target. Connaway, three lookouts, and Cromwell were on the bridge at the time and turned their binoculars in the direction of the target. But in the darkness, they were unable to pick it up. Lt. Joseph Defrees, the officer of the deck, made his way topside, relieving Cromwell, who went below so as not to get in the way. Defrees was electric, eager for action. He had spent all of his free time working with the torpedo data computer (TDC) and the torpedoes, and studying the history of every attack by the *Sculpin*. So great was his enthusiasm that he had earned the nickname "Little Napoleon." In many ways, Defrees had a vested interest in the boat as the son of Adm. Joseph Defrees Sr. And it was his mother who had christened the boat in 1938.

As the *Sculpin* attempted to close, Connaway sent Defrees down to the conning tower to the TDC to prepare for battle. Radar determined the ship was pulling away to the north at 14 knots. The skipper calculated the submarine could run parallel to the vessel at 21 knots and then take position ahead of it in a classic end-around approach that would take nearly seven hours. During the surface dash, radar revealed the target was accompanied by seven smaller ships, possibly destroyers. Connaway concluded the largest blip had to be a transport because of its slow speed. By the morning twilight, the *Sculpin* had arrived ahead of the convoy undetected. As the battle stations alarm was sounded, the boat dove and waited. All was in readiness.

Shortly, the target came into view. Connaway took a quick look through the periscope and then lowered it to avoid detection. What he saw was a single freighter with five destroyers and a cruiser. The setup was perfect. But as Connaway raised the scope once more for final bearings, the convoy suddenly zigged toward the submarine. "Down scope! Emergency, 200 feet!" the captain shouted.

The boat plunged to the prescribed depth as the convoy passed over without dropping any depth charges, leading Connaway to believe the sub had not been detected. But Lt. George Brown, the diving officer, noted the ships had picked up speed. The noise of the negative buoyancy tank used in the quick dive must have given away the boat's location.

After an hour at deep submergence, Connaway brought the *Sculpin* back to periscope depth for another look around. He reported the convoy moving away, almost out of sight in heavy haze. The skipper and Cromwell conferred, deciding the transport must be very important to draw such heavy protection. They agreed the *Sculpin* should surface and go after it in another end-around.

Connaway made a periscope sweep as he gave the order to surface. At 0730, the *Sculpin* burst from the ocean, and quartermaster Billie Minor Cooper (QM2c) hurriedly flung open the bridge hatch so he and

Lt. John N. Allen, the boat's executive officer, could climb topside for a look around—Cooper going aft on the bridge and Allen facing forward. "I said to Allen, 'I don't see a thing,'" recounted Cooper. "And he says, 'Look at this. What is that? Is it a crow's nest I'm looking at?'" Cooper squinted intently at what appeared to be a ship's staff just over the horizon, some seven miles away. He agreed with Allen that it looked like the top of a crow's nest on an unidentified vessel. "We couldn't tell what kind of a ship it was, so Allen says, 'We better take her down.'"

The two quickly dropped through the hatch to the conning tower as the boat commenced a dive, Cooper dogging the hatch behind him. Connaway meanwhile raised the periscope to take a look and soon made out a destroyer moving rapidly toward the boat. "It looks like they left a sleeper up there. Now he's on our tail!" he exclaimed.

In fact, a large flotilla leader destroyer, the *Yamagumo*, had dropped back five miles, hoping to catch the submarine off guard. The warship now bore down as the submarine sought the depths. The *Sculpin*'s sound operator reported screws of a fast-approaching vessel as the boat leveled off at 300 feet, rigged for silent running. In the quiet, the crew listened to the swish of the destroyer's propellers moving steadily toward them, growing so loud it seemed the destroyer would ram the submarine. Keller, as the after battery talker, was on the battle phones. "I want to tell you the screws sounded like a freight train coming through a tunnel. You could hear them coming from a long ways off. I looked around and saw Tom Brown [S2c] on his knees, blessing himself. Brown had made one patrol before, so he knew what to expect."

After the destroyer passed overhead, crewmen heard the unmistakable splash of depth charges catapulted from the *Yamagumo*. Seventeen 600-pound depth charges began ripping the depths at 30-second intervals. Immense shock waves battered the boat. Broken glass and shattered instruments showered the compartments. Chunks of cork fell from the overhead, and water began to spew like a fountain from a ruptured exhaust valve in the engine room. Packing around the starboard propeller shaft was blown loose, compounding the leaks. George Rocek and his fellow motormacs tried desperately to control the flooding but they couldn't.

Meanwhile, the destroyer began another run. "On the telephone, I can hear the sound man and tracking team," said Keller. "They would say, 'He's at 145 . . . 150 . . . 160 . . . 170 . . . 180 . . . he has turned towards us . . . he's coming in.' At that point I got scared. Then you heard propellers coming . . . swish. . . swish."

The *Yamagumo* dropped eighteen depth charges directly over the boat. The bombardment knocked out the boat's lighting system and worsened the leak. "The hands of the depth gauges fell off in front of my face," recounted Lt. George Brown. "The pressure gauges near the diving station commenced flooding and there was other minor damage about the ship." The boat groaned and creaked with every detonation. Attempts to evade were useless. Weather conditions were perfect for the destroyer's sonar, which had locked onto the *Sculpin*. Furthermore, the boat could find no thermal layer to hide under.

Brown stepped into the galley briefly where Keller and the cook were alone. "I say to Brown, 'When do we lose these bastards?' Keller recalled. And he says, 'We're not going to lose them. They have us.' I thought he was lying. After all, we were Americans and we can get away from them. I told him, 'You've got to be kidding. If they hadn't gotten us on the past two runs, how're they going to get us?'"

At 0930, the *Yamagumo* made a third run, dropping another accurate string of explosives. The disconcerted crew worked feverishly to control mounting damage. At a depth of 400 feet, the boat was barely under control. She took a large up-angle from the weight of water taken in. Connaway had to race the propellers to keep the boat from sinking to crush depth. The acceleration caused a whine to emanate from the boat, easily picked up by the *Yamagumo*.

Mercifully, the sound operator on the *Sculpin* located a squall on the surface. The boat headed for it, knowing the *Yamagumo* would lose contact in the noise of the storm. Connaway used the reprieve to start up bilge pumps so water could be pumped out of the boat to regain the trim. But the pumps failed to take suction and burned up. Now there was no way to pump water out of the compartments.

The skipper relieved Brown at the diving station in the control room so he could assess damage in the boat. Ens. William Fielder, a reservist making his first war patrol, took over as temporary diving officer while Connaway stood over him. Before going aft, Lieutenant Brown warned Fielder of the faulty depth gauge and the risk of accidentally broaching the boat if he wasn't careful.

In the after engine room, severe flooding made it impossible to level the ship without shorting the motors, the only thing now keeping the submarine afloat. Brown quickly organized a bucket brigade. In 115° heat, the men bailed water forward until the boat could be trimmed without danger to the motors. "All this time, the air is getting worse, the heat is terrific, and still he [the destroyer] doesn't let up on us," said Rocek, who manned the bucket line.

Connaway kept the submarine deep for several hours until it seemed the destroyer had left the area. No screws could be heard. Keller thought the submarine was home free. Even the cook began warming up chipped beef for breakfast.

The skipper decided to come up to periscope depth to determine if the destroyer was still around. At Connaway's command, Fielder began blowing the ballast tanks. The troublesome depth gauge began to move—from 200 feet to 190. From 190 to 180. And then 170, where it stuck fast. Neither Fielder nor Connaway noticed, as Fielder continued blowing the ballast. Suddenly, without warning, the submarine's bow shot into the air and splashed heavily onto the surface.

"Again I'm on the phone and I hear someone in the forward torpedo room screaming, 'What are we doing on the surface?! The bow is out of the water!'" recalled Keller. The boat wallowed in full view of the *Yam-agumo*, sitting 5,000 yards away. It was a near hopeless predicament for Connaway who ordered, "Take her deep! All ahead full!!"

The boat fell toward the bottom as the *Yamagumo* raced forward to deliver the *coup de grace*.

15

The Loss of the *Sculpin*

The crippled *Sculpin* fell slowly, nose down, toward the floor of the Pacific, five miles below. Her pressure hull was distorted and leaking. The after engine room was dangerously flooded. The motors, turning at high speed to keep the boat from sinking, were rapidly draining the batteries. And the crewmen bailing water in the engine rooms were exhausted in the nine-hour buildup of heat and stagnant air. Keller braced for the inevitable.

"I thought, 'Oh, my God. How can this be happening to me?' My heart was in my throat for 30 minutes. I remember hearing reports from the forward torpedo room that we were at test depth, and then a steady count in tens as the sub sank. And then a report we were below crush depth."

A pressure gauge registered 700 feet. The immense weight of the sea squeezed the vessel from all directions. The boat's hull plates and superstructure groaned, threatening to tear loose from the welded seams holding the ship together. The end would come quickly now, in darkness and a thunderclap of water.

But just as all hope seemed lost, Lieutenant Brown put a bubble in the bow buoyancy tank. The release of compressed air raised the bow enough to stop the downward plunge. Now the boat planed upwards, steeply, toward the surface where the *Yamagumo* awaited. Connaway turned to Brown. "Vent bow buoyancy!" The crew was finally able to regain control over the boat at 100 feet.

Immediately, the skipper turned his attention to the boat's worrisome batteries. He called the maneuvering room. "How much battery do I have left?" he inquired. "Sir, I give you just a few minutes to live," came the terse reply.

The *Sculpin* could do no more to save her crew. A surface shootout with the destroyer seemed the only option short of suicide. "Well, boys, we've done our best," Connaway said with finality to the men in the control room. "We'll have to surface while we can still bring her up." He instructed Brown to make sure the boat was scuttled if the battle was lost. The enemy could not be allowed to capture the submarine. Then Connaway cried out, "Battle stations! Gun action!"

Lieutenant Brown teamed up with others on the stiff, hand-turned diving planes, managing to nudge them enough to put the boat into a slow ascent. The gunnery crew sloshed through puddled water at the rear of the control room, ready to race topside to man the three-inch gun and two 20mm antiaircraft batteries aft of the bridge. In the after battery, others prepared to shuttle ammunition from a storage locker to the deck. Rocek and the black gang stood by to restart the diesels once the boat surfaced. Yet no order was given to prepare the ship to fire torpedoes once she surfaced. Quartermaster Cooper was baffled. "[Weldon E.] Dinty Moore [CSM-AA] asked the skipper, 'Don't you want to make ready the [torpedo] tubes?' And he said, 'No, just battle surface.' The tubes weren't opened because they were never ordered to be opened, forward or aft. I think the skipper had just given up. He knew we didn't have a chance with the little three-inch deck gun we had. I think he just wanted to give as many as wanted off a chance to get off once we surfaced."

Cromwell, returning to the control room from the wardroom, approached Connaway. The destroyer, he argued, had to be running out of depth charges. The crew had counted fifty-seven explosions. Even if the warship made another run, it would be unable to drop more than one or two. And it was quite possible the destroyer had no depth charges left. Although it was still more than six hours to sundown, if the *Sculpin* could somehow remain safely submerged, she could use the darkness to surface and escape. But Connaway stood his ground. "Cromwell was telling the skipper, 'Keep her down! Keep her down!' He says, 'No, we're going to battle surface!'" said Cooper who overheard the disagreement.

At that moment, the *Yamagumo* relocated the submarine from the noise of her propellers and dropped another depth charge. It exploded with a staggering roar slightly below the boat, cracking the hull around the torpedo tubes at both ends of the ship. The forward torpedo room began taking water. Sound heads below the boat were driven upwards, shearing clamps that held the sonar gear, leaving the boat with no means of tracking the destroyer or finding another squall under which to hide. In the dimness of emergency lights, the skipper knew the end had come. Connaway told Cromwell his crew deserved a chance to surface, to attack the destroyer. If the *Sculpin* lost, as he reasonably expected, at least the men could abandon ship and hope for rescue.

At 1330, the submarine burst to the surface in a frothy upheaval. As she bobbed there, Connaway still hadn't issued the order to open the hatch. With the submarine in extreme peril, others pleaded with Cooper to open it to give the gunnery crew a fighting chance. He finally did so, letting the men dart for the 20mm batteries and the deck gun. From the bridge, Cooper was the first to see the *Yamagumo*. It appeared to be stationary, about a half-mile away on the port side and vulnerable to a quick torpedo hit. "All we would have had to do is aim the boat," Cooper said. "We both were going in the same direction. All we would have had to do is aim the boat and let three fish go and we would have gotten him instead of him getting us."

The order to turn the boat and fire never came. But as Lieutenant Brown later explained, "No one was sure that the boat could open the outer torpedo doors. We couldn't get anything going."

The gunnery crew, meanwhile, squinted into a bright sun. "The day was a pretty one, with whitecaps coming over the deck," recalled Cecil Baker (F1c). "At first, we couldn't see the destroyer. Then one of the men spotted it right against the sun. He was about 3,000 yards off. Immediately we went to our stations on the gun and began to fire at him. We got off the first shot, which went over him. The second fell short."

Still, the destroyer didn't return fire. Cooper was surprised. "I think the Japanese were stumped, were wondering what we would do next because they could have gotten the fire out quicker than we did. When we surfaced, we didn't even go topside at first and they were dead in the water." With its superior firepower, the *Yamagumo* took no chances. It moved aft of the *Sculpin*'s conning tower, out of view of the boat's deck gun. Then it let loose with its powerful five-inch guns. The first salvo straddled the boat, sending geysers skyward but scoring no hits.

In the after battery compartment, crewmen were terrified. They knew the submarine was no match for the destroyer. Keller observed the shuttle crew opening an ammunition locker to pass reloads to the deck gun. "They start singing, 'Praise the Lord and pass the ammunition' and then we hear shots being fired from our sub," said Keller. "You hear our guns going 'boom . . . boom . . . boom.' Suddenly, there is this terrible, large explosion. They pass the word, 'What's the damage?' The word comes back, 'The conning tower has been hit.' "

The *Yamagumo*, zeroing in on the *Sculpin* after its first round, had fired a perfect second shot. The shell pierced the conning tower, scattering a blizzard of shrapnel that demolished the main inductions. Connaway, Defrees, Lt. John Allen, and Lt. (jg) G. R. Embury were killed instantly.

On the bridge, Cooper had been helping a gunner with a jammed machine gun. "I said, 'Let's go forward' and about this time the shell hit the conning tower and took the gunner's left arm clean off at the shoulder." Both men leaped from the wreckage into the ocean just as another shell hit the deck above the forward torpedo room, killing and injuring several men on deck. Alexander Guillot (F1c) tried to defy massive injuries. "I still remember how he looked with blood streaming from great rips in his chest, passing ammunition to the three-inch gun until he fell over the side," said Baker.

The *Sculpin* now was defenseless. The *Yamagumo* moved in, pouring gunfire. In the control room, Brown was shaken as the death toll was counted and he heard, "Sir, you are in command." He now worried the destroyer's next volley might incapacitate the boat's hydraulic system, preventing him from scuttling as Connaway had directed. He informed Cromwell that he could wait no longer. "He told me to go ahead, that it was the right thing to do," Brown later recounted. "He said he could not come with us for he was afraid the information he possessed might be injurious to his shipmates at sea if the Japanese made him reveal it by torture." Despite Brown's urgings, Cromwell stood fast by his decision to sacrifice himself.

The lieutenant ordered the engine room to power up to maximum speed. The big diesels roared to life, pushing the *Sculpin* ahead with a surge. Brown passed word over the intercom to abandon ship, as Cromwell sat down on an empty ammunition box, gazing at a photograph of his wife that he carried with him. Brown sent Richard Hemphill (CMMA) forward and William Haverland (MoMMA) aft to inform everyone to leave, in case the PA system had failed. But it hadn't and Keller, still on the phones in the after battery, would never forget Lieutenant Brown's last words on the line: "Abandon ship and God have mercy on your souls."

In the forward compartments, Hemphill encountered Fielder, distraught for his role in broaching the boat. He and Cromwell's steward, Eugenio Apostol (CK1c), refused Hemphill's admonition to hurry. "We do not choose to go with you. We prefer death to capture by the Japanese," Fielder replied, seated at the wardroom table.

Hemphill and Haverland returned to the control room where Brown and Philip Gabrunas (CMoMM), who volunteered to stay behind to help the lieutenant, prepared to scuttle the ship. Brown waited exactly one minute to give the survivors a chance to escape. The hatches were open and men were pouring out to be met by strafing gunfire from the *Yamagumo*.

In the after battery, Delbert Schroeder, the yeoman who had replaced Reese, was distraught as he made his way aft. "He came through and he was crying," said Keller. "I says to him, 'What's the matter?' He replies, 'I can't find my life jacket and I can't swim.' I say, 'I can swim but I don't think we'll be up there too long.' So I gave him my jacket. At that time, you could hear shells hitting the water. I got up and I was so scared I ran without taking the phones off." Yanked backwards, he fell flat on his back, got up, and hurried to join Schroeder and others making the climb to the deck from the engine room.

"There was no panic. No pushing and shoving. As I waited my turn, [Robert] Carter, a seaman second class, was going through the hatch with motormac [Duane] White right behind. Carter got shot and fell back down into the engine room. White caught him but his head had been blown off. He lowered him to the deck and then walked over to the engines.

"The next man going up was [George] Goorabian [S1c]. He notices I don't have a life jacket and says he'll wait for me on deck. I say, 'For God's sake, don't wait for me.' I then turn to White and say, 'Come on, Whitey! It's time to go.' He says, 'Them sons of bitches have got me this far. They can take me the rest of the way.' And he lights up a cigarette.

"I then went up the hatch. As I got almost to the top, Goorabian was hit and half his body was blown off. At that point, there was an explosion in the boat and I was blown out the hatch and over the side."

Meanwhile, George Rocek was going through a door at the base of the conning tower when a shell hit. "The blast just stunned me. I looked to make sure I had everything. I just couldn't feel anything," he said, describing how he jumped overboard with shrapnel wounds all over his legs.

With no more time to spare, Brown and Gabrunas opened the vents to take the *Sculpin* down for the last time. The lieutenant exited the boat by climbing the ladder into the conning tower where he slipped through the wreckage. "As I left the conning tower door, water was coming waist deep over the door sill and I am certain no one left the ship after me. I last saw Gabrunas going up the conning tower hatch. He either became fouled in wreckage or was killed by machine-gun fire."

Brown stepped into the sea as it rolled over the deck. He now was adrift. The *Sculpin* raced ahead with the destroyer in hot pursuit. Purposefully, the boat settled into her dive and disappeared, leaving a whirlpool of white foam. To the survivors, it was as pretty a dive as the boat had ever made. Moments later, a tremendous concussion rocked the ocean as the boat's 252 storage cells short-circuited, shattering the submarine. A giant waterspout erupted a half-mile from the survivors and then the sea closed over the *Sculpin* forever.

It had been exactly five years and 115 days since she had come down the ways in Portsmouth. In her time, she had helped save the trapped crew of the *Squalus;* had survived the Japanese onslaught in the Philippines; had defended Australia when a Japanese invasion seemed imminent; and had scoured more than 65,000 miles of the Pacific on nine war patrols, sinking three cargo ships and seriously damaging one enemy aircraft carrier, a light cruiser, a destroyer, five cargo ships, and one oil tanker. She had done her part to win the war, and now she was no more.

On the surface, Brown collected the survivors in one group. Stronger swimmers aided the wounded and the weak swimmers. Fortunately, the *Yamagumo*'s depth charges had cleared the area of all sharks.

Keller, who had been blown out of his clothes exiting the boat, recalled the peace that came over him. "I remember looking up and seeing how beautiful it was in the water and how beautiful the sky was. I just rolled over and said, 'Oh . . . ' Then, I became conscious of someone shooting at me. I rolled over again and saw the destroyer was very, very close. I was looking up at it. The bow was already by me and the aftergunners were machine-gunning those in the water. I could see them on the guns. I was too scared to notice anyone else in the water. But Julius Peterson [RM2c] had seen me and noticed I wasn't wearing a life jacket. He told me to come over and hang onto him and Schroeder. I swam over and then saw that Schroeder was dead. He had been shot, with at least two wounds in his chest."

At 1500, the destroyer ceased fire and began a pass through the survivors. "He only made one pass," explained Keller. "They threw out the lines and if you caught it you were very lucky. If you didn't, you were gone. But the destroyer was traveling very, very slow. Actually, he gave everybody a chance." But some chose to swim away.

"Me and Peterson grabbed the lifeline. I came up the [rope] ladder on the side of the ship where we were motioned by men with rifles to go forward to the bow. That's when I thought, 'Oh, my God. They want to tie us to the anchor and drop us overboard.'" Keller flashed back to the night before when the movie *Black Swan* had been shown in the forward torpedo room. It told the story of a sailing ship overtaken by the British who suspected it was carrying illegal slaves. During the pursuit, the crew of the suspect ship tied the slaves to anchors that were dropped overboard to hide the evidence.

There were no such plans on the *Yamagumo*. Rather, the survivors were ordered to sit on deck. Most were seriously injured. And two were in grave shape when they came aboard. "This guy who was striking for quartermaster, Claiborne Weade, had been hit in the stomach," said Cooper. "I grabbed him around the chest and another man grabbed him around the feet. We start forward when the guards motioned us to drop Weade on deck. Then they rolled him back into the sea. He was conscious, but he was bleeding from the stomach. They might have figured they just didn't want to fool with someone bleeding that much." The other badly mangled crewman wrenched free of the guards who intended to throw him overboard and hid among the other prisoners.

Later a large tarpaulin was draped over the survivors. A head count revealed there were three surviving officers and forty enlisted men out of a crew of eighty-four.

"Of course there was blood all over the place," said Keller. "I would estimate that out of forty-three of us, thirty-five had to be wounded severely. It was sometime later that someone said to me, 'How bad you hurt, Ed?' I said I wasn't hurt. But then I looked down at my chest and saw blood everywhere. It was dry, but right then I thought I was going to die."

With the prisoners under guard, the destroyer got under way for Truk, 200 miles to the west. Lieutenant Brown thought about Connaway, and how it had been almost unfair for the Navy to put Cromwell aboard when the skipper was making his first fleet boat patrol. He thought about the debate between the two over surfacing, Cromwell wanting him to hold out because the destroyer was running out of depth charges. And in fact, the *Yamagumo*'s racks contained only three more explosives when the survivors boarded the ship.

Incredible thirst gnawed at the survivors, dehydrated from the heat and exertion inside the *Sculpin*. Several tins the size of tuna cans were passed around with barely enough water to wet their lips. It would be the last they would have for three days. As night fell, the ship plowed ahead through a rainstorm and rough seas. The men were in agony from their untreated wounds and thirst, and they worried about their fate. "If I had known how hard it was going to be on Truk, I'd have gone down with the ship," said Cooper.

Indeed, Japanese intelligence officers were eager to get their hands on the *Yamagumo*'s cargo. For months, the naval fortress had been operating under tight restrictions because of diesel oil shortages caused by the submarine blockade. From his super battleship *Musashi* at anchor in Truk Lagoon, Vice Adm. Mineichi Koga, commander-in-chief of the Imperial Combined Fleet, had been unable to send out sufficient aircraft or ships to scout the area for signs of the U.S. fleet. By early November, he was certain something was up. American air strikes were occurring from the Kuriles in the extreme North Pacific to Rabaul in the extreme south. General MacArthur's forces had invaded Bougainville to liberate Papua New Guinea, and Admiral Halsey's South Pacific Fleet had won the Battle of Empress Augusta Bay. Koga responded by racing a cruiser-destroyer task force from Rabaul to help out at Bougainville. Sensing a trap, he simultaneously dispatched another cruiser-destroyer force plus 173 warplanes from Truk to protect Rabaul.

On November 13, American B-24 bombers began hammering the Gilberts and Marshalls, 1,500 miles to the east of Truk. For Koga, the question remained: Where would the invasion come—at the Gilberts to threaten Rabaul, or at the Marshalls to take Truk?

The *Sculpin* captives seemed likely to provide some answers through torture. However, as dawn approached and the destroyer entered Truk Lagoon at the foot of an imposing volcanic island and military fortress, Operation Galvanic—whose details Cromwell took to his grave—burst into the open. A Japanese reconnaissance plane on routine patrol glimpsed the advance elements of a carrier-assault fleet of 200 American warships moving on the Gilberts from the east—the largest amphibious attack force the world had ever seen. As the *Yamagumo* set anchor and guards blindfolded the *Sculpin* prisoners, U.S. marines stormed ashore on the soon-to-be famous beaches of Tarawa and Makin.

Meanwhile, far to the north, the *Sailfish* had taken up station off the southeast coast of Honshu, prepared to intercept and sink any enemy vessels on the sea lanes between Japan and Truk. In little more than 10 days, she would make a rendezvous with history and the *Sculpin* survivors.

Terror on Truk

The *Yamagumo* docked at Truk's Dublon Island, a bustling seaplane and submarine base. The prisoners' hands had been tied behind their backs and they were blindfolded so they could not see the battleship *Musashi* and other warships at rest in the lagoon. After being off-loaded from the destroyer, the men were prodded with bayonets toward waiting trucks. Many struggled to walk because of their wounds. All had lost blood and were in various degrees of agony. Rocek's legs were open wounds, covered by tiny coiled slivers of metal embedded under his skin. Another man grimaced from a hole the size of a silver dollar through his hand. Two others—one with a badly broken arm and the other losing blood from the calf torn from his leg—were in excruciating pain. Nonetheless, they were kicked and beaten with sticks as they moved toward the trucks.

Tales of Japanese brutality were well known to the men, and they were certain they faced torture. Already, on the *Yamagumo*, Herbert Thomas (TM1c) had been beaten during an interrogation. Anxious to avoid further injury, he "confessed," revealing that American submarines were refueling at a secret island between the Gilberts and Truk. His inquisitors laid out charts dating as far back as 1820, demanding that he pinpoint the island. He was vague about the location because, of course, it didn't exist. Taken back to the bow, he briefed his shipmates so they could give consistent accounts. Now they faced the same inquisition as they were driven to the other side of Dublon to a small stockade at the foot of a 1,500-foot peak.

For the next 10 days, the prison was their home, "a living hell for everyone concerned," said Cecil Baker, the *Sculpin* fireman. The captives were divided into three groups of fourteen men each and jammed into three cells, measuring less than eight feet square. Below a small ventilation window at the back of each room was a hole in the floor used as a toilet. The only other window was a foot-wide opening used to pass food to the men—and club them. "There wasn't much conversation because if there was, a hand would come through the window with a club like a baseball bat, only longer, and just swing," recalled Keller. "I happened to be in a room with a man named Baker [Joseph Baker, F1c]. We were all walking wounded. Baker cried all night from thirst and the pain. He would yell, 'I need water! I need water!' and that hand with the bat would reach in and whomp! whomp! whomp! We had to gag him to keep from being clubbed. Everybody took a blow. . . . The club could reach just about the whole length of that room. I got hit in the shoulder and the head. It hurt but didn't knock you unconscious. You learned to put your hands over your head and turn to protect yourself."

The survivors received bare sustenance. "Our food rations consisted of one rice ball a day and a few ounces of water," said Rocek. The rice, about the size of a softball with a very bitter fruit like a persimmon in the middle, was salty, inducing even greater thirst among the men. To receive a drink, the men lined up outside their cells and cupped their hands. Guards would move down the line with quart bottles and pour, not caring how much they spilled. "Anyone who didn't get any would be without until the next meal," said Keller.

Interrogations began immediately. The men were summoned individually for sessions ranging from 20 minutes to several hours. The Japanese wanted to know the answers to many questions: Where had they come from? How many submarines were operating and where? What was the U.S. plan of attack? What kinds of ships had they seen in Pearl Harbor? How fast could the submarines travel? How deep could they go? And who was the radar officer? "One of our radarmen [John Parr, RM3c] survived," said Keller. "The officers informed all of us he was to be considered a gunner, not a radarman."

Keller was among the first to be grilled. Still naked, he was taken blindfolded to a small room where he stood in front of five officers in white fatigues, seated on folding chairs behind a long table. A guard stood next to the prisoner while others were posted at the door. Some of the officers understood English but only one directed the interrogation, in a very polite manner. "I was asked my name, rank, serial number, and where I lived. After that they addressed me as Edwin." They wanted to know whether the battleships sunk by the Japanese at Pearl were still on the bottom. Keller responded he had not seen the battleships, or anything else unusual. "I was rapped one time in the groin with a stick between the legs during the interrogation," said Keller, "but I don't know why."

For him, the inquisition took only 20 minutes. But for others, whom the Japanese believed knew more, the sessions were much tougher. "If you hesitated in answering a question," said Rocek, "you received a whack across the rear with a piece of wood larger than a bat. I learned to bide for time by saying I didn't understand the question." The officers had it worse. All three—Brown, Ens. J. W. Gamel, and Ens. C. G. Smith Jr.—were beaten with fists and clubs in an attempt to extract secrets. But none broke.

"I do know they found out that Parr was the radarman because one day they came in and asked for him by name and rank," said Keller. "No one was supposed to have told. Nobody answered them. But they finally found out who it was and took him away. He was gone several hours. When he came back, he was beaten badly in the shoulders and arms."

The interrogations went on for five days. Lieutenant Brown over and over demanded medical care for the men but was rebuked or ignored every time. The Japanese harbored complete disdain for the prisoners, believing they should have sacrificed themselves on the *Sculpin*. Japanese troops rarely surrendered, preferring death. It was this understanding of the enemy that convinced the *Sculpin* survivors they would never leave Truk alive.

"I still believe that on Truk, they had no intentions for us to survive," said Keller. "There was no treatment for the wounded. And there was the terrible harassment with bats. We all felt they wanted information and then they would kill us." But on the fifth day, conditions changed when a group of well-dressed officers made a visit.

"They could smell the gangrene," Keller continued. "The leader asks us who was in charge. George Brown says he is. The officer asks him who are the wounded. Brown says just about everyone. The officer asks if they were treated. Brown replies he hasn't even been given an aspirin. The officer then turns around and rants and raves at another officer. And then, to punctuate his comments, he punches him in the face and knocks him backwards. He then turns to another group of men and they leave."

Two hours later, ambulances and buses arrived. Eight of the most seriously injured, including Rocek, were put in the ambulances. The others boarded the buses and were blindfolded for the ride to a small medical office. There doctors amputated Charles Pitser's (TM2c) arm, and another man's hand. The others were treated with fish oil and bandaged, but no medicines or shots were administered.

The amputees remained at the hospital for the next several days. For the rest, the interrogations ceased. Food and water improved. The men also were allowed out of their cells for longer periods of time, where they could sit in the sun. No talking was allowed except when native girls appeared on the slopes above the compound. "They'd allow you to laugh and talk between yourselves when the girls appeared as long as they thought you were talking about the girls. They appeared on the slope about 100 feet high behind the compound. The guards would holler at them but wouldn't chase them away," said Keller.

Japanese commanders at Truk were absorbed in what to do about the U.S. invasion of the Gilberts. The large carrier *Zuiho* and two smaller aircraft ferries, the *Chuyo* and *Unyo*, had arrived from Japan, loaded with airplanes but not nearly enough to mount an effective counterattack. Admiral Koga was fearful of sending his four remaining battleships and heavy cruisers into the fray, knowing they wouldn't have a chance against U.S. carrier-based aircraft. He chose instead to send fast cruisers, loaded with troops and protected by destroyers, to reinforce the islands.

It also was decided that the *Sculpin* survivors were serving no useful purpose. Orders were received to ship them to Japan to a secret prison for captured aviators and submariners near Yokohama. Subsequently, the forty-two survivors were lined up so their heads could be shaved, and then issued Japanese navy undress blues, plus small, flat, wooden blocks with Japanese writing to hang around their necks. By that time, the two amputees had returned to the compound. "They told us the amputations were done without any anesthetic and they were questioned at the same time," said Rocek.

Trucks arrived on the morning of November 30 to pick up the survivors—the tenth day of captivity. Again blindfolded, they were driven to the harbor where they were divided into two groups and put aboard two small boats. "We could only look down," said Rocek. "The launch

I was on, we tried to look up but each time the Nips would clobber the hell out of us with bats they were carrying. But one shipmate of mine had gotten a glimpse and said that we were heading for a Japanese aircraft carrier." Rocek and those with severe injuries, including the *Sculpin*'s two ensigns, boarded the carrier *Chuyo*, where they were led below deck and packed into a small compartment. Lieutenant Brown, Keller, and the other group boarded the *Unyo* and were locked in a similar hold below the waterline. The two vessels, plus the large carrier *Zuiho*, the cruiser *Maya*, and two destroyers immediately embarked for Yokohama, 2,000 miles to the north.

By then, the *Sculpin* had been officially reported overdue and presumed lost. In another development, ULTRA codebreakers picked up news of the convoy's departure. Lockwood immediately positioned submarines on patrol all along the route to intercept and sink the carriers. But one after another, they were unable to make contact. For three days, the Japanese convoy sped north, zig-zagging radically to successfully outmaneuver the hidden boats.

Aboard the *Unyo* and *Chuyo*, conditions were miserable for one group of prisoners and adequate for the other. The compartment that held the men on the *Unyo* was well ventilated. Rations were brought in three times a day. And two intelligence officers distributed cigarettes daily, and began teaching the men Japanese. "They taught us certain phrases, for instance, the words for attention, permission to go to the bathroom, and how to say thank you and good morning," said Keller. Incredulously, the men were told to view themselves as "guests" of Imperial Emperor Hirohito.

On the *Chuyo*, it was quite a different scene. Straw mats were strewn around the compartment for the men to sit or lie on. Ventilation was nonexistent, leaving the room hot and very stuffy. In one corner was a small hatch toward the ceiling. Through it were passed food and very little water. "Every time we would bang on that hatch for water, the guard would open it, spit on us, and slam the hatch closed. That was it," said Rocek.

On the night of December 3, the fast-moving convoy was nearing the end of its voyage when it encountered a typhoon. "It was a very rough storm," explained Keller. "We could feel the ship rolling and could hear waves outside and something thrashing about." Winds in excess of 50 knots threw mountainous seas at the *Unyo*. Despite the ship's 591-foot length and 77-foot beam, it heaved and rolled. As midnight approached and the storm worsened, the convoy commander on the *Maya* decided to suspend evasive maneuvers, thinking them unnec-

essary. No submarine could possibly strike under such extreme conditions, he reasoned.

For the *Sculpin* survivors and the Japanese, it was a costly mistake.

At 0016, an explosion jolted the *Unyo*. "We thought we had been hit.
We didn't know what had happened. No battle stations were sounded.
Then we feel the ship pick up speed," said Keller. "It was then that one
of the other prisoners said, 'Christ, a submarine must have gotten in!'" In
fact, it was the *Sailfish*. She had put a torpedo into the side of the *Chuyo*
and another into her propellers.

Now, as the *Unyo* slipped away with twenty *Sculpin* prisoners in her
hold, twenty-two others on the *Chuyo* began a desperate struggle for life.

PART THREE

The Valley of Darkness

Come listen, my son, and I'll tell you of one
  Of the battles we fought by the sea.
On the morn' of the fourth, we came out of the north
  In search of this battle to be.

MOLDY ROLFS, "ATTACK,"
USS SNOOK (SS-279), APRIL 7, 1943

The *Sailfish* Strikes

The *Sailfish*'s attack on the *Chuyo* the night of December 3/4 epitomized the future of the underseas war against Japan. So astonished were the Japanese at the tenacity of the submarine that, in a general order to the Sixth (Submarine) Fleet, Vice Adm. Shigeyoshi Miwa cited the attack as an example of what persistence and courage can accomplish. "We did not expect such skillfulness," he said after the war. "That carrier was attacked in the night, wind speed at 20 meters, just a single submarine and the same one attacked twice again the next morning."

The skirmish drew attention on both sides of the Pacific—for what it achieved and for the irony it left behind, embodied in the *Sculpin* prisoners trying to escape death on the doomed carrier.

DECEMBER 4, THE *CHUYO*, 0020

In the pandemonium following the two torpedo explosions, a fire broke out in the forward crew's quarters, filling the passageways with smoke. The prisoners, left unguarded, undogged the compartment door but found it was locked from the outside. Together, they put their shoulders into it but it wouldn't budge.

On the deck below, the ship was taking water. 145

Although damage-control men succeeded in plugging the hole, the makeshift bulwark soon began to cave in because of the storm. "We could hear the sloshing back and forth of timbers and wedges. Then, there was banging. We could hear the hollering and jabbering of the sailors below, banging sledges. But heavy seas kept breaking through," said Rocek. "After the third time, we never heard any more attempts. Apparently, they sealed off that area of the ship as she settled down in the water. By that time we could feel seawater starting to seep into our compartment. We had to get out."

The prisoners banged loudly on the door to get attention, but no one responded. One captive managed to free a long iron handle attached to the compartment's toilet. "Using the pump handle, we pushed and pushed that door wide enough to wedge the handle in. Then on the count of three, we all pushed and pulled. On the second attempt, we broke that door open," said Rocek. With a triumphant whoop, the survivors poured into the corridor, knowing their feat would have been impossible on an American ship.

Meanwhile, the *Chuyo* radioed a distress signal to Tokyo, which in turn ordered the destroyer *Urakazi* to return to the ship. But the message wasn't received and the destroyer with the rest of the convoy proceeded toward Japan, leaving the *Chuyo* alone.

THE *SAILFISH*, 0152

The rearmed submarine surfaced among towering waves and a driving rain. Despite the rough ride, the crew was jubilant. They realized they had a rare opportunity to finish off a major enemy warship. But the storm made the approach tricky. Although visual contact could not be made, Captain Ward pressed the assault from the bridge, exuding quiet confidence despite the wild battering of the boat.

THE *CHUYO*, 0215

In the smoky passageway, Weldon Moore, the *Sculpin*'s chief of the boat, organized the twenty-one survivors while wondering which way to go. "We didn't know where to head for," said Rocek. "Moore designated one of the men who had served on a service craft to lead. He thought he would have the best chance to get us topside. We all held hands. We put the wounded men [the amputees] closest to the lead. We had to backtrack a couple of times when we ran into a dead end."

THE *SAILFISH*, 0230

Radar finally located the carrier, apparently circling at 8,500 yards.

The submarine eased in cautiously as the *Chuyo* resumed a northerly course at two to five knots. Ward decided to stay on the surface, get as close as he could, and then fire three torpedoes from the bow tubes. If that didn't sink the ship, he would submerge and deliver a final salvo. On the bridge, the captain and the lookouts squinted into the night with seas rearing above them. But they still couldn't see the target.

THE *CHUYO*, 0430

The prisoners groped in the dark, trying to find an escape path to the flight deck. It was their only hope. Frenzied Japanese crewmen ran past at times, completely ignoring them.

THE *SAILFISH*, 0515

The rain had stopped but the bridge was still shipping water. Morning twilight had improved visibility, convincing Ward that he had to fire soon or risk being spotted. Still, he could not make out the target, now 3,500 yards to starboard by radar reckoning. At 0552, the *Sailfish* fired three torpedoes. Five minutes later, the captain noticed a "puff" of flames. Seconds later, a second explosion sent a brilliant ball of fire into the gray dawn. The hit "looked and sounded like a battleship firing a broadside—even with the locomotive rumble so characteristic of sixteen-inch shells," noted the captain. He could see star shells exploding overhead and heavy antiaircraft tracers from at least a dozen guns firing in all directions. "It's a good show, but despite the illumination, I can't see the target," he said into the bridge speaker.

THE *CHUYO*, 0550

Staggered by the torpedo explosions, the *Sculpin* survivors continued on with renewed urgency, coming to a compartment filled with life jackets, which they immediately put on. Then they followed another passageway to a small galley where they discovered wooden crates filled with bottles of soda. The men broke them open and guzzled the contents, relieving their parched throats.

"From there we proceeded to a gangway that led to the flight deck," said Rocek. "We saw Japanese sailors in a human chain passing pine logs, 4 to 6 inches in diameter and 15 to 20 feet long, from storage beneath the gangway. Once on the flight deck, they were being lashed together into rafts. I also saw an open boat in the water, about 14 feet long. Three high-ranking Japanese officers were in it. The boat kept circling the carrier." A deck officer saw the prisoners and put them to work passing timbers. "Then he had us brought to the center of the flight deck where we were kept in a circle. A few minutes later, he had about four of his men strip us of our life jackets."

Meanwhile, the *Chuyo* radioed a second SOS, this time picked up by the *Zuiho*, which dispatched the cruiser *Maya* to tow the vessel to port.

THE *SAILFISH*, 0748

While submerged to reload, the boat came to periscope depth where Ward finally got a glimpse of the carrier. It was dead in the water with nothing else in sight. But the view was intermittent because of heavy seas. "When we are at 60 feet," noted the captain, "there is nothing but green waves with the scope looking into or under a wave most of the time. At 55 feet, we damn near broach and still can only see about 20 percent of the time." The submarine passed down the carrier's port side from aft to forward from a range of 1,500 yards. "He has many planes on deck forward and enough people on deck aft to populate a fair size village," Ward noted. "The only visible evidence of previous hits is a small list to port and a small drag down by the stern. The number of people on deck indicates they are prepared to abandon ship—a reassuring picture." Ward began to maneuver the *Sailfish* abeam of the carrier where he could aim the stern torpedo tubes from point-blank range.

THE *CHUYO*, 0800

The officer who discovered the prisoners on the flight deck returned with men carrying 30 feet of rope. They began tying the survivors to one another, looping the rope around their waists until the rope ran out. Rocek noticed that most of the enemy sailors were not wearing life vests, despite a roomful of gear below deck. Each officer, on the other hand, wore one over his overcoat, with his prized samurai sword stuffed in between. Before too long, a warrant officer began gesturing to the prisoners, indicating a ship was en route to tow the carrier to safety. "We heard a lot of excited talk and pointing toward the horizon," said Rocek. "Visibility was still very poor, but we could make out a vessel of some sort coming into view."

THE *SAILFISH*, 0940

Ward gave the order to fire three more torpedoes from 2,700 yards away.

THE *CHUYO*, 0941

As the enemy crewmen were distracted by the sight of the approaching cruiser, the prisoners used the occasion to untie themselves—just as the *Sailfish*'s torpedoes exploded. A huge cloud of smoke rolled over the flight deck. "She just shuttered and shook. You could feel the vibration," said Rocek. "She had a slight list to port. But after that torpedo hit, she started getting a more pronounced list and the bow started going downward."

The *Sculpin* survivors and the ship's crew scrambled to the high starboard side of the carrier. "Me and Moore, we were holding onto a collapsible searchlight," Rocek continued. "We didn't go over to where all the people were. We thought that when in the water with so many on top of you and below you, fighting your way back to the surface would be almost impossible. The smartest thing we could have done is jump over the side and start swimming away. But no one did.

"The carrier was going down at a 45-degree angle and the sea was raging. Every now and then a geyser of water would shoot up. I turned to Moore and said, 'Let's go!'"

THE *SAILFISH*, 0946

The crew celebrated as the screech of metal bulkheads collapsing could be heard throughout the submerged boat. There was no doubt now that the huge ship was headed to the bottom. Ward, at the periscope, watched a skyful of tracers signal the carrier's last hurrah.

THE *CHUYO*, 0948

"Perhaps it was instinct. Perhaps I wanted to get it over with," said Rocek. "I let go and slid down the deck with Moore toward that boiling water. I kept taking deep breaths as I slid. Then I hit the water. I was being tossed around like a little boat. I was stroke, kicking . . . stroke, kicking with all my power. But the suction caused by the carrier going down was so great. I just couldn't make any headway. I was getting so tired and weak I actually gave up. I thought, 'This is it.' I started letting seawater trickle into my mouth. My life flashed before me like a high-speed camera. The most minute things came to mind. Things I had completely forgotten about. It's kind of an eerie and serene feeling, all at the same time."

THE *SAILFISH*, 0951

At 55 feet, Ward raised the periscope to confirm the carrier had vanished. It had. But in its place loomed a heavy cruiser, the one sent to tow the carrier. Ward chastised himself for not taking more time before the third attack to track around the target to make sure no other ships were standing by. Had he seen the cruiser, the *Sailfish* could have sunk it before finishing off the *Chuyo*. But now the cruiser was making emergency speed toward the boat. The *Sailfish* went deep as the cruiser passed overhead, sailing away to the north. Ward returned to periscope depth where he could see no other surface craft. Thus he cleared the area, noting in his log, "One full day's work completed."

But what he had no way of knowing was that shipmates off the *Sculpin* were adrift and floundering on the surface above.

Deliverance

All seemed lost for George Rocek, trapped in a whirlpool in a typhoon. The maelstrom left by the sinking *Chuyo* pulled him downward amid the shrieks of the great ship's metal plates collapsing. Internal explosions wracked the ocean as the carrier plunged to the ocean floor. In his exhaustion, he gave in to the forces around him just as a large air pocket, rising from the ship, caught him and broke the vortex's hold.

"All of a sudden the sea seemed to quiet all around me. Then the suction subsided. I looked up and could see a little light above me. I thought to myself, make one last try." He flailed with his remaining strength and broke through to the surface, choking and spitting seawater. Eying a raft 20 feet away, he swam for it, where he hung on, gasping for breath. "I looked around and the carrier was completely below the surface. I wedged my hand between the opening in the binding and a log just in case I lost my grip."

Among scores of survivors clinging to the raft were two other *Sculpin* prisoners—the boat's Philippine mess cook, Maxiso Barrera (CK1c), and Ens. C. G. Smith Jr. Three other rafts bobbed in the storm, too far away to make out their passengers. High winds continued to lash the ocean, causing huge waves to crash down on the men. Occasionally, they lost their grip and were borne away. Most managed to swim back, but others disappeared.

After a short while, the destroyer *Urakazi* appeared out of the storm. "We could see the can," said Rocek. "She circled our area but she wouldn't stop. She was like a cork in that sea. You could just about see her bottom as she pitched and rolled. But she was afraid to stop and pick anybody up for fear the American submarine was in the area. If she did, she would be a sitting duck."

For four hours, the flotsam bearing the survivors cast about until the destroyer slowed to attempt a rescue. The ship dropped a Jacob's ladder and ten single lines over the side and made a pass close to each raft.

"When they came along our raft, I grabbed the closest line to me. As the can rolled, my body cleared the sea and all my weight was on that wet line. I couldn't pull myself up and slid right back down into the sea. Another swell pushed me closer to that Jacob's ladder. About the time I was about to latch onto it, a [Japanese] officer who was on the raft stood up and, in order to get to the ladder, stepped right on me, forcing me down under. I thought I was done for. But that Man up there was looking out for me. I got back to the surface and another swell pushed me back over to the Jacob's ladder and I threw my arm through it. As bad as I wanted to crawl up, I just didn't have the strength. I just hung there. Everybody had gone up the ladder. Then they pulled it and me up together."

Rocek was dumped face down on deck, where he was mistaken for a *Chuyo* crewman until someone turned him over. "When they saw I was not [Japanese], they got excited, jabbering and hollering." *Urakazi* crewmen began carrying him aft to throw him back into the ocean. "But apparently they got a change of orders and stopped. While we were there at the fantail, I saw about ten sailors with bamboo poles about 10 or 15 feet long, jabbing down and pulling up. I couldn't tell if they were trying to keep people away or trying to help them aboard."

Guards whisked Rocek to midships and plopped him in a small compartment off the main deck. The door was left open and he lay motionless on deck for hours as the ship headed for port. "Of course, I didn't realize I was the only *Sculpin* survivor. I figured they had picked up others and kept them in various portions of the ship so we couldn't get together."

That night, cold winds swept the open compartment. No one came to check on the prisoner, let alone give him food, water, or blankets. He started to shake uncontrollably. "I tried to do exercises to keep warm but didn't have the strength. At one end of the compartment, I saw a little water-filled metal tank, three to four feet long, two feet wide and four feet deep. I put my hand in and the water felt so damned warm. So I crawled in with just my head above. I felt comfortable and stayed there all night."

Early the next morning, he climbed out of the tank and put his clothes back on. As it started to get light, a young sailor came in, gesturing that he worked in the engine rooms. "I managed to convey that I did the same thing, only in submarines. He seemed to understand. He left and came back about 15 minutes later and slipped a few hard crackers into my hand. He motioned to me with his finger over his lips to be quiet and not say anything or it would be bad for him. I was so dehydrated, I couldn't work up any saliva to eat in a normal manner. I took a few bites at a time. I kept chewing and chewing. It took half an hour to eat those two little crackers."

Rocek's next visitor was a drunken petty officer. "I could smell the alcohol. He stuck his face in front of mine and he yelled and laughed and then slugged the hell out of me with both hands." The tormentor left but returned every 30 minutes to repeat the routine.

The storm broke as the destroyer entered Uraga Bay off Yokohama later that morning. The ship proceeded along the city's waterfront where damage to ships at anchor startled Rocek. "They had damaged top sides. Some sunk by the bow, some along the port side. Some had a port list. Some had starboard lists. All kinds of damage about the superstructure. In fact, I can't recall one ship in there that wasn't damaged in some way."

After the *Unukagi* docked, the petty officer returned with three men carrying 40 feet of rope. They used every bit of the rope to completely hog-tie the prisoner and blindfold him. He couldn't move for 30 minutes. Then another petty officer, very tall and husky, came in, took the blindfold off, and untied him. He then retied just his wrists, leaving a two-foot tether. He put the blindfold back on, but left it open at the bottom so Rocek could see where he stepped. Using the tether, the officer led the captive down a gangway to a small launch, which motored to a dock some distance away. Embarking from the boat, the two walked briskly through a business district, where Rocek could hear much commotion. Colorful women's kimonos appeared around his feet as he passed. The two arrived at a commuter rail station where they waited on a bench. "We sat there for a few minutes and I could hear the chief talking to a young lady. Next thing I know, he took my blindfold off. She was a doll. She was cute as a button. Dressed State-side. Makeup on. Silk stockings and high-heel shoes. And short skirt and a white blouse.

She was pretty. Apparently, she must have inquired that I was an American prisoner. She talked him into letting her look. He left the blindfold off for 10 or 15 seconds."

A southbound passenger train squealed to a halt and the two men got on. Since it was crowded with civilians, both had to stand, hanging from overhead slings. After an hour-long ride, they disembarked in a rural area and set off at a trot down a small gravel road. "I had to stop several times. I just couldn't run as fast. I pointed to my shoes and his. He got the message but conveyed to me that if we didn't get to a camp on time, I would not get anything to eat. Well, we ran off and on for 20 minutes."

Finally, they arrived at a large compound, surrounded by a 12-foot-high wooden fence set in the middle of flat farmlands with a high mountain visible to the west. At the main gate, Rocek's blindfold was removed and he was motioned inside where two Japanese intelligence officers greeted him. Both were dressed in American business suits and spoke perfect English, claiming to have attended universities in the States. "One asked me where I was from and I told him I came off a carrier that was sunk. He got highly indignant. He asked what American ship I was off of and I told him I was off the *Sculpin*. He apparently knew what had happened because he didn't say anything more and led me into a bath."

The room contained a large, concrete tub filled with warm water. Two other men were bathing. To Rocek's delight, both were mates off the *Sculpin*. But because of the presence of guards, they were unable to converse—a camp rule. "I crawled in and I almost fainted since it felt so good, so warm and so relaxing," he said of the effect of the water on his badly injured legs. Afterwards, he put on fresh clothing and was escorted to a large barracks.

On both ends of the structure were interrogation rooms connected by a long central hallway. Thirty cells—each about four feet by eight feet—lined the sides of the corridor. Each room contained a single electric light, a bunk with a bamboo mat, and a door with a small window from which guards could look in. The prisoner was shown to his cell and locked inside, but not before he realized twenty other *Sculpin* survivors off the *Unyo*, including Lt. George Brown, the only surviving officer, were bivouacked in rooms next to him. Inside his room, Rocek discovered a plate of fish cooked in soy sauce, which he hungrily ate.

The next morning he was able to whisper the details of the *Chuyo* sinking to his shipmates when the guards weren't looking.

The kindness extended Rocek on arrival was deceptive. Unknowingly, he and the other survivors had entered Ofuna, a secret prison camp that would come to be known to captured aviators and submariners later in the war as the "Torture Farm." Built in 1942 to extract military secrets from POWs, the prison was located 29 miles southwest of Yokohama and contained three barracks enclosing a large field the size of a football gridiron. The camp was designed to hold no more than 100 POWs in individual cells. To make room for the *Sculpin* prisoners, nearly the entire crew of the USS *Perch* (SS-176), scuttled after a depth-charge attack in the Java Sea in March 1942, moved out to distant labor camps.

The Ofuna captors' intentions became clear on the first morning after arrival. "Three interrogators came in. They had us line up in a small room," said Ed Keller. "Two guards were holding small-caliber machine guns. Then one of the interrogators addressed us in English: 'You have survived the sinking of a submarine. No one survives the sinking of a submarine. No one knows you're alive. We are going to ask you questions. This man and this man are going to shoot you if you don't answer the questions. And no one will ever know you were alive.' I was scared. But I didn't think it was the end of the world. We had survived Truk Island after all."

The men were summoned individually, and faced the same questions they were asked on Truk. "We all said the same thing, that we were captured while on our first patrol run. We filled in with bullshit on our time in the Navy until the sinking. We played dumb. In a way, that's the way they treated their own personnel. They didn't tell them anything," said Rocek. "The only thing we had to make sure we did was answer each question quickly. If you started stumbling around, they would feel you were trying to lie to them."

The interrogations were repeated every two weeks, with the inquisitors comparing notes to determine if any of the men had changed their stories. "If you did," Rocek said, "you got the hell beaten out of you." The men were slapped, hit in the face with fists, or beaten with four-foot-long clubs swung by a guard using both hands. Punishments were frequent at Ofuna. The most severe were formal beatings for refusing to answer questions, suspicion of lying, disrespect to an interrogator, sitting on blankets, whispering to a fellow POW, or spilling a dish of food. Other forms of punishment were rendered on the spot—for speaking to a guard in English, not showing proper respect, being late to formation, not counting properly in Nipponese, or taking food without permission.

Men suspected of any of these were beaten about the face with a curled fist, took two to three blows with a club, or faced physical drills and/or standing at attention for long periods.

Guards slapped the prisoners in the face incessantly. They were slapped for not asking permission to go to the head; slapped for not bowing; slapped for not saying "thank you" in Japanese; slapped for violating a new regulation unknown to the men. The prisoners often were forced to stand stationary for as long as an hour in what came to be known as the "Ofuna crouch"—heels together, toes pointed in opposite directions, knees bent, back straight and arms held high. The effort to maintain this position left the men trembling all over.

Officers by far endured the harshest treatment. Lieutenant Brown was beaten violently, put on reduced rations, and threatened with death. Yet, he disclosed only information contained in the book, *Jane's Fighting Ships*, which he was allowed to consult freely. Eventually, he convinced his tormentors that as the engineering officer on the *Sculpin*, he knew nothing about U.S. strategic plans.

Daily, the prisoners had to get up early, muster outside, and bow in the direction of Emperor Hirohito's palace. "The Americans, when they bowed down, would spit and say, 'Pituee, the hell with you!'" Keller said. "And the [guards] would turn around and yell, 'Don't do that! It's not right!'"

For the most part, the survivors sat on benches in the sun every day. "No talking was allowed between the prisoners. They clobbered the hell out of you if they caught you talking," said Rocek. "When sitting on the benches, we had these signals made up. If you were sitting there soaking up the sun and feeling good and closing your eyes, the guards would draw their bayonets and put them right up to your eye. If you moved or repositioned yourself, you could poke your eye right out. So, if you felt pressure of another prisoner's leg against yours, you knew not to move. You knew a bayonet was close to you and you just froze. The guard would finally move away. The guy next to you would cough and you knew it was okay."

But not all guards were sadistic—just weird.

One, known to the prisoners as "Fatso," spoke half English and would offer a cigarette, light it, and stand guard outside a prisoner's cubicle. "When he felt you had smoked enough, he'd take it from you, snuff it, and then hit you," said Keller. "He was just a weirdo. We had one fellow in there we called Smiling Jack. Japanese Zeros would practice simulated attacks in the sky over the camp. We could see them.

They appeared to be having gun fights. Well, Smiling Jack would always walk around and be going, 'Arroom! . . . arroom!' making like a plane."

Those who had suffered injuries in the *Sculpin*'s gun battle with the destroyer received little medical attention. The shrapnel wounds on Rocek's legs festered, hobbling him. The guards offered an ointment made of fish oil and one set of bandages, which had to be washed frequently by the prisoner. But the infection persisted, turning gangrenous. Rocek feared he might lose his legs. "I recalled my dad telling me when I was a kid that, if I ever was cut and couldn't get treatment, to urinate on my wound." He turned to Edward F. Ricketts (MoMM2c). "We were both from the black gang on the boat and were pals. When I asked him, it didn't bother him at all because he was a hunter and fisherman himself and had heard that urine could heal wounds. He did it every day. You know, every one of the wounds healed up after that except for one on my shin bone in my left leg."

The *Sculpin* survivors soon discovered that crewmen from two other U.S. subs were in camp: eight from the *S-44*, sunk in the Kuriles in September 1943, and nearly the entire crew of the USS *Grenadier* (SS-210), scuttled off the Malay Peninsula in April. They included Lt. Cdr. John L. Fitzgerald, the skipper of the *Grenadier*, who had been mercilessly tortured in Panang where splinters were driven under his fingernails to get him to talk.

At Ofuna, the enforced silence gradually eased. The crews got to know one another as Fitzgerald kept up spirits through the winter months. "He was a very enthusiastic man. A natural leader," said Keller. "He would come around and talk to you. Everybody got to know him. He was very happy-go-lucky. He would come over and smile and talk with you. Being he was the skipper of a submarine, it made your day a little better."

Part of the routine at Ofuna was enforced laps around the barracks every morning, although any prisoner could get out of doing so by feigning illness. "Forty of us would be running at a time around the compound," said Keller. The [guards] liked to run with us because there was a famous miler in Ofuna, a man by the name of [Louis] Zamperini. They used to like to run against him. They knew his reputation. We would let Zamperini through and block the Japanese out. And they'd be yelling, 'Make way! Make way!' and they would end up chasing him." The men also engaged in baseball games to fight the boredom. The teams would consist of twenty men on a side, hitting a ball that could only go about 10 feet. The winners got two cigarettes. The losers got one. The guards, looking on, wagered on the outcome. Fitzgerald frequently organized and participated in the contests.

The International Red Cross began delivering boxes of rations, cigarettes, chocolate, cans of corned beef, coffee, and jars of jelly. Prison officials parceled out the supplies, and occasionally issued new clothing, including Red Cross–issue leather shoes, many of which were later stolen by guards.

The men ate three times a day at the entrance to their cells. Sitting on the raised floors, they could converse freely down the hallway. Often, each was allowed a second helping of soup or stew, containing fish or pork, dished out of a tub. Despite the variety of the food, most prisoners lost weight, as much as five to ten pounds over a month's time.

Much of the meat arrived spoiled and had to be cooked thoroughly. One evening, Zamperini, a U.S. Army Air corpsman, peered into a wagon loaded with fish. "The fish were covered with maggots which were swarming all over. As I was looking at this," he said in a deposition after the war, "[a guard] came up and intimated that I wasn't supposed to be doing this. He beat me twelve times with his fists. Later that same night, fish was served as a meal but I lost my appetite. The guards forced me to eat it."

Women from a nearby village entered the prison periodically to shave the prisoners' heads to combat the camp's serious lice problem.

In February 1944, the Japanese decided there was no point in keeping most of the enlisted men off the *Sculpin, Grenadier,* and *S-44;* they had disclosed little of value. Summoned before the camp commandant, they were made an offer. "They asked if we wanted to move up to a work camp," explained Keller. "They said we would be registered as prisoners of war. They made it sound like we had a choice since one of the things they warned us about was it was going to be hard work.

"We knew what we had at Ofuna—leisure time, regular meals, and Red Cross supplies. But we took the chance to go because we would be officially recorded as prisoners of war and our families would be told. That meant a lot to us. We knew everybody back home thought we were dead. They had been told we were presumed lost at sea. There is nothing like 'presumed lost at sea' when it was a submarine. You *were* lost at sea."

On the day of departure, guards called out the names of those to be transferred. The men picked up their belongings and marched from the camp a half mile to the train station, where their blindfolds were removed. When the electric train arrived, a section of one car was cleared of civilians so the prisoners and their guards could board. The train took a northerly route to Tokyo where the men remained overnight at Omari, a mammoth POW camp operated by the Japanese army. The next day, the journey continued on a steam train through rugged mountains northwest of Tokyo, an area known as the Japanese Alps. In the late afternoon, the prisoners arrived at the high mountain village of Ashio.

"It was a unique looking town. Very picturesque," said Keller of the tiny wooden rowhouses that lined the main street. "None of us had ever seen a Japanese town. It looked like a real quiet, clean town." The men stepped from the train, carrying their belongings loosely in their arms. The street had been cleared of all pedestrians, in accordance with the Geneva Convention that forbad parades of captives. The POWs were led to the far side of town where they crossed a footbridge over a deep river gorge. They marched another quarter mile up a hill to an internment camp at the base of a high cliff.

"When we walked in, I remember seeing a whole bunch of very thin, brown men wrapped in something like Friar Tuck would wear," said Keller. "It was a one-piece robe over the head. Not sinister looking but desperate in appearance.

"I thought to myself, 'Oh, my God, what have we come to?' "

Ashio

Nothing had prepared the *Sculpin* survivors for what faced them in the bleak prison at the headwaters of the Watarase River in Ashio.

At an elevation of 2,000 feet, Japanese Army Camp 9B was covered by a foot of snow. More than 100 Javanese and Dutch prisoners huddled against sub-zero temperatures. Most bore unmistakable signs of exposure and malnutrition—pronounced limps, swollen limbs from beriberi, and pneumonic coughs.

A 15-foot-high wooden slat fence with three strands of barbed wire at the top encircled the prison, some 300 feet wide and 500 feet long. Inside the entrance were two small buildings—the camp headquarters and a guard shack with an attached storage room and sick bay. Behind them stretched the two largest structures in the camp, twin buildings, parallel to one another and built to house 300 prisoners. The low barracks resembled oversized chicken coops lined with windows with loose-fitting glass panes. To the back of the barracks, sitting between them, was a fifth building, containing a general purpose room, the camp kitchen, and a wash house with a water trough and a tub for twenty prisoners at a time. But since it was February, the plumbing was frozen, making cleaning clothes and taking baths impossible. Guards led the new arrivals into one of the barracks, where four pot-bellied stoves struggled vainly to heat the uninsulated building. Rising 18 inches off the dirt floor were two tiers of wooden sleeping pallets astride a central corridor. The tiers were divided into sections, with twelve prisoners assigned to each. Woven grass mats were provided as thin mattresses. Each POW received five wood-pulp blankets, no thicker than a baby's receiving blanket, and was instructed in how to fold them into makeshift sleeping bags. No extra clothing was available; the men had the clothes they were wearing from Ofuna and one threadbare Japanese army overcoat each. No underwear was provided, and only one pair of canvas shoes. At the far end of each barracks was an enclosed room containing two open pits, used as latrines.

The ninety new prisoners—survivors of the *Tang*, *S-44*, *Perch*, *Grenadier*, and *Sculpin*—were taken to the meeting room adjacent to the galley. As they sat on the floor with two guards posted nearby, an Australian pilot captured in China in the late 1930s stood before them. During two years of solitary confinement, Geoffrey Lempriere had taught himself to speak fluent Japanese and was now the camp interpreter. He explained what was expected of the POWs: to help the Japanese produce copper from a nearby mine for which they would be paid 10 cents a day. The prisoners would be divided into work teams. Some would dig ore in the back of the mine and load it into railcars. Others would unload them into hoppers, which would be shunted to a copper smelting factory three miles downriver. A third group would work the copper smelters amid intense heat and soot. Keller, Rocek, and most of the *Sculpin* survivors were assigned to the mine. The prisoners were expected to work 10-hour shifts, seven days a week, except on special *toshiban* ("for the emperor") days when the shifts were stretched to 17 hours. It was necessary, in the Japanese view, in order to produce enough copper from a mine that had seen better days. The men would be allowed two days off per month.

For many centuries, Ashio had been a preeminent mining center. In fact, rich veins of bluish-green copper discovered in 1610 were responsible for 40 percent of all copper produced in Japan until the 1920s, when the ore began to dwindle, forcing a closure in 1936. But in 1943 the mine reopened because of a dire need for raw materials to support the war. Initially, the Furukawa Company, which owned the mine, employed civilian residents of Ashio and Korean immigrants. But younger men were needed for the back-breaking jobs at a time when the draft had drained the mountains of potential workers. The Japanese army responded by building the prison camp at Ashio from where it could farm out POWs to Furukawa. Captured submariners seemed ideally suited for claustrophobic conditions in the multilevel tunnels that by now stretched more than a mile into the mountain that Ashio rested on.

The men were divided into eight teams and were blended with Dutch and Javanese. After receiving instructions that first afternoon, the men were sent back to the frigid barracks for the night. Most lay on the pallets, unable to sleep because of the cold. "The Javanese were already sleeping together, two or three in one bag made of the blankets," said *Sculpin* survivor Keller. "We learned to do that, too, in order to share body warmth. But it was totally alien to us. Americans were different and had a hard time adjusting to that."

At 0500 the next morning, a guard roused the prisoners with the demand to "moveskay!" They folded their blankets as some POWs went to the galley to bring back tubs of cooked rice and grain. The daily ration was 650 grams (about three cups) plus hot tea. After eating in the barracks, the prisoners assembled before the camp commandant, a 47-year-old former grammar school principal and father of three.

Shigeru Numajiri was rather tall by Japanese standards, about five feet, seven inches. Stoop-shouldered with a thin mustache and a pinched face, he had a small, pronounced pot-belly, graying hair, and a frozen smile. Neat in appearance, he wore a gray bellyband and a red-banded cap and spoke with an effeminate voice, demanding fanatical punctuality and military courtesy. From the outset, many prisoners viewed him as harboring a rabid hatred for Americans.

The son of a farmer, Numajiri served a one-year stint in the army before paying a stipend to move into the reserve corps. He began a 20-year career as a grammar school teacher, principal, and youth group leader. In 1943 he was recalled to duty but did not acclimate well. He was afraid to ride on horseback and did not mesh well in the officer ranks. As a result, he was transferred to Ashio in November 1943 where he assumed command of ten guards supervising the prison camp.

"At the time," Numajiri said after the war, "the entire nation, regardless of occupation or sex, pledged to fight the last battle on Japan proper. The leaders of the nation spread propaganda by means of magazines, broadcasting, and lectures. The common people worked from morning till late at night and every man, woman, and child in Japan was in a state of frenzy."

Under the circumstances, he said, he and his guards were ill-equipped to deal with foreign prisoners. "None of us realized that the POWs were people whose civilization was far advanced than ours, I know for sure. There were no instructions or books or pamphlets to read. The only information we could obtain pertaining to the Allied nations pointed out the shortcomings of those people and that they were our hated enemies."

The guards shared Numajiri's view. They were ex-soldiers who, because of injuries, had returned to Japan and detested the POWs. None spoke English, so the prisoners knew them primarily by their physical characteristics. Four of them were to make the prisoners' lives miserable: "Four Eyes" (Shigeo Eizumi), a 30-year-old, bespectacled former army lieutenant; "Three Fingers" (Imajira Kira), 29, who had lost two fingers in the premature explosion of a hand-grenade; "Blue Coat" (Takayoshi Shinkae), 37, who was a miner by vocation; and Takashi Neishi, a former infantryman.

That first morning, carbide head lanterns were issued to the prisoners for use in the mine. Then a group of eighty were led by four guards across the narrow river bridge and into Ashio where they trudged down the middle of a residential street. "The typical home was no larger than a single garage of an American home," said Billie Cooper, the *Sculpin*'s quartermaster. "Each had a dirt floor, a tile for cooking rice, and a straw mat like ours to sleep on, sit on and eat on." There were between eight and ten people living in each single-room house. The mat was rolled out when people were at home and rolled up when they weren't. Shoes were left outside to keep from soiling the mat. A communal toilet existed outside each home, with the excrement regularly scooped out and put on gardens. As the prisoners passed the homes, police kept adults off the street. "The only ones allowed near you were preschool kids," said Keller. "They would holler at you while running in little groups alongside."

The men walked in the middle of the streets with the civilian guards flanking them, moving downhill about three city blocks to the mine entrance, a squarish hole with railroad tracks disappearing into the darkness. The mine was near the river bank, opposite the prison camp that perched on the hillside. Just inside the entrance was a small shrine in a niche in an eight-foot wall where fresh flowers, an offering of rice, and lit candles were displayed. Most able men in Ashio worked the mine. When a child was born, wheat was placed on the altar for a boy and corn for a girl. Every worker who went in or exited bowed at the shrine. "We bowed down to the shrine on the way in every morning," said Keller. "You asked the shrine to protect you from disasters in the mine each day and [gave] thanks on the way out for having given protection. You never spit. You got used to the idea that maybe you were in the presence of a God. When you bowed down to Tokyo, you would spit but not at the altar." The constant peril posed by rock slides was frightening. "Considering the earthquake tremors you felt on the inside, we said our own prayers at the shrine," said Rocek.

The men would light their lanterns and strap them to their foreheads before walking about a mile into the mine to what the prisoners called a "kitty hall"—a large cavern about 40 feet high and 60 feet across where ore was blasted from the walls and ceilings overnight. The ore sat in rough piles, sometimes as high as 30 feet, before being loaded into rail-cars. In the "osmay" room—a resting area off the kitty hall—the prisoners lit their lamps and changed from their prison clothes into small sashes wrapped around the groin. The heat inside the mine made no other clothes necessary.

After tea and a bit of bean curd, the men were approached by the mine's "honcho" (civilian foreman), a huge, chubby man weighing 210 pounds and five feet, ten inches tall. He assigned the prisoners to the various work details. The *Sculpin* survivors became "muckers," breaking up the ore and shoveling it into small railcars, which were pulled out of the mine by a General Electric locomotive. The quota was eight tons per man per day. The men were given a triangular hoe, a shovel, and a "queenamee," a dustpan-sized tray. After breaking up the ore, they raked it onto the queenamee and dumped it into a railcar until it was full.

The men worked in teams of two, four, six, or eight. Each man had a number and the honcho kept a running count of the team's production on a slate board. Every man was known by his number, not his name. The honcho frequently argued with the men when he passed through to check their production. "If you said you had filled thirteen cars, he would say ten and you would settle on twelve," explained Keller. "He had a weird way of punishing you. He would put his fingers on your forehead and pull one back and snap it. It would whack you one. You could feel it. Both he and you would laugh."

The prisoners were allowed one half-hour break at noon in the osmay room where they could eat, sit, and talk. The work resumed for the rest of the afternoon until around four o'clock when the men returned to change and make the trek back to the barracks.

The routine was repeated day after day. Inevitably, there were accidents, some serious. Although the mine entrance was shored up, no timbers were used in the tunnels. Earth tremors, as many as four or five a day, and the overnight dynamite blasts weakened the ceilings. "One day, about five of us were sitting down taking a break and felt sand drifting down from above," Rocek said. "We scattered quickly but one man had his leg broken by a huge rock that fell from the overhead."

The prisoners did what they could to foil the mine operators. "We learned to arrange some flat rocks in the copper cars to make them appear full. After months of getting away with this, they caught on and they began tapping the side of the car," said Rocek. "If it sounded hollow, they dumped it over and made us refill it."

That first winter in the mountains took its toll on the POWs, particularly the Javanese who could not adjust to the cold weather. Through February and March, deaths were common. "When you came up to camp at night," Keller said, "if there was a dead man, everybody would stand death parade. The body would be loaded onto a rickshaw pulled by a human volunteer, usually a Japanese. The POWs would be in two rows and the cart was pulled between them and you would know who died. The bodies were taken up to a temple and cremated. I remember one Javanese, an older man of 45 who never worked the entire time I was there. He was like a zombie. He never talked. His eyes reminded you of the devil. They had a weird glow to them. Any hour of the night or day, you'd go by his pallet and he would be sitting there staring at you. One day, Mondo, a Javanese I worked with says to me, 'He's going to die tomorrow.' He lay down the next day and died. I remember him more than the others. I swear he willed himself to die."

The food supply continued to be inadequate, and the prisoners steadily lost weight. The grain mixture was tough to digest, causing many to develop dysentery, although some believed the Japanese practice of using their own excrement as fertilizer contributed to the illness, since most of the food was grown locally. Frequent bouts with diarrhea at times caused prisoners to soil their pallets, as well as the latrine area. Lice and fleas nested in the bedding mats and blankets. Insect bites left the prisoners' backs inflamed. Rats also ran wild in the barracks. Despite frequent demands to disinfect the camp or at least provide bug spray, Numajiri and his guards refused to do anything. Drafty conditions inside the barracks also affected the POWs' health. Many contracted serious colds that turned into walking pneumonia. The only treatment provided was tiny punk sticks inserted in the skin and set on fire by a Japanese medical officer—a practice the Americans viewed as a form of voodoo.

Hunger was a constant obsession. The prisoners foraged for anything they could find, although they risked punishment. One man was beaten severely when he was discovered trying to cook the carcass of a snake he had killed. And three Javanese POWS were found dead, the result of a hunger-related murder. "On the way back from the mine one night," Keller explained, "the Javanese found a puppy the size of a big cat. They were going to keep it as a pet, giving up a bit of their food to keep it alive. Well, the dog disappeared. The Javanese found blood indicating it was killed in one of the latrines. They went out and found three men cutting up meat and putting it in a pot to make stew. It was the dog. They took the men out behind the latrine, tied them up and gagged them, and then poured water over them. They left them outside where they froze to death, all because they killed that dog. The Javanese thought nothing of it."

As winter turned into spring, desperation grew. The latrines filled to overflowing. Maggots and flies thrived by the millions in the excrement. Fleas overran the barracks. And food for the prisoners was pitifully rationed. Grain meals, occasionally pickled shark's heads and the bones of slaughtered horses, plus soup flavored by radishes were all that sustained them. Those who didn't work due to illness were given even less.

Although there wasn't much to be thankful for in Ashio, the *Sculpin* survivors had gotten one wish: The Japanese had registered the men as POWs and the Red Cross had gotten word back to families in the United States. Rocek's parents had just about given up hope. In quick succession, they received a Western Union telegram reporting their son was missing in action and a letter from the Navy Department expressing condolences. But in April 1944, news arrived that he was alive after all in a prison camp in Tokyo. Nothing else was learned until early summer when they received the one letter Rocek was able to send during his captivity: "Dear Mother and Dad. Hope you are in best of health. Don't worry about me. I am alright. Thinking a lot of you and everybody. Hoping very much to be with you soon. And home cooking. Think and dream a lot of you and of times past and the future. It is possible to receive packages. Am sure we will be together soon. So cheer up. George Rocek."

He was deliberately upbeat. But he knew the prospects for surviving Ashio were not good. He and his shipmates clung tenaciously to life, many heartened by the sight of high-flying U.S. bombers passing over Ashio and dropping tiny bits of tin foil to deflect radar prior to bombing raids on large, distant Japanese cities. The prisoners pondered the possibility of imminent liberation. But the weeks and months dragged on, with conditions only getting worse.

Cooper, who had been working the mine alongside Keller, hatched an escape plan. The POWs believed U.S. submarines were strangling

Japan and that many boats, perhaps even the *Sailfish,* were operating daily just off the coast. "We thought we could easily scale the fence at the prison camp at night. After all, we were young," Cooper said of the men, whose average age was 23. "We thought we could walk over the mountains, hiding under the bushes, and head toward the coast. Once there, we would steal a sampan and head out to sea and hope and pray we could find us a submarine."

Indeed, the U.S. underseas fleet had taken up position all around Nippon. The tightening blockade had isolated Japan, and the *Sailfish* was at the forefront, wreaking havoc under her new captain.

An Enemy in Retreat

For the men of the *Sculpin* and the *Sailfish,* the afternoon of July 8, 1944, was a study in irony.

As *Chuyo* survivor George Rocek struggled to load copper ore into a railcar under a mountain in Japan, the crew of the *Sailfish* stood proudly on deck at Pearl Harbor to receive the nation's thanks for sinking the carrier. The Navy's top-ranking Pacific officers, hundreds of sailors, a band, and war correspondents crowded around the submarine for the ceremony. Naval circles still were abuzz over the boat's tenth war patrol, particularly the sinking of the *Chuyo.* In an assessment sent to the commander-in-chief of the U.S. fleet, Admiral Lockwood described it as "one of the most outstanding patrols of the war. . . . This is the first known unassisted sinking of an enemy carrier by a submarine of this force." President Roosevelt was so impressed that, for the second time since the war began, he went on national radio to hail the success of the former *Squalus* and authorized a Presidential Unit Citation to the crew.

It was an incredible honor for the men since fate had placed so many obstacles in the way of the boat prior to the attack on the carrier in December of 1943. One by one, the crew overcame them all—as if destiny manifested the *Sailfish* sink the *Chuyo.*

First, a torpedo hot-run filled the sub with suffocating steam, forcing her to surface for an hour in daylight and risk aerial attack off the coast of Japan. Then the weather worsened, and the boat's dead-reckoning indicator broke down, making it difficult for the crew to navigate. And finally the real drama: The radar failed just when it would be needed most. The boat's electronics technician, Frank Dieterich (RT1c), a 37-year-old oil-field engineer trained in surface radar, was stumped. He had never been on a submarine before and groped for three days to understand what was wrong and how to fix it. He poured over blueprints and read and reread instructions. He pleaded for help. Yet, no one—not the captain nor the electricians nor the engineering officer—had any idea of what to do. At the last possible moment, though, on the afternoon of December 3, Dieterich managed a near miracle by fixing the radar unit just as the *Chuyo* and her convoy came into range.

Dieterich was one of the heroes of the tenth patrol. But there were others, like the skipper, Lieutenant Commander Ward, whose aggressiveness was just what the Navy had been looking for in its move to younger commanding officers, and William Lyon (CMoMM) and chief electrician Lester Bayles, both of whom were credited with averting disaster after a terrifying encounter with a Japanese dive bomber three days after the *Chuyo* went down.

At the time, the submarine had surfaced in daylight 500 miles southeast of Honshu so crewmen could get a navigation fix on the sun. Ward impressed on the lookouts the need to keep alert in case an enemy plane homed in on radar pulses from the boat. Still, the men didn't hear or see a fighter bomber until it was almost too late. "This plane was not picked up on radar nor was he seen until he dove out of low hanging clouds with his wing machine guns chattering," Ward noted in his patrol log. One of the lookouts heard bullets whizzing by and then looked up. "Plane!" he yelled, dropping to the bridge, where he landed on top of the quartermaster, who was left dazed. Seven others quickly dove through the hatch, pulling the quartermaster after them as the boat dove for safety. "The pilot of that [Japanese] plane was a little too anxious and started shooting too soon, thus giving us time to almost completely submerge before the bombs landed," said Ward.

The first missed. But the second, with its delayed action fuse, landed near the boat's deck above the after compartments. "The water apparently caught its forward motion, with the submarine going down past it before it exploded," said Bayles. A tremendous concussion pushed in the starboard side of the hull, jerking the nose of the boat upwards. Nuts and bolts shattered in the maneuvering cubicle in the after engine room. Deck gratings jumped, and a secured heater flew six feet into the air. Ominously, all power to the boat's motors was knocked out, and water gushed into the submarine from a ruptured motor fitting. Men stumbled around in shock from the blast as Bayles and Lyon entered the compartments from the forward battery.

"The motors weren't running. I never heard anything so loud in my life. The silence was eerie," Bayles said. He was one of the few aboard who knew what to look for in the intricate maneuvering cubicle that controlled the motors. Bayles traced the problem to a faulty switch and quickly reset it, restoring power. Meanwhile, Lyon organized machinist's mates to stop the leak by jacking the faulty motor off the keel, exerting enough force to reseal bolts and gaskets damaged in the explosion. The jack, however, had to be left in place for the rest of the patrol.

The quick action by Bayles and Lyon enabled the *Sailfish* to go on to sink the cargo ship *Totai Maru* six days later; sustain a very heavy, accurate depth charge counterattack; sink another transport, the *Uyo Maru*, a week later; and outwit a destroyer that dropped thirty depth charges on the boat near the end of her patrol. By the time she headed home after 49 days on station, the submarine had sent 29,571 tons of enemy shipping to the bottom.

The *Sailfish* returned to San Francisco for repairs and was nearly destroyed on her return trip to Hawaii when a U.S. bomber mistook her for an enemy boat as she cruised the surface. The plane dropped two bombs, which straddled the submarine and exploded. Fortunately, the boat escaped with no damage. Now, on July 8, the *Sailfish* was back at Pearl with her seventy-two-man crew about to receive the Presidential Unit Citation from Admiral Nimitz. In praising them, he predicted details of the submarine war would someday be revealed and "they will prove to be a story of intrepidity and devotion to duty that will inspire Americans for generations to come." After the ceremony, final preparations were made for the boat's departure the next morning on her eleventh patrol in a war that had moved decidedly in the Allies' favor.

In Europe, U.S. and British forces had taken Rome and landed on the beaches of Normandy while Russian infantry swept into Hungary and Rumania to obliterate German forces. In the Pacific, the Japanese had evacuated New Guinea and U.S. planes had begun bombing the Japanese mainland.

Still, in mid-1944, the submarine force bore major responsibility for stopping the flow of oil and strategic materials to Japan from Southeast Asia. More than 140 boats were on patrol from bases in Hawaii, Midway Island, Brisbane, and Perth. How they were to be used, however, hung in the balance that summer in an emotional debate between General MacArthur and Admiral King. The general favored an island-by-island offensive aimed at fulfilling his vow to return to the Philippines. But the admiral proposed bypassing the islands altogether so the U.S. could take Formosa. From there, heavy bombers could easily blast Japan. Under the plan, every submarine would be used in an impregnable blockade around Nippon. King believed that Japan would be starved and bombed into surrender within a matter of two or three months.

MacArthur, fearing the Navy would have its way, appealed to Roosevelt, who flew to Hawaii to mediate the dispute. The president took no sides as the general presented his case eloquently, arguing the United States had a moral obligation to rescue their Filipino allies first. Because Nimitz was lukewarm to a direct assault on Formosa, he did not argue strongly against MacArthur's plan, and consequently, the submarine force was denied a single mission of quarantining Japan. From that point on, according to naval historian Clay Blair, "the submarine force was called upon more and more to provide support for Allied invasion forces—guerrilla activity in the Philippines, photographic reconnaissance, lifeguard duty [picking up downed aviators], scouting for enemy fleet units—all of which reduced the number of submarines on anticommerce patrol and needlessly prolonged the war."

Against this backdrop, the *Sailfish* embarked from Pearl Harbor on July 9 in league with two other submarines—the *Greenling* (SS-213) and *Billfish* (SS-286). Under Cdr. S. P. Moseley in *Greenling*, the mission for "Moseley's Maulers"—the twelfth wolfpack of the war—was to prey on the shipping lanes between Formosa and Luzon.

Even at this point in the war, the *Sailfish*'s reputation as the former *Squalus* lingered. Her past loomed in every dive, as Lockwood noted in a postwar memoir: "One [sailor] who could not forget said to me, 'Admiral, I never dive in that ship without the haunting fear that I will hear the crash of water coming in through the main induction.' I recommended a transfer for him." That kind of premonition nearly came true on the first day of the boat's eleventh patrol. She was about to make her initial trim drive to check the distribution of weight in the boat, but the diving officer miscalculated the distribution of weight, not accounting for two torpedoes in the forward tubes. "We made our first dive and Holy Christmas! I think we're heading for Davy Jones's locker. We're going down like this," recalled Larry Macek (F1c), holding his hand in a near vertical position. "Spare parts were flying all over the place in the engine room." By blowing all ballast, the boat narrowly averted disaster as she passed 500 feet. Afterwards, Ward reamed out the officer responsible for the mishap.

Despite the incident, the men retained supreme confidence in the officers, particularly the captain who, like the *Squalus,* was a survivor. As one of only three men to survive the sinking of *S-26* in 1942, he later became executive officer of the *Gurnard* (SS-254), where he was known as a skilled strategist who remained cool under fire. Much of the credit went to him for the sinking of a Japanese freighter and damage to at least five other vessels, including a destroyer and a carrier during a single patrol in 1943. Thus the Navy decided to give him command of his own submarine. "In fact," said his wife Billie, years after the war, "Bob was given the opportunity to pick his first sub from several and chose the *Sailfish* because he felt that because the sub had sunk on its maiden run as the *Squalus,* it would prove to be a challenge."

The crew bonded with the ruggedly handsome captain from the start. A thin, wiry man, the son of a California judge, he was known for even-handedness in his dealings with the rates, and had a keen understanding of submarine warfare. He was assertive without being unreasonable, aggressive without being reckless. "The main thing which attracted you to Ward was his smile," explained Macek. "He was outward, friendly. Also a submarine skipper has to convey to the crew his character. Everybody on board has a need to know that *he* knows what he's doing. With Ward you always had the feeling you would be coming back. He had charisma, always with that wry smile of his." The captain's youth helped him identify with the crew, whose average age was just 23, and his daring tactics left an impression on them. "I knew this skipper was different," said Bayles, thinking back on the *Chuyo* attack. "I could see daylight coming down through the conning tower hatch. I had never seen that before in a surface attack. We never risked a surface attack in daylight before."

With all the fanfare that the tenth patrol produced, the *Sailfish* crew was eager on the run to Formosa. But two weeks passed with no action, the crew whiling away the hours doing maintenance, studying, reading, watching cowboy movies, and playing round after round of poker.

On July 23 a lookout spotted a man clinging to a shipping buoy and in great distress from badly ulcerated legs. Mistaking him for an American aviator, crewmen pulled him aboard before realizing he was Japanese. "At first the Old Man was talking about shooting him and throwing the body overboard," Bayles said. "Then they talked about taking him close to some island and letting him swim ashore. We feared initially that he might be gung ho and, if he got loose in the boat, he might attack the crew. But then we began to realize that he was just happy to be alive and was harmless."

The prisoner, in his late 30s, was a fisherman whose vessel had been sunk by another sub during the American invasion of the Bonin Islands. He initially was kept under armed guard, shackled to a torpedo skid, where his leg wounds were treated by the pharmacist's mate. Later, after his wounds began to heal, he was released and put to work in the galley washing dishes. He slept on a mess-hall bench for the rest of the patrol. Crewmen treated him as a passenger. Frequently, he and a seaman engaged in friendly arguments over the gestation period of women and whether Pearl Harbor was part of Japan or the United States.

Two weeks passed. On August 7 the *Sailfish* encountered an enemy minesweeper accompanied by a small patrol craft. The boat fired a spread of three torpedoes at 1749 from a submerged position. The captain watched through the periscope as the target completely disintegrated. Nine days later, a Japanese battleship escorted by three destroyers came into range. From 3,600 yards at 0132, Ward fired four torpedoes that left brilliant phosphorescent wakes. One of the destroyers apparently saw them coming and intercepted the fish, sacrificing itself to spare the larger ship, which sped off. On August 24, the *Sailfish* spotted four transports escorted by two smaller vessels. At 0333, the boat fired four bow tubes at the leading ship, the *Toan Maru*, which was hit and split in two. Ward had hoped to attract the *Greenling* and *Billfish* into all three skirmishes, but communications problems thwarted him.

As August came to an end, the *Sailfish* headed for Midway, where the patrol was terminated. Sacks of mail, crates of fruit and vegetables, and the traditional canister of fresh milk awaited the crew as a gangplank was put over to the boat and marines came for the prisoner. At the same time, Bayles, who had been on the boat from the beginning of the war, left for the States for new construction, as did several other rates.

Midway, which the Japanese failed to take at the opening of the war, was now a bristling U.S. naval fortress 1,200 miles west northwest of Hawaii and 2,200 miles from Japan. It consisted of two sandy islands, about two square miles in area, covered with dunes and groups of tall coconut palms. Midway had been used before the war as a refueling stop for Pan American Airlines' China Clipper service. A large, ramshackle hotel, built to serve passengers, had been converted to officers' quarters and rechristened the Gooneyville Hotel after the island's ungainly gooney birds.

Near the hotel were barracks to serve enlisted men who viewed Midway as world's end. There was nothing to do but play cards, baseball, football, and volleyball, drink beer and whiskey, and watch drunken gooneys who were addicted to beer. At night, wedge-tailed shearwaters, whom the men dubbed "moaning birds," wailed like grieving women from tunneled sand nests. There were no women on Midway, the last one getting off when Pan Am pulled out. This lack of female companionship understandably frustrated the men, in part inspiring the "Midway Hymn" popular at the time: "Beautiful, beautiful Midway, Land where the gooneybirds grow, Beautiful, beautiful Midway, The goddamnedest place that I know!"

The *Sailfish* embarked from Midway on September 26 for her twelfth patrol. Unsealing his orders en route, Ward described the unusual mission facing the men: U.S. carrier aircraft planned to bomb Formosa for three days beginning October 12. The raids would be a diversionary tactic to the main event—the U.S. invasion of Luzon in the Philippines on the sixth day. *Sailfish*, like a number of other submarines, would stand off Formosa to rescue any pilots who were shot down. The plan was fraught with risk. The sub would have to stay on the surface at all times so U.S. pilots could spot her before crashing. That meant she would be vulnerable to attack by Japanese fighters and shore-based artillery. Ward had no choice but to count on high surface speed to dodge any strikes.

During the two-week voyage, the crew rehearsed the rescue plan, which involved a life-ring tied to a rope, a rope ladder, a strong swimmer, and a three-man deck party. As Ward conceived it, "We approach at high speed until close aboard, throw the life ring to the aviator who catches the line and hangs on while the rescue party pulls the aviator into the Jacob's ladder. Then the swimmer helps the aviator onto the ladder, sees that the rubber boat is knifed and started sinking and then everyone down the hatch as speed is immediately built up again."

The *Sailfish* arrived on the morning of October 12 after battling a typhoon the previous day. Japanese Admiral Toyoda, then at Formosa, feared something was up and sent 600 planes to counterattack, just as Admiral Bull Halsey, commander of the U.S. Third Fleet, launched his carrier-based planes against the island. At 0925, more than 100 U.S. planes passed over the submarine on the way to Formosa. "We can tell they are friendly carrier planes but don't feel too happy about their ability to identify us," noted the skipper. "We've been running at high speeds on the surface with planes all over the sky and are just hoping that all the [Japanese] are too busy to sneak in on us." Ward sent out a steady stream of identifying radio signals until an air escort showed up later in the morning to protect the boat. By then, the terrific bombardment of Formosa could be heard from great distance.

At 1210, *Sailfish* lookouts observed a U.S. plane trailing smoke and crashing to the north in a heavily mined "forbidden zone" that all submarines were ordered to avoid. Ward headed for the site at once. As he later explained to Lockwood, "What else could I do?" The submarine came alongside a life raft 25 minutes later, rescuing a grateful pilot and navigator. Just then, another plane crashed nearby. A naval ensign was pulled aboard.

At 1314, the boat rescued another pilot and his radioman, who later told the crew he had outlived seven pilots since the attack on Pearl Harbor. And at 1353, another pilot radioed, "I'm hit! I'm going to crash!" The two-man crew was spotted bobbing in the surf with a large Japanese patrol boat attempting to outrace the submarine to the men. The *Sailfish* opened fire with her three-inch gun, holing the vessel. U.S. planes also strafed it, leaving it afire and sinking.

The nonstop action continued at 1430 when a plane that was out of gas made a spectacular landing close aboard the bow, forcing the *Sailfish* to back down at emergency speed to keep from ramming the aircraft. The pilot barely managed to climb out before the plane sank. Fifteen minutes later, another crippled fighter bellied to a landing alongside the submarine and two more aviators were pulled aboard.

In all, six officers and five crewmen had been saved at the rate of one man every 10 minutes. No other distress calls were made in the vicinity of the boat. But the next day, the boat plucked another aviator from the shark-infested waters, bringing the total to twelve. Since the boat's radio transmitter had broken down, Ward decided to head for the nearest U.S. base for repairs and to debark the airmen. The *Sailfish* rendezvoused with the submarine *Parche* (SS-384), which accompanied the boat to Saipan, 1,200 miles to the east in the northern Mariana Islands. The *Sailfish* moored alongside the USS *Fulton* (AS-11) for repairs. Five days later, she, *Parche*, and *Pomfret* (SS-391) steamed from the island as a newly formed wolfpack to continue the patrol off Formosa.

On November 3, the *Sailfish* made an unsuccessful attack on a transport. The following day at 0822, she made contact with a submarine "killer" group of seven warships. At 1544, she set out to sink two destroyers in the flotilla. Salvos of new electric wakeless torpedoes were launched at both targets. Through the periscope, Ward watched as the after end of the first target "blew sky high." Simultaneously, an enemy plane dropped a half-dozen bombs over the boat. Explosions close aboard caused a fire in the after torpedo room and ruptured an inboard vent on one of the torpedo tubes. Water surged into the vessel from the tube. The boat immediately took a large up angle. Fearful the nose would broach, Ward sent all those not on duty—thirty-five men—running to the forward torpedo room where they jammed themselves in front of the torpedo racks to stop the ascent with their extra weight. The boat's screws also reversed, catching the submarine at 170 feet. Precision teamwork extinguished the fire quickly and stopped the flooding. A bucket brigade transferred water forward where it was pumped overboard, returning the boat to an even keel. With enemy vessels pinging the depths all around the boat, Ward snaked a course toward open water under silent running.

At sunset, the men reloaded the torpedo tubes—four forward and one aft—and at 1913 burst to the surface in the center of the convoy. By radar reckoning, the submarine headed at emergency speed for the widest gap between the vessels. Just before midnight, safely out of range, the captain and several crewmen went topside to inspect the boat for external damage. What they found confounded them: A pair of underwear caught on the forecastle and a pair of pants on the forward gun. "We hereby claim to be the first submarine to not only catch a [Japanese] with his pants down but also to actually take them off," Ward declared in his log.

For the next several days, the wolfpack patrolled off Formosa with little result. Again, poor communications between the boats caused considerable confusion. But on November 24 at 2000, the *Sailfish* encountered a group of four cargo ships led by a destroyer, which Ward decided to pursue. When the destroyer veered toward the submarine, the captain responded by firing three bow tubes in a "down the throat" shot from 3,000 yards away. An explosion enveloped the target in smoke as radar reported the ship had sunk. But as the *Sailfish* turned toward the cargo ships, the destroyer emerged from the smoke screen, its forward deck guns lobbing shells at the sub. One was a near miss, delaying the boat's dive momentarily until Ward was sure there was no damage. The vessel then plunged to 300 feet. A severe depth-charge attack jarred her, forcing her down to 345 feet and causing much minor damage. The warship stayed on the track for the next $4\frac{1}{2}$ hours, dropping very accurate depth charges intermittently, causing Ward to wonder if the boat was leaking tell-tale oil. But finally at 0135, the enemy lost contact and the *Sailfish* surfaced to clear the area.

The boat headed for Pearl Harbor, arriving on December 11. Headlines made Ward and the crew celebrities for the dramatic rescue of the twelve aviators off Formosa. But for them, it was a last hurrah as *Sailfish* crewmen; Lockwood had decided the boat had done enough. She was too worn out, too outmoded to make another run when so many new submarines were being sent to the front. Furthermore, there was demand for target and training vessels back in the States, and the *Sailfish* was ideal. The admiral ordered the boat to return to the Atlantic under a new commander after a refit in Pearl Harbor. In a final note to Admiral King, Lockwood expressed admiration for what the *Sailfish* had accomplished in her three years of combat: The sinking of a carrier, an aircraft ferry, five cargo ships, a tanker, and a destroyer, plus damage to many other vessels. "Her illustrious combat record will long be remembered," he wrote.

On December 26, 1944, the *Sailfish* embarked for the last time from Pearl Harbor, bound for the submarine school at New London. For her, the war was finally over.

On the other side of the Pacific, the conflict raged on. The submarine war had turned the sea lanes into a massacre zone in 1944. By the end of the year, Lockwood's forces had sunk one battleship, seven carriers, two heavy cruisers, seven light cruisers, thirty destroyers, seven submarines, and an incredible 548 merchant ships, including seventy-two tankers carrying much-needed fuel to Japan. Nowhere could Tokyo find encouragement. Italy had fallen and Germany was being battered from east and west, teetering on the edge of collapse. The United States had retaken the Philippines and had obliterated what remained of the once-vaunted Japanese fleet. In the pivotal Battle of the Philippine Sea, Japan lost three carriers and 219 of 326 carrier planes sent against the U.S. fleet. Two of the flattops were sunk by American submarines, permanently ending Japan's carrier capability.

To most, defeat for the Empire seemed inevitable as the year ended. Still, the Japanese government struggled on, unwilling to accept Allied terms for an unconditional surrender. Rather, it began massing kamikaze fighters and suicidal midget submarines to prepare for a final Armageddon. The nation had entered what came to be known as a "valley of darkness"—an epoch of firebombings and mass starvation. Seventy-five million Japanese coped daily with unparalleled desperation. Fish and other staples were unavailable. Electricity and gas were severely rationed. Matches, soap, thread, coal, charcoal, firewood, shoes, leather, nails, paper, and other daily necessities were almost impossible to come by. Yet the government urged citizens to persevere with the slogan "yase-gaman"—"strength through skinniness." The army goaded the nation to fight to the last man, to stave off American forces at all costs. Robert Guillain, a French author trapped in Japan, foresaw the coming holocaust. "It seemed to us it [the war] would go on forever, would last long after the fall of Germany and that it would leave none of us alive, that it already promised us a slow, suffocating death."

That seemed likely for the forsaken *Sculpin* survivors, reduced to animal existence in the mountains at Ashio.

The Last Year

Dreams of a daring escape from Ashio were quickly abandoned by the *Sculpin* survivors. The camp guards made sure of that. "They told us that if any of us escaped, they'd kill his friends," said Billie Cooper. Besides, George Rocek said, where would you hide in a place like Japan? "It would have been pretty hard for us to escape and mingle with the people. We would have stood out like a sore thumb. It wasn't like Germany or Europe where you could mingle and look like the other people. So the guards felt pretty comfortable with the fact that we would not attempt an escape."

It was clear the prisoners' only hope was an Allied invasion. But as the days and months passed, many wondered if salvation would ever come. Long hours toiling in the mine sapped their strength. Lack of food took their health. Pellagra, beriberi, and other vitamin-deficiency illnesses were rampant. And the great killer, pneumonia, was a constant threat. Starvation and hard work caused most to lose a few pounds every month. Unsanitary conditions didn't help. Lice and fleas infested the barracks. "The Americans tried always to get rid of them. But the Javanese wouldn't bother. They saw them as pets," said Ed Keller.

Somehow the *Sculpin* survivors endured. They

hung together against all odds. "You got used to the long hours and the lack of food," said Cooper. "We were thin and weak, and we lived on barley, maize and worms. But we survived." Added Keller, "We were tough, very tough. We developed kinship in Ashio. We always tried to team up together to ease the workload. We would rehash old stories. You heard the same fifteen stories about fifteen times each from fifteen guys. About the girl they picked up in Chicago on the Loop, or the girl in San Francisco." It was that kinship that sustained them at a time when many other POWs lost all hope.

Ashio was one of 175 camps handling thousands of Allied captives imported to Nippon. As Japanese workers went to the frontlines, POWs replaced them—in steel mills, in shipbuilding yards, on railroads, in coal, copper, lead, and nickel mines, in foundries and on farms. Quotas were demanded of the men and punishments meted out if not met. Japan, which had signed but then renounced the Geneva Convention before the war, handled the captives with brutish contempt. One out of every four of the 95,000 Americans, Britons, Canadians, Australians, and New Zealanders taken prisoner perished in captivity. By the late summer of 1944, twenty *Sculpin* sailors—all but the boat's only surviving officer, George Brown, who was still at Ofuna and not registered as a POW—were in Ashio. They had been mucking ore for months and now saw an opportunity for lighter duty as drillers, assisting Japanese civilians who placed explosives in the overhead to blast fresh ore from the tunnels. "I knew the man who had been doing the job was not doing much work. So I said, 'You're damned right! I'll do that work,'" Rocek said of the offer made to him. Drillers used air guns fixed with five-foot drill bits to carve holes in the ceilings above the muck piles. "The object was to get about twenty-four holes into the bulkhead," said Keller. Dynamite with gunpowder fuses was inserted into each hole and packed with clay. As the fuses were lit, the men ran from the chamber. From a distance, they listened while the honcho counted the blasts. "If we set twenty-two fuses and there were twenty blasts, the honcho would know there were live fuses up there and leave a note for engineers to check," Keller said. "One day we came back into the mine and learned one of the engineers had been killed."

Rock falls were a constant threat. On one occasion, a very large boulder fell to the top of a 30-foot-high muck pile. Keller was detailed to the top to blast it apart. As he stood on one edge of the rock, it suddenly split in two, hurling him down the side of the pile with a table-sized boulder following behind. "I tried to get out of the way because I knew the rock was coming after me. I tried to land on my feet, tried to roll with it. My chin knocked my teeth out when my knees hit it. The same instant the rock hit my hand. When I finally got to the bottom and looked at my hand, I thought it was mangled. It was all bloody. I cursed those Japanese up and down because I thought I had lost my hand." But the injury looked worse than it was and Keller recovered.

In mid-August 1944, some Javanese and Dutch prisoners were transferred out of Ashio to make room for 150 American Army prisoners, survivors of the Bataan Death March who had been incarcerated in Singapore. When it appeared Southeast Asia would be lost, Japan feared the Bataan survivors and thousands of other POWs would be liberated. Thus they crammed the POWs into the holds of every available freighter in a frenzied attempt to move them to Nippon. Many died en route from thirst and heat. Nearly 5,000 others perished when American bombers and submarines unwittingly sank the unmarked "Hell Ships."

The new arrivals were quite a sight in Ashio. "They looked better than we did," said Keller. "And they came in with books, instruments, accordions, violins, clarinets, mouth organs, guitars, bongos. There was entertainment in the camp every night after that. We just couldn't believe it. They came in with whole chests full of things. They all came in at once and there was a very jovial feeling. These men were used to prison camp and they set up gambling and card games. They knew how to get along."

Since no officers were among the new POWs, the men set up their own police and provost marshal to maintain internal order and control thefts. A court presided over by the provost marshal—a "kangaroo court" to the *Sculpin* survivors—dispelled instant justice, putting men in solitary (the cold vestibule of the barracks) overnight or flogging them for such things as stealing a pair of socks. The tightly knit *Sculpin* prisoners managed to avoid such accusations.

The new POWS were put to work in the mine alongside the submariners and did not shirk from the task. Many were to suffer injuries from rock slides and other accidents, leaving a few permanently disfigured. One, Pvt. Basillio Rodriguez, was buried while standing beneath an ore chute. His skull was fractured and he later died in convulsions. The prisoners suspected murder because of bad blood between him and a prison guard who had ordered a railcar dumped into the chute. But no action was taken.

In October, malnutrition caused beriberi to flare up alarmingly. "My legs swelled up to about twice their normal size," said *Sculpin* petty officer William H. Haverland. "My face would swell up, and my joints

would get rather stiff. Many of the other men periodically were paralyzed from their hips on down and didn't have control over their muscles. When my legs would swell up quite a bit, they'd let me off for two
or three days and the swelling would go down. When I would go back
to work, they'd swell up again and I would get off for a couple more
days."

In November the Japanese army command in Tokyo decided to step
up production by putting each of the camps in competition to meet
higher quotas. At Ashio, the mine company instituted more frequent
toshibans—an extra production quota. "To meet this we had to work 16
hours a day, and for doing so, we got a little extra rice," said *Sculpin* survivor Paul L. Murphy (MM3c).

Inevitably, beriberi and other illnesses worsened. Japanese civilian
medics treated all the symptoms with a kind of acupuncture and occa-
sional B_1 vitamin shots. "We were permitted to have B_1 vitamin shots
only if the beriberi was in an aggravated condition," said Bataan Death
March survivor Joseph Roy LeBlanc Jr. The Japanese preferred burning
small areas of the legs, stomach, and back as a cure for virtually any ailment including piles, the common cold, and pneumonia. "The treatment took the form of applying a small portion about the size of a
match head of a substance which resembled spun glass," recounted
Eldon Wright (EM3c), *Sculpin* survivor. "This substance would then be
lighted and it would burn slowly. The treatment consisted of three
applications in the same spot each day for a period of 20 days, and it
ultimately resulted in a festering sore." Wright received the treatment
on his back as a "cure" for a hernia. Likewise, Rocek received repeated
burning treatments all over his legs as a remedy for chronic beriberi.
Those with diarrhea were burned on the stomach.

Despite their woeful condition, the prisoners were forced into the
mine. "If a man said he was sick and could not work and was still able
to stand up or walk without the typical malnutrition limp, this Medico
would remove his slippers, which were made by cutting the top out of a
pair of tennis shoes and slap him several times across the face with the
rubber sole of the slippers," said Jack J. Jones, a machinist attached to
the Cavite naval station prior to the Japanese conquest of the Philippines.

What the men really needed to overcome their illnesses was more
food. However, rather than increase the rations to the laborers, the
camp administration reduced them in mid-November. "This continued
until every man in the camp had beriberi and malnutrition," Jones said.
"There were 230 men in the camp who were sick and unable to work

by the approval of the [Japanese] medico. That meant that they were unable to walk or could not walk at a normal pace. Thirty of these men were unable to move at all, other than moving their hands and to roll over. These were cared for by three or four Americans assigned to do this job. I was one of the seventy men who were still working even though my left arm was paralyzed and I had malnutrition so bad I could not feel pins that were stuck in my leg by the [Japanese] medico. I could still walk and I had to work."

Reports of a slowdown in production at Ashio resulted in a Japanese army physician being dispatched from Tokyo to check the condition of the prisoners. He ordered them to run inside the compound for 10 minutes. Those that passed out were taken for treatment at a hospital near Tokyo. The others were forced to disrobe completely and line up for examinations. "It took all morning and part of the afternoon," recounted Jones. "He decided about every third prisoner was not sick and proceeded to slap them several times, at the same time making the remark, 'You came to Japan to kill Japanese. You shall work in the mines until you die.'"

Soon after, however, food rations improved somewhat. Intestines and heads of sand sharks were shipped from Tokyo to supplement the diets. Also, quantities of ground grasshoppers, cabbage, and seaweed arrived. "This put most of the men back to work for a short time, which is proof that food was all we needed," Jones said.

Secretly, some Ashio civilians helped sustain the prisoners. One of them, Kiichi Katoku, a camp interpreter and civilian medical assistant, was credited with saving many. "At a time when more than half the prisoners were unable to work owing to illness, he personally produced extra food for the beriberi patients," said one Army POW, Maj. H. J. Kinzell. Other civilians smuggled food to the POWs in the mine. One was a man known to Keller and Cooper as "Smiling Charlie," a disabled Japanese veteran who wished the war would end. "He would draw pictures in the dirt to explain how the war was going," said Cooper. "He walked like Charlie Chaplin. A bag on his back and straw mat strapped on his butt. He treated me better than any [Japanese] the whole time I was a prisoner." Smiling Charlie brought small portions of beans, Chinese spaghetti, meat, and fish to the men from his home in Ashio. "He would always say, 'Your house very poor. My house we share with you.' That meant he stole it from his wife. Otherwise he said his wife sent it in to me," said Keller.

A civilian guard the men nicknamed "Pappy" was another benefactor. "While Pappy was in camp, he would put on an act and shout and rave at the POWs like all the other guards," said one prisoner. "Just as soon as he got his unit alone, he did everything in his power to make it easy for the men. He would let the sick rest, gave them food and cigarettes if he had any, even helped them fill their quota of work."

As November came to an end, Red Cross food and clothing began arriving, boosting morale. But the guards kept tight control on the packages, dispensing some contents before Christmas but otherwise inexplicably stockpiling them at a time when the men desperately needed them. Twice a month, the POWs in Ashio didn't have to work. At such times, the guards would hold inspections, with the prisoners kneeling on the pallets. "If they saw your fingers on the railing, they would whack you with a gun butt. [*Sculpin* survivor] Herb Wyatt [GM2c] couldn't stand it so he came out of the second tier and jumped on the guards' backs. He convinced them he was crazy. So, from then on, they went down the barracks on the opposite side from Wyatt. Herb, in order to reinforce it, would jump out at them anyway," said Keller.

January descended on the grim barracks with the coldest temperatures in 20 years. Readings of 18° below zero were recorded. Inside the compound, misery reigned as the guards continued to hoard the Red Cross blankets, clothing, and boots. Holes in the roofs were left unpatched. Snow filtered down, falling on the blankets of prisoners, huddled together in twos and threes to preserve body warmth. Only enough fuel was distributed to the men to keep stoves lit for two hours a day. "We stole anything which would burn," said one POW. Often, a detail of thirty men returning from work was searched at the main gate. If any wood or coal was discovered on any of them, all would have to stand at attention in the cold for an hour. Some were clubbed by the guards. When a theft of coal was discovered from a camp supply in mid-January and no one confessed, they banned any heating for three days.

"Our big trouble in wintertime was getting enough clothes to wear to keep warm," Ralph E. Shuping, an Army Air Force corporal, testified after the war. "They gave us Japanese uniforms which were about like burlap and about as warm as a piece of burlap would be. If you worked down in the mine about 2,000 feet where I worked for awhile, it was very hot. We had to work in the heat all day and when you came out of the mine, your clothing would be wet with perspiration and you would be hot and dirty, and you would have to come out into the cold wintry weather and wash in cold water. We had colds all winter and a lot of men had pneumonia."

One of them was Pfc. George F. Gallion, 26, of the 803rd Engineer Battalion, who turned to cigarettes to fight off hunger, sometimes bartering bits of food for additional cigarettes, which were rationed by the guards from Red Cross supplies. Gallion suffered greatly from beriberi and was hospitalized for a time. On returning to Ashio in January, he was accused of taking a turnip-like radish from a storeroom in camp. He was confined to an unheated guardhouse for three days during which the temperature dropped to 16° below zero. Suffering from frostbite, he finally confessed and was ordered back to work. After about two weeks, he developed a 105° fever and asked to be relieved. Because he was recognized as the radish thief, Numajiri, the camp commandant, refused to allow him medical treatment and ordered him back to the mine, despite vigorous protests from American medics.

On January 29, Gallion and a crew including Keller completed a normal shift loading eight ore cars and drilling holes for dynamite. The men took a break to eat before starting a second shift of four hours. By then, Gallion was trembling from exhaustion, feverish, and unable to eat. But "Blue Coat," one of the guards, demanded he work. He did so until he could do no more and sat down, later passing out.

Keller and the other prisoners took turns bringing him out of the mine on their backs. "All the way out, I belittled him because he had traded meals for cigarettes. He was dying of malnutrition. I carried that man on my shoulders, across my back, sometimes piggyback, sometimes laying on my shoulders. I had the compassion to carry him but I was very angry that he was dying," recalled Keller. At 2200, Gallion was delivered to the camp medical office. "He was cold as ice and unable to talk or walk," said Basil B. Dulin, an Army surgeon. "His chest was full of coarse bubbling rales which could be felt as well as heard." Despite efforts to revive him, Gallion died at 0807 on January 30. Noted Dulin after the war, "Prisoners [at Ashio] were driven to the limit. There was no increase in the quality or the quantity of the rations. The final demand on Private Gallion's energies was too much."

On returning to camp the next day, Keller and others stood death parade as Gallion's body passed in a rickshaw, headed for the crematorium. "I felt very bad for scolding him," said a tearful Keller. "I thought he would get strength from it, not die."

Through teamwork, the prisoners managed to survive the winter without further deaths. The Army medics, given some medicine delivered in the Red Cross packages, helped nurse those suffering the greatest through the winter freeze.

Meanwhile, the POWs did what they could to sabotage the Japanese.

They poured carbide dust into the pneumatic guns to disable them when the guards weren't looking. And they caused equipment in the smelter to break down.

Trains began arriving with scrap metal, cartridge cases, and millions of dollars in Chinese pennies—all to be smelted into ingots for the military. But it was all in vain. Japan steadily lost ground to Allied forces.

The United States had invaded Iwo Jima in February and was about to launch an all-out assault in April on Okinawa, the final objective before invading Japan itself. Gen. Curtis LeMay, commander of the XXI Bomber Command in the Mariana Islands, conceived employing new long-range B-29 bombers in nightly fire bombings of factory neighborhoods of Japanese cities. The initial target was Tokyo, the most heavily populated city on earth and made almost entirely of wood. On March 9, 325 B-29s took off from the Marianas for Tokyo. Wave after wave of the bombers flashed across the city, dropping nearly 2,000 tons of firebombs. The attack created a conflagration so intense that updrafts ripped violently at the planes. On the ground, city residents suffocated from lack of oxygen or were burned alive. In that one night, 83,000 people died. Nightly, the planes returned to renew the terror. By the end of the month, nearly 50 percent of the city was in ruins and millions had fled to the countryside.

In Ashio, little was known of outside developments, although Korean laborers with relatives in Tokyo told of the destruction of large parts of the city. Still the war dragged on. Occasionally, the POWs received postcards from home. And they were allowed to write. But the charred remains of their efforts were found at one point behind the guard shack.

The men constantly dreamed of sumptuous meals back home. On books of rice paper, used to wrap cigarettes, the *Sculpin* survivors recreated hundreds of recipes, trying as a group to remember the ingredients for each. The books were divided into categories, such as jams and jellies, pies and cakes, and main courses. Entries included "Bridge Club Salad," "Maple Peanut Ice Cream," "Noodles a la Genevoise," "Baked Manicotti," "Strawberry Chiffon Pie," "Raspberry Surprise," and "Veal Cutlets Curried." The men envisioned the joy of actually tasting their creations—someday. But inevitably, they faced the reality of shark-head soup for dinner after a hard day at work. "One of the things that kept me alive," said Keller, "were ammonia-filled shark heads. A lot of them were for sale. Some of the men couldn't stomach them when they ended up in their soup. Not me. I ate those shark heads. It cost you one cigarette for each head." Bones from a horse or cow sometimes were given the men, who smashed them open and ate the marrow. One prisoner ate more than he should have; a bone fragment got caught in his rectum, causing great pain. A camp medic had to go in with a fork in order to dislodge the splinter.

In March, Tokyo sent an officer—Lt. Cdr. Arthur G. McIntyre—to take command of the Americans. McIntyre, a survivor of the *Grenadier*, was appalled on arrival, as he later testified: "When I entered that camp, I viewed one of the most dismal sights I have ever seen. Snow was about one or two feet deep, the barracks were cold and dirty, and I was barely able to recognize men whom I had known well only a few months previously. . . . The prisoners there looked like wild men. They were not shaven, their hair was extremely long, and both their bodies and their clothes were filthy." McIntyre spent his first night in the barracks in misery as lice feasted on the midsection of his body. With the coming of warmer weather in April, fleas added to the discomfort. "The fleas increased to an unbelievable and unbearable number," he said. "If I walked at a normal rate from one end of the barracks to the other end inside the building my legs to a point above the knees would be covered with fleas in a concentration of about one per square inch of my skin. After walking through the barracks, I would have to stop and scrape the fleas off my legs with my hands very much as if they were beads of perspiration."

McIntyre vigorously protested conditions. Yet nothing was done as spring turned into summer.

By June, the Allies were closing in on Japan. Victory in Europe had been declared on May 8. Preparations began in earnest to shift American troops and equipment to the Pacific for a final assault on Japan. Laying out Operation Olympic, the Allies intended to first seize Japan's southernmost island, Kyushu. Thirteen divisions of American troops would be mobilized for the assault on November 1, 1945. This would be followed by Operation Coronet, an attack by twenty-five divisions on Tokyo in March 1946. Gen. George C. Marshall estimated the Allies would lose 500,000 men. Japan, girding for the inevitable, began hoarding more than 5,000 kamikaze bombers and hundreds of midget suicide submarines in a final effort to stave off defeat. The military trumpeted the slogan, "One Hundred Million Die Together," and rallied the populace for one last stand, "Ketsu-Go"—Operation Decision.

In June in Ashio, none of this was known to the POWs. The biggest news was the opening of a second POW camp near the smelter. By then most of the captives weighed 100 pounds or less, "just skin and bones," as one put it. Attempts to combat the lice and control the fleas failed. Flea powder distributed by the Japanese proved to be ineffective. The warming weather also caused an explosion of flies. "Maggots about $1\frac{1}{2}$ inches long with horns overran the toilets and crawled around the yard adjacent to the toilets," said McIntyre.

A sadistic Japanese medical sergeant put some prisoners to work producing fertilizer for his garden. According to McIntyre, he had the prisoners stack rice bags made of straw outside the camp gate. They then fetched excrement from the toilets and dumped it atop the rice bags. "He then made these prisoners pull off their shoes and tramp around on top of the rice bags tramping the waste from the toilet into the bags. [The guard] seemed to derive great joy from the operation."

Occasionally, small portions of the Red Cross parcels were rationed to the men, who knew that the camp guards were appropriating the supplies as well. Some of the prisoners, anticipating a cutoff in food should the United States invade, hoarded some of what they were given—with grave consequences for three of them. In early June, a theft was discovered in the storeroom. The Japanese searched the barracks and found items belonging to three Army POWs. Believing they were the stolen items, the guards led the three to the prison gate where they were strung up and beaten to extract confessions. "They beat them bad," recalled Keller. "They hung them up by their fingers, almost off the ground, and beat them with rubber shoes. They were beaten unfairly and almost to the point of unconsciousness. It was the worst beating I ever witnessed. No one was forced to watch but nobody turned their backs."

Of the three, the guards singled out Wallace Hall, an Army sergeant, as the true thief. Taken to the brig where Gallion had been confined, he was beaten and strung up by his wrists and his ankles so his body was two feet off the ground. Despite the torture over a four-day period, he would not break and finally was released.

The real culprit, it turned out, was another POW who was accosted in the barracks by his fellow captives. "He was put in a circle of men, hands tied behind him. One of the beaten men was given the first crack. He punched him right in the face. Each time the man staggered against the circle, the man who caught him hit him back to someone else," explained Keller. "They beat that man unconscious. It almost killed him."

By the summer of 1945, the POWs were worried they would not survive another winter. Then, on August 7, one day after an American B-29 dropped a single bomb on the city of Hiroshima, Keller was working in the mine when Smiling Charlie approached him. "He came in and said, 'Very soon you go home to America. The war will be over.' I asked him why. He told me the Americans had bombed a city and he kept saying, 'One bomb . . . one bomb!' had destroyed the city and killed tens of thousands of people. The city was on fire. I could not understand this concept—one bomb. I kept asking him, 'One bomb?' He kept saying, 'Yes!'"

22

Back from the Deep

The last day of the war arrived without warning in Ashio on August 15, 1945. As usual, the first shift of POWs left for the mine at sunup while others languished in camp, many asleep. Just before noon, the guards unexpectedly left their posts, gathering around a radio in the commandant's office where the Japanese national anthem blared. Then an announcer said the emperor would speak to the nation.

In a quavering, high-pitched voice that none in Ashio had ever heard, Hirohito began by defending Japan's declaration of war on America four years earlier, saying it was the only way to ensure Japan's self-preservation. But the war had gone badly. And now, he said, "the enemy has begun to employ a new and most cruel bomb, the power of which to do damage is indeed incalculable, taking the toll of many innocent lives. Should we continue to fight, it would not only result in an ultimate collapse and obliteration of the Japanese nation, but would also lead to the total extinction of human civilization." There was no alternative to surrender, he said. For the first time in 2,600 years, Japan would submit to a conqueror. He appealed to the nation to resist no further. "The hardships to which our nation is to be subjected hereafter will certainly be great. We are keenly aware of all ye, our subjects. However, it is according to the dictate of time and fate that we have resolved to pave the way for a grand peace for all the generations to come by enduring the unendurable and suffering what is insufferable."

The Ashio guards, faces in their hands, were stunned. Some grieved openly, tears rolling down their cheeks. The POWs, witnessing the scene from the barracks, couldn't understand what was going on. "We sent a man up onto the roof of the building," explained Keller. "We thought the emperor had died and if flags were at half-mast, we would know. But half an hour later, there was no indication this had happened. Then someone mentioned maybe there's an armistice. We waited and then the first shift of workers was brought back from the mines at about one o'clock in the afternoon. Normally, they didn't return until between four and five. This really stirred up excitement."

"We knew something was up," said Rocek. "We thought the Allies had made a landing and the Japanese wanted to keep us in camp to keep an eye on us just in case we tried to rebel or escape."

The prisoners sought out the Japanese camp interpreter, who told them that since winter was coming, mine officials wanted to give them extra time off to build up their bodies. "Is the war over?" asked one. "No! The war isn't over!" he replied. But the captives didn't believe him. They decided to break a camp rule to see what would happen. "The worst thing you could do was to smoke on your rice mat. Fire could destroy the barracks," explained Keller. "So a couple of POWs took cigarettes and sat on their mats smoking when the guard came through. These men had taken a great chance of being severely beaten. But when the guard stopped, all he screamed was 'Danger! Danger!' The POWs hollered back, 'We know! We know!' The guard then ran out and got the interpreter who returned with him and told the POWs, 'Please don't smoke on the beds!' We then knew the war was over."

Work was suspended permanently at the mine for the POWs. Several days later, the guards brought in cans of yellow paint and directed the survivors to paint "PW" letters 20 feet high on one barrack roof. Still, no one would confirm the surrender. Rather, the men were told the lettering would keep U.S. planes from bombing the barracks. Numajiri began distributing beef and horsemeat, plus stores of Red Cross food, clothing, and other items that had long been withheld.

On August 27, three fighter planes from USS *Shangri-La* (CV-38) located the cliffside prison. One pilot swooped down just over the barracks, tipping his wings in a salute as the prisoners cheered from the ground. Then the fighters zoomed in, dropping with pinpoint accuracy seabags loaded with candy, cigarettes, and other supplies. Clearly, liberation was at hand. On August 30, a B-29 roared low over the river valley. Ten large parachutes blossomed in the sky, dangling crates filled with clothing and food, which fell gracefully to earth close to the camp. One, however, damaged a house and another the town hall. The euphoric POWs rushed the containers, devouring the food as fast as it could be unpacked.

Ashio was too remote for freedom to come quickly. But the POWs knew it wouldn't be long. As they waited, they were grateful for deliverance. A certain nobility came over them, a spirit of benevolence, even to a woman who lived near the camp and had caused one POW to be severely beaten earlier that summer. The men gave chewing gum and candy to her children. "Upon witnessing this, the Japanese woman burst into tears," said Lt. Cdr. Arthur G. McIntyre. "She could not understand why these prisoners would give her children these things after she had caused one of them to be punished for taking a vegetable from her garden."

The survivors summoned to the barracks all Korean and Japanese civilians who had aided them, including Smiling Charlie and Kiichi Katoku, lavishing on them blankets, food, and other materials. They asked them to share them with their families or those in need in the village. In a note to the Katoku family, Major Kinzell reassured them. "Please do not worry, although the Americans are taking over here. There is nothing to fear. You will not be mistreated. I am very happy that these two nations have quit fighting. I have many Japanese friends in America, so please write to me at any time. I should be very happy to hear from all of you. Thanks, Mr. Kato, for all you have done for us boys here in camp."

The camp commandant, Numajiri, watched in astonishment from a window in his office. "The PWs took the Japanese into their barracks and gave them food and blankets, clothing, shoes, etc.," he later wrote. "When the Japanese returned to the mine, the PWs carried those articles for them to the gate to bid them farewell. . . . I watched all this from the window of my room. Suddenly I became speechless and felt tears in my eyes."

Pappy, the civilian guard who had befriended the prisoners, was likewise repaid for his kindness. He was summoned to the prison camp from his home in Ashio. "When Pappy entered our compound, you could see the fear of death on his face," recalled one POW. "That is, until the Americans started shouting, 'Pappy, Pappy Tomodachi

[friend], Nakayoshi [good friend],' and rushed up to him offering cigarettes, candy, and cigars. At one time he had five cigarettes lit by Americans in his mouth. . . . Pappy was loaded down with blankets, shoes,
clothing, food, cigarettes, medical supplies, candy, etc. The one cart
assigned to our camp was rolled out and loaded so high, Pappy could
not budge it. We had the [Japanese] commander assign four guards to
help him pull it. Along with the cartload of supplies went an inventory
of the supplies and a letter to American and Japanese authorities, stat-
ing that Pappy had been good to the prisoners and all that he had was a
gift. This letter was signed by all the officers and most of the 300 men
in camp. Pappy went out the gate a relatively wealthy man with a broad
smile that did justice to that one and only gold tooth."

Later, the POWs drew up a list of those who had mistreated them, to
be turned over to American authorities for prosecution. At the head
was Numajiri's name.

On September 5, twenty Japanese marines under the command of a
lieutenant came into the camp with orders from the Americans to
escort the survivors to the Ashio train station. Japanese police cleared
civilians from the streets as the POWs packed their few belongings.
Then they left together, making their final trek across the bridge over
the Watarase River. Many took a last look back at the bleak barracks,
fixing in their minds the view of what had almost taken their lives. They
marched in silence through the city for three-quarters of a mile. Children ran alongside, begging for candy, which some of the POWs
handed out. No one came to cheer or boo. Residents hung back,
crowded into alleys, watching as the Americans passed in the street.

The survivors quickly boarded a waiting train and it rumbled away
to the south out of the valley toward Yokohama. From the windows, the
men watched as the spiny mountains gave way to the Tokyo plains. The
train skirted the city, out of sight of the firebombings that had leveled
most of it. As men who had barely survived, they felt no remorse for the
enemy. "Maybe if we had seen Hiroshima, we might have felt sorry for
them," said Keller. POWs on other trains applauded when a devastated
city came into view. "By the time we had passed a dozen such cities and
towns, we stopped cheering," said Army Capt. Kenneth Day. "The dev-
astation was so total that it overpowered our senses. . . . We said little
but stared out the windows. . . . I began to feel sorry for them. I still
wanted to kill them, but a feeling of sympathy crept in alongside the
hatred."

The *Sculpin* survivors arrived in Yokohama and were greeted by an

Army nurse, offering cigarettes and candy bars to the men. "What a beautiful sight! She was the first American female we had seen in two years," said Rocek.

The men boarded buses that shuttled them to the city's wharf where a decontamination center had been set up. There they bumped into George Brown, who had just arrived with forty-three small wooden boxes and his own incredible story. The *Sculpin*'s only surviving officer had been a prisoner at Ofuna until March 1945, when he was transferred to Omari to make room for Capt. Richard H. O'Kane and other survivors of the USS *Tang* (SS-306). Brown was put to work sewing canteen covers. One morning he overslept and was punished by standing at attention all day in the compound in 35° weather. "I was soon freezing," he recalled. "Finally another POW walked by me and whispered, 'Get permission to go to the head.' I did and when I entered one of the stalls a bowl of hot soup came over the partition from the next stall. I got soup three times that day and it literally saved my life. However, I did get a severe case of pneumonia and still have scars on my lungs as a result."

In April, Brown was transferred to the Matushima prison camp about 125 miles west of Tokyo. The camp was home to 200 American and British enlisted men forced to excavate a sluice for a hydroelectric plant at a nearby dam. In his $4\frac{1}{2}$ months at Matushima, Brown presided over the funerals of forty-three Americans who died of pneumonia. "About six men would carry the dead man in a big poled box about one-half mile up the mountain side to a spot where the Japanese had an incinerator. We started a fire and placed the body in the oven. I, as the senior American officer, would say prayers which I had to make up since there was no Bible or prayer book available. Then the coffin bearers took the box back down the mountain while I waited with a guard to collect the ashes in a tin can. I would later transfer the ashes to a small wooden box properly identified with the name, rank, and serial number."

After liberation, Brown caught a train to the coast with the forty-three boxes and then hopped a U.S. destroyer, which took him to the reunion with the other *Sculpin* survivors. Some, including Brown and Keller, flew back to the States, while others, including Rocek, embarked on a hospital ship.

Miraculously, all twenty-one who arrived in Japan in December 1943 came out alive on September 5, 1945. Mike Gorman (S2c), one of the youngest, sank to his knees in prayer on the fantail as the hospital ship steamed out of Tokyo Bay. He watched as the mountains hiding Ashio slowly sank below the horizon.

For the next few days, the survivors feasted aboard the ship. "We ate whatever we could and it was just like putting food down an acid bath," said Rocek. "We were still hungry at night and the captain broke out K rations. That's all you heard all night long—guys munching." Now in safe hands, the men relaxed and began to think about what they had endured. Troubled by nightmares, some snapped, shouting and punching the air, requiring medics to calm them with tranquilizers.

The ship stopped in Guam and Pearl Harbor before sailing on to San Francisco, arriving in early October. "All the submarine men were the first to depart," said Rocek. "The Submarine Force had individual cars, with an officer assigned to each, and they took us to a hotel for a large welcoming dinner. We were all impressed and proud and knew that we were not forgotten."

After a brief stay at Oak Knoll Hospital in Oakland, Rocek and others received orders to transfer to hospitals closer to their homes. "They put us on a train to Chicago. That's when I called my sister to meet me. It was heart-wrenching, with all the crying and sobbing . . . " said Rocek, trailing off. She hardly recognized him when he arrived. After visiting a few hours, he continued on to the Great Lakes Naval Hospital just outside the city. Then, a few days later, he headed home, taking a bus to Chicago and an elevated train west to Cicero. The train dropped him two blocks away. "I came in unannounced. My dad was working in the tailor shop. I could see the look on his face. I could see he was happy to see me but I also saw the look of surprise that I was so thin. My mother heard the commotion in the shop and came running out, crying."

For Rocek and his fellow *Sculpin* survivors, the long rehabilitation had begun. For many, the scars of their ordeal never quite healed, particularly for Rocek. At night, haunting memories catapulted him back time after time to his harrowing escape from the sinking *Sculpin*, to his near drowning on the *Chuyo*, to the torture on Truk, and to the years of starvation in Ashio. But at least he was home.

The people of Maine and New Hampshire had hoped for a homecoming of their own—for the *Sailfish*. But the Navy had other plans. For the last six months of the war, she had been used as a training boat in New London and at Guantanamo Bay, Cuba. On the day the war ended, the boat arrived at the Philadelphia Navy Yard just as city church bells, factory whistles, and sirens celebrated Japan's surrender. The Navy, faced with a huge inventory of submarines, decided the boat would be decommissioned and scrapped at the yard. But when word filtered back to Portsmouth that the *Sailfish* would not be coming home, shipyard machinists bitterly objected, asking President Truman to intercede. Soon the Portsmouth Chamber of Commerce, the city's Elks and Kiwanis clubs, and others swamped Secretary of the Navy James V. Forrestal with telegrams, letters, and petitions. The congressional delegations of Maine and New Hampshire joined in. The world's most famous submarine, they argued, could not simply pass into oblivion in Philadelphia as so much useless nautical junk to be made into refrigerators. She should be returned to her home to become a permanent memorial to the *Squalus* rescue and all World War II submariners.

After initially resisting, the Navy gave in amid a torrent of press coverage. Thus, on October 1 the *Sailfish*'s crew reassembled and the boat embarked from Philadelphia, steaming up the Atlantic coast for the last time.

In a poignant two-day voyage, she sailed past the benchmarks of her early life . . . New London where all her crews had been trained through the war years . . . along the ragged coast of New England where divers from Washington, D.C., raced with a police escort through barricaded cities in the spring of 1939 to reach the stranded *Squalus*; . . . past Cape Cod where the captain of the *Falcon*, the naval tug bearing the McCann rescue bell, opened the throttle wide, wondering if he could possibly reach the boat and her survivors before their air ran out; . . . and further up, to the barren Isles of Shoals where Captain Naquin and his crew were trapped 40 fathoms down, a depth no one had survived before.

For the young sailors now serving on the *Sailfish*, men like Laverne "Bud" Pike (Y1c), who had been aboard since the attack on the *Chuyo*, it was an incredible journey. He was just a kid when the *Squalus* went down, and he remembered the newspaper headlines well. "We hung onto that news," he said. "And never did I dream that I would be the last one off that boat." Yet here he was, six years later, bringing her home to Portsmouth.

At the Isles of Shoals, the *Sailfish* turned inland past a lighthouse, toward the mouth of the Piscataqua River. The familiar numbers "192" loomed large on her conning tower, like a mirage to coastal residents who remembered the *Squalus* and now watched the gallant boat enter the river, three miles from Portsmouth. They stood on beaches and hillsides, cheering or in silent wonder as the tiny boat slid by. She cut a narrow wake against the heavy tide, which was doing all it could to slow her fade into history.

To those watching, those who had waged the fight to bring her home, the boat seemed a part of them as she passed. The "ghost ship" of the fleet, the boat always referred to as the "ill-fated *Squalus*," the one that many predicted would never survive the war, had overcome all the odds. She had criss-crossed more than 132,000 miles of the Pacific and Indian oceans, sailing into battle alone from Pearl Harbor, Manila, Perth, Albany, Brisbane, Java, Midway, and Saipan. Although attacked by destroyers and dive bombers, she somehow persevered. "She was like a cat," one crewman said. "SS 192 seemed to have many lives." In her time, she had redeemed herself from the disaster of 1939 to touch the lives of a great general, several admirals—on both sides of the war—two presidents and one grateful nation.

Now she turned into the home stretch, battling the rip tides as she rounded Pull-and-be-damned Point and came into view of Portsmouth. With a surge of power, she came alongside a drydock at the navy yard to the wild ovation of yard workers who turned out in force to welcome her back.

For the next three weeks, they bent to the task of readying the boat for her formal decommissioning on October 27—Navy Day at the yard.

More than 30,000 people packed into Portsmouth for the event. Men and women from throughout the region, workers from the naval yard, and officers of the line stood with tears welling in their eyes as the great boat settled into the river for the final time at 1100. Near the pier where she was born, with the cruiser USS *Portsmouth* (CL-102) standing by, she roared with blasts of compressed air, dipping below the river in a ceremonial last dive. Her deck tipped to port just beneath the waves, leaving her conning tower jutting above the water. Then she surfaced and returned to the dock.

As the end approached, her crew stood at attention on deck, hugging her rails in two straight lines of white hatted officers and enlisted men. A silent throng pressed forward around her, from every vantage point in the yard. Among them was Margaret Batick, the widow of John J. Batick (EM1c) who died on the boat. His daughter, Betty, now 7, held tightly to her mother's hand, her eyes fixed on the submarine. And on the deck of the boat, below the bridge and standing back from the crewmen, was the solitary figure of an older man, dressed in a long overcoat—Harold Preble, the only civilian to survive the *Squalus* sinking.

The boat's last skipper, Lt. Cdr. Berkeley I. Freedman, stood before his crew and the world and summed up what the *Squalus/Sailfish* had come to represent. "Those who served aboard her and those who helped to build her know deep in their hearts that she is an eternal symbol of what courage, fine workmanship and faith in God and one another can accomplish."

In the eerie silence that followed, the boat's commissioning pennant was lowered as the last act of her existence. Winds stiffened, roaring in off the ocean as gulls cried, cartwheeling in the sky above the *Sailfish*. An aging CPO, fighting back tears, stood near the drydock and raised his hand in a firm salute. Beneath his breath, he whispered the thoughts of many.

"May God let her rest in peace."

EPILOGUE

Forever a Vigil Keep

To those who have hunted
And been hunted in the deep.
Who in long iron homes
Forever a vigil keep.
That muster among sunken ghosts
Piped by Neptunial hosts.
Whose tread on hulks beneath the sea,
Is logged by bells tolling silently.
We lift our hearts to honor you,
And drink quietly to you of the sea.

CHARLIE L. WILLIAMS, "SILENT TOAST"

After the *Sailfish*'s decommissioning, the Navy briefly considered sending her back to the Pacific as a floating target for an atomic bomb test. Naval officials wouldn't support a plan to turn the entire boat into a shrine. But they eventually agreed on a compromise with the people of Portsmouth: The bridge, conning tower, and a small portion of the boat's deck would be cut away and preserved as a memorial on the central mall at the shipyard.

On Veteran's Day, November 11, 1946, Undersecretary of the Navy John L. Sullivan presided over the dedication, saying the memorial would be a permanent reminder of what the submarine navy had accomplished. Because of secrecy, the public knew little of the underseas war. The submarine force consisted of 50,000 officers and men, about 1.6 percent of the entire Navy. Yet, it sank 55 percent of Japan's merchant fleet and 29 percent of its warships. Through 1,570 patrols covering 16.5 million miles (4 million submerged), the boats sank hundreds of ships, including a battleship, fifteen cruisers, forty-two destroyers, twenty-six submarines, and eight aircraft carriers.

The *Sailfish* earned nine battle stars during the war under four skippers: Morton Mumma, Richard Voge, John Moore, and Robert Ward. Mumma, recipient of the Navy Cross for the *Sailfish*'s first patrol, retired after the war to become managing editor of a newspaper in West Virginia. He returned to active duty during the Korean War and then retired with a physical disability, later becoming vice president of the National Rifle Association. Voge, also a recipient of the Navy Cross, completed a detailed historical analysis of the submarine war for the Navy prior to his retirement in 1946.

Hiram Cassedy, the boat's executive officer under Mumma and Voge, went on to a distinguished career as commander of the *Searaven* and *Tigrone* (SS-419). After his death years after the war, fellow submariners placed his ashes in a special container and put them in the forward torpedo tube of an experimental submarine, the *Barracuda,* at Key West. At a designated place in the Caribbean, the tube was fired to fulfill Cassedy's request to be buried at sea.

Capt. Joseph R. Tucker made the first eight patrols on *Sailfish* and ended the war as a prospective commanding officer on *Carbonero* (SS-337). He later served in a variety of command positions in the Navy and capped his career in the 1960s as Commander Service Force Sixth Fleet and U.S. Naval Attaché Rome. He retired in 1968.

The *Sculpin* earned eight battle stars under two skippers: Lucius Chappell and Fred Connaway. Connaway was posthumously awarded the Silver Star and the Purple Heart. Cdr. John P. Cromwell, who was promoted to captain during the last war patrol of the *Sculpin,* was awarded the Congressional Medal of Honor for sacrificing his life when the submarine was scuttled. The boat's lone surviving officer, George Brown, retired from the service and became a successful businessman.

The *Sculpin* was among fifty-two boats lost during the war, claiming the lives of 374 officers and 3,131 enlisted men. After the war, 11 officers and 157 crewmen were recovered from Japanese POW camps.

The *Squalus / Sailfish* memorial was the first of many established throughout the United States by submarine veterans. Monuments also were erected in Perth and Albany, where citizens annually honor the memory of American submariners who served there.

KEY WEST, FLORIDA, 1946

After the war, Lieutenant Commander Ward became captain of the *Sea Leopard* (SS-483). Many *Sailfish* veterans were assigned to the boat, as well as *Squalus* survivor Gerald McLees. The lone American survivor of the *Chuyo* sinking, George Rocek, almost completed the circle. "After I got out of the hospital," he recounted, "I decided to go back into submarine service. I had to requalify to get back in. So I went to New London to school and then transferred down to Key West to a submarine squadron. They sent me to report aboard the *Sea Leopard*. Talk about a twist of fate, on board was McLees, the electrician off the *Squalus*, and [Albert] Kasuga, the first-class electrician on the *Sailfish* when she sank the carrier." But Rocek just missed serving under Ward, the man who sank the *Chuyo*. Because of illness in his family, Ward received a transfer a month before Rocek arrived.

ASHIO, JAPAN, OCTOBER 1946

Lt. Cdr. Arthur McIntyre, the *Grenadier* survivor and senior officer in Ashio, returned. He walked through the deserted barracks, recalling the men who had passed through. He revisited the guard shack and the galley and stepped inside the brig, where he found an inscription left by a POW who didn't make it home: "G. F. Gallion Nov 27, 1944 Dec 3, 1944 No blankets only the clothes on my back 'Onion thief' Come on Uncle Sam "

YOKOHAMA, JAPAN, JULY 10, 1947

Shigeru Numajiri was a shattered man when he went on trial. The Ashio camp commandant and seven guards stood before a military commission at the headquarters of the U.S. Eighth Army.

In a rambling sworn statement, he reviewed the accomplishments of his earlier life as a respected school teacher and principal. Now at age 51, remorse had set in. "This two-year army life—the last two years of my life up to now—made [me] a notorious war criminal of the twentieth century and to be tried by an international tribunal—alas! What a misfortune and calamity."

During the month-long trial, depositions from scores of POWs sealed his fate. On August 7 he was sentenced to 18 years at hard labor. Imajira Kira—"Three Fingers"—received a term of 15 years. Shigeo Eizumi—"Four Eyes"—and Takashi Neishi were sentenced to five years. "Blue Coat"—Takayoshi Shinkae—received a term of three years. Three others were acquitted.

Two commission members urged a reduced term for Numajiri, saying he "was neither malicious nor vicious in his actions, but rather a commanding officer with little or no knowledge of how to command or carry out the duties for which he was responsible." But Lt. Col. Winston L. Field, in reviewing the sentences, concluded that Numajiri could have done far more than he had to improve conditions in camp. Therefore the sentence would stand.

PORTSMOUTH, NEW HAMPSHIRE, JUNE 18, 1948

The remains of the *Sailfish* were sold at auction to the Luria Brothers of Philadelphia as scrap for $43,167.

ASHIO, FEBRUARY 28, 1973

The mine closed after producing more than 700,000 tons of copper over a 400-year period. It is now a tourist attraction, where mine trams convey visitors through the many tunnels, passing mannequins and antique trains illustrating its centuries of operation. In a guide to visitors published in the 1980s, no mention is made of the POWs who once worked there.

MOBILE, ALABAMA, AUGUST 1–5, 1979

Forty-seven *Sailfish* and *Squalus* veterans from twenty-three states convened at the Brave Bull Restaurant. It marked the first reunion for what was to become the *Squalus/Sailfish/Sculpin* Association.

Through the hard work of two of the *Sailfish*'s yeomen—Bud Pike, an Iowa banker, and Aaron Reese, a Washington, D.C., lawyer—a special guest had been invited to the reunion. Robert Ward, in spite of recuperating from open heart surgery and advised not to make the trip from his home in California, came with his wife. As six of Ward's shipmates stood at attention, flanking the closed door to a banquet room, the skipper arrived. Larry Macek, the former *Sailfish* fireman, sounded a boatswain's pipe as Ward made a grand entrance to sustained applause. He then was led around the room, greeting each of the veterans until he came to a tall, lanky man with a gentle demeanor, still affected by war injuries to his legs. It was George Rocek, located by the men in Illinois and coaxed to the reunion without Ward's knowledge. "The two threw their arms around each other. Everyone was watching. There was not a dry eye in the room," said Macek.

The survivors of the *Squalus*, the veterans of the *Sailfish* and their skipper, and the survivor of the *Sculpin* relived the war that day. In the morning Ward returned to the airport for the flight back to San Francisco. Unbeknownst to him, the men at the reunion got there first, forming two lines on the tarmac leading to the steps of Ward's plane. The skipper walked between them with a wide grin, saying his goodbyes and stopping to embrace Rocek for the last time. Macek then piped Ward aboard.

ARLINGTON, VIRGINIA, APRIL 18, 1980

Retired Rear Adm. Robert E. M. Ward, 66, victim of a fatal heart attack at home in Santa Cruz, California, was buried with full military honors at Arlington National Cemetery. The funeral procession was led by a horse-drawn caisson with a riderless horse. The former *Sailfish* captain was laid to rest in a stand of white dogwood trees on a knoll overlooking the capital city. Among those attending were five of his Annapolis classmates. One expressed surprise that five enlisted men from the *Sailfish* also came. "That's how much he meant to us," said Macek, who was one of them.

PORTSMOUTH NAVAL SHIPYARD, KITTERY, MAINE, MAY 23, 1989

In his eighty-fifth year, Oliver Naquin stood before all that remained of the submarine he once commanded.

As the boat's first captain, the old man had outlived all who followed him through four years of battle in the Pacific. Now in ill health, less than six months before his own death, the retired admiral steadied himself on deck with a silver-handled black cane and gazed upward at the rounded conning tower of his old boat. A half-century had passed and still the USS *Squalus* looked as she did in 1938, sliding down the ways to become the most famous underseas boat in the world.

To an unwary visitor rounding the square in the bright morning sunlight, past the yard's former red-brick administrative building with its white cupola and large clock, the scene was extraordinary: A submarine with "192" painted in large numbers on her side, half submerged in the earth. Three hundred VIPs looked on, many dressed in blue satin vests and broad-brimmed "digger" hats with white feathered plumes, designating wartime service in Australia. Two honor guards flanked a large memorial wreath positioned against the conning tower. Officers and enlisted men in dress whites stood at attention, poised in the superstructure as "The Stars and Stripes Forever" resounded over loudspeakers.

It was the very portrait of a commissioning party for a new warship.

But it was a remembrance for an old one, a retelling of the unusual events that link the *Squalus* to the *Sculpin,* lying half a world away on the Pacific Ocean floor. As a ship's bell sounded in the cupola, the hands of its clock came to rest at 1000 . . . 50 years to the second that the sleek new *Squalus* with Captain Naquin at the helm disappeared in the Atlantic 20 miles away. Now, one by one, the survivors—"my survivors," as Naquin liked to call them—assembled alongside him. William Isaacs from Maryland. Jud Bland from California. Leonard de Medeiros from Massachusetts. Danny Persico from New York. Carol Nathan Pierce from Mississippi. Eugene Cravens from Florida. Carl Bryson from Connecticut. And Gerald McLees from New Hampshire.

Admiral Naquin dabbed at his eyes with a handkerchief, fighting for composure before the shipyard workers, naval officers, townspeople of Kittery and Portsmouth, reporters, and submarine veterans from throughout the country. Time had reduced him to a wisp of the man who survived the sinking of the *Squalus.* Now he and eight of his crewmen settled on folding chairs before the *Squalus* memorial as 1100 arrived in the blast of a shipyard whistle. In the ensuing silence, broken only by the squeak of a slow-turning pulley, a seaman lofted the boat's red, white, and blue commissioning pennant to a position alongside the periscopes where it fluttered for the first time in a half century.

Naquin surveyed the crowd, thinking back on all the years and all the stories that the war produced for the men of the *Squalus/Sailfish* and the *Sculpin.* Many of them were there. They each had incredible stories to tell that morning in the square, including *Sculpin* survivor Edwin Keller who had arrived from his home in New Jersey. But none was more amazing than that of Naquin himself.

As chief engineer to the *California* at Pearl Harbor, he was ashore when Japanese dive bombers attacked and sank the battleship on December 7, 1941. One torpedo pierced midships, exploding near his cabin where he had kept mementos from his days aboard the *Squalus.* With the battleship out of commission while repairs were made, Naquin transferred as navigator to the cruiser *New Orleans* (CA-32), which saw duty in the Battle of the Coral Sea. Afterwards, the ship returned to Pearl Harbor for a refit, putting in near the *California,* which was in dry dock. Draglines were at work, scooping out debris from midships. "As I walked down the dock, one of these scoops dumped its load right in front of me. And there was a little silver sailing ship given me by the people on *Squalus.* Right at my feet. I think that's the most extraordinary thing that's ever happened to me."

Later in 1942, Naquin was aboard the *New Orleans* when she intercepted a Japanese convoy at Tassafaronga on its way to relieve troops at Guadalcanal. During the ensuing battle, the cruiser was hit by a torpedo. "We lost a third of the ship. The bow was blown off and the strands of armor plate left sticking out looked like a cat's whiskers," Naquin later said. In the pandemonium, he rallied the crewmen to save the ship.

Now in the twilight of his life, Naquin solemnly gazed at the scene in Portsmouth from his old boat as a choir sang the Navy Hymn and a bell tolled for each of the twenty-six men who lost their lives on the submarine in 1939. After a moment of silence, he stood up with the help of a naval aide and moved in a labored shuffle to the podium where he unfolded a prepared text.

"It is difficult for me to realize that it has been fifty years since the *Squalus* sank to the ocean floor 240 feet down off the Isles of Shoals," he began in a lilting Southern accent, just above a whisper. "It is quite fitting that the Portsmouth Naval Shipyard, the building yard of the *Squalus*, should set aside this day of remembrance for that unfortunate occurrence with the loss of so many of our fine crew, our shipmates."

The admiral noted how all the survivors volunteered to sail the renamed submarine before the war, or reenlisted on other boats. He told of how the war claimed four: Lt. R. N. Robertson in *Argonaut*. Basilio Galvan (MA1c) in *Runner* (SS-295). Charles Powell (RM2c) in *Pickerel*. And Lloyd Maness, one of the heroes of the *Squalus* rescue, in *Growler* (SS-215). Naquin then paid tribute to his men.

"In my report to the Secretary of the Navy," he continued, "I wrote, 'My officers and men acted instinctively and calmly. There were no expressions of fear or complaints about the bitter cold. Never in my remaining life do I expect to witness so true an exemplification of camaraderie and brotherly love. No fuller meaning could be possibly given to the word shipmate than was reflected by their acts. They shared their blankets, the crowded floor space. They lay in each others' arms in an effort to keep each other warm.'

"The divers displayed extraordinary heroism in the performance of their hazardous duties, making our rescue by the diving bell possible. The Medal of Honor was awarded to four of them and forty-five received the Navy Cross. The nation was grateful and we owe our lives to them. We were lucky."

The statement hung in the air, a testament not only to the *Squalus* survivors, but to the men who went to war on the *Sailfish* and the *Sculpin*. To those on both boats who endured unimaginable horrors faced alone at sea. To the *Sculpin* survivors, whose caring for one another brought them through torment and starvation as prisoners of war. And to the *Squalus* survivors who came face to face with doom off the Isles of Shoals.

Abbreviations

The following ranks do not include class (1c for first class and so on).

B	Boatswain's mate
CB	Chief boatswain
CE	Chief electrician
CEM/AA	Chief electrician's mate/Acting assignment
CK	Steward
CMM	Chief machinist's mate
CMMA	Chief machinist's mate acting
CMoMM	Chief motor machinist's mate
CPO	Chief petty officer
CQM-PA	Chief quartermaster–Permanent assignment
CRM-PA	Chief radioman–Permanent assignment
CSM-PA	Chief signalman–Permanent assignment
CT	Chief torpedoman
EM	Electrician's mate
F	Fireman
GM	Gunner's mate
MA	Mess attendant
MM	Machinist's mate
MoMM	Motor machinist's mate
MoMMA	Motor machinist's mate acting
PM	Pharmacist's mate
QM	Quartermaster
RM	Radioman
RT	Radar technician
S	Signalman
SC	Ship's cook
Sea	Seaman
TM	Torpedoman
Y	Yeoman

Bibliographic Essay

PREFACE

The toll of submarine fatalities between the world wars comes from Prof. A. M. Low, *The Submarine at War* (New York: Sheridan House, 1942). The toll on U.S. submarines during World War II comes from numerous sources, including Theodore Roscoe, *United States Submarine Operations in World War II* (Annapolis, Md.: U.S. Naval Institute, 1949).

CHAPTER 1. THE SURVIVORS

I reconstructed the attack on the *Chuyo* from the *Sailfish*'s tenth war patrol report (U.S. Archives, Washington); numerous interviews with *Sailfish* veterans and *Sculpin* survivors; Capt. C. Raymond Calhoun, *Typhoon: The Other Enemy* (Annapolis, Md.: Naval Institute Press, 1981); and Keith Wheeler, *War under the Pacific* (Alexandria, Va.: Time-Life Books, 1980).

CHAPTER 2. THE VOLUNTEERS

My portrait of the Depression era came from interviews with *Squalus/Sailfish* veterans and from Donald Worster, *Dust Bowl: The Southern Plains in the 1930s* (New York: Oxford University Press, 1979). The quote from Charles Lockwood concerning attributes of American submariners is from his book with Hans Christian Adamson, *Through Hell and Deep Water* (New York: Greenberg, 1956), 79. The background on New London comes from personal visits; research at the library of the submarine school in Groton, Conn.; and from Robert Hatfield Barnes, *United States Submarines* (New Haven, Conn.: H. F. Morse Assoc., 1946).

· CHAPTER 3. SPRITZ'S NAVY

My profile of Charles Spritz was pieced together through interviews with submarine veterans and three magazine articles: Gordon A. Bowker, "Spritz's Navy" (*Polaris*, December 1987); "Shaky Jake" Jacobus, "What's All This about Chief Spritz?" (*Polaris*, October 1989); and Charles Wigle, "Spritz's Navy" (*Polaris*, December 1985). The training regimen at the submarine school is drawn from personal interviews and four books: Barnes, *United States Submarines;* Henry Felsen, *He's in Submarines Now* (New York: Literary Guild of America, 1929); Capt. Edward E. Hazlett, *"Rig for Depth Charges!"* (New York: Dodd, Mead, 1945); and Henry B. Lent, *Submariner* (New York: Macmillan, 1962). Details on the "Long Island Express" hurricane are from the *New York Times* of September 22–24, 1938.

CHAPTER 4. THE BIRTH OF TWINS

My account of the *Squalus* launch is from interviews with the crew, plus press accounts in the *Portsmouth* (N.H.) *Herald* newspaper. Historical perspective on Portsmouth, the navy yard, and the Isles of Shoals was obtained through personal visits; from Neal R. Peirce, *The New England States* (New York: W. W. Norton, 1976); from William G. Saltonstall, *Ports of Piscataqua* (Cambridge: Harvard University Press, 1941); and from the pamphlet "Cradle of American Shipbuilding," published by Portsmouth Naval Shipyard. Biographies of Oliver Naquin and Warren Wilkin were obtained from the Navy Biographies Section, Military Records Center, St. Louis, Missouri. My understanding of what motivated submarine officers to volunteer in the 1930s is primarily through correspondence with Capt. Frank Wheeler (Ret.), Los Altos Hills, Calif., who graduated from the Academy in the 1930s. In recreating a tour of a fleet submarine, I visited the preserved fleet sub *Becuna* (SS-319) in Philadelphia several times and the *Silversides* (SS-236) in Chicago, in addition to consulting the following sources: John D. Alden, *The Fleet Submarine in the U.S. Navy* (Annapolis, Md.: Naval Institute Press, 1979); Barnes, *United States Submarines;* and Harley Cope and Capt. Walter Karig, *Battle Submerged* (New York: W. W. Norton, 1951). My encapsulation of Japan's motives for going to war comes from a variety of sources, including Ray F. Downs, *Japan Yesterday and Today* (New York: Bantam Pathfinder Editions, 1970); and *Life* editors, *Japan at War* (Alexandria, Va.: Time-Life Books, 1980). The incident on the *Snapper* (SS-185) comes through interviews with *Squalus* survivors and a written account of the incident by *Squalus* survivor Lawrence Gainor as told to him by his brother, who was on the *Snapper* at the time.

CHAPTER 5. THE LAST DIVE OF THE *SQUALUS*

The sinking of the *Squalus* and the rescue of her crew are examined in depth in two excellent books: Nat A. Barrows, *Blow All Ballast!* (New York: Dodd, Mead, 1941), and Peter Maas, *The Rescuer* (New York: Harper and Row, 1967). Barrows was a *Boston Globe* newspaper reporter who covered the event; Maas's book focuses on Lt. Cdr. Charles E. Momsen, who supervised the divers during the rescue/salvage. Quotes used in this chapter were drawn from the *New York Times* of May 26, 1939; testimony before the naval court of inquiry (Office of the Judge Advocate General, Dept. of the Navy, Alexandria, Va.); and correspondence and interviews with many survivors conducted by the author.

CHAPTER 6. THE RESCUE

Background is from Barrows, *Blow All Ballast;* Wilbur Cross, *Challengers of the Deep* (New York: William Sloane Assoc., 1959); Maas, *The Rescuer;* and depositions by the survivors for the naval inquiry board. Additional information comes from the *New York Times* (May 25, 1939) and various other newspaper press clippings collected by *Squalus* survivor Carl Bryson. The author also drew information from Momsen's lecture to the Harvard Engineering Society on October 6, 1939. The author interviewed survivors Bland, Bryson, Cravens, de Medeiros, McLees, Persico, Pierce, Lieutenant Commander Naquin, Lieutenant Doyle, and Lt. Albert R. Behnke of the U.S. Navy Medical Corps, who was attached to the rescue team.

CHAPTER 7. BIRTH OF THE "GHOST SHIP"

Details on the *Thetis, Phenix,* and *I-63* disasters and reaction to them are from Capt. W. O. Shelford, R.N., *Subsunk: The Story of Submarine Escape* (Garden City, N.Y.: Doubleday, 1960), and C. E. T. Warren and James Benson, *Only Four Escaped* (New York: William Sloane Assoc., 1959). The salvage of the *Squalus* is explored in depth in Barrows, *Blow All Ballast,* and Maas, *The Rescuer.*

CHAPTER 8. WAR GAMES IN PARADISE

Historical background on Japan's decision to go to war comes from Robert C. Christopher, *The Japanese Mind* (New York: Linden Press/Simon and Schuster, 1983); Joseph C. Grew, *Ten Years in Japan* (New York: Simon and Schuster, 1944); Robert Guillain, *I Saw Tokyo Burning* (Garden City, N.Y.: Doubleday, 1981); Saburo Ienaga, *The Pacific War, 1931–1945* (New York: Pantheon Books, 1978); and Col. Roy M. Stanley II, *Prelude to Pearl Harbor* (New York: Scribner's, 1982). Biographical information on Morton Mumma is from the Military Records Center, St. Louis, and interviews with *Sailfish* veterans.

I drew on the same interviews and the following in describing Hawaii in the prewar years: Gwenfread Allen, *Hawaii's War Years* (Honolulu: University of Hawaii Press, 1952), and Forest J. Sterling, *Wake of the Wahoo* (Philadelphia: Chilton, 1960). My exploration of how the submarine force prepared for the war is from Clay Blair Jr., *Silent Victory* (New York: Lippincott, 1975); Edwin P. Hoyt, *Submarines at War* (New York: Stein and Day, 1983), which details Admiral Withers's strategy; Charles A. Lockwood, *Down to the Sea in Subs* (New York: W. W. Norton, 1967); and Roscoe, *United States Submarine Operations in World War II*. The breaking of Japanese military codes is from Peter Calvocoressi, *Top Secret Ultra* (New York: Pantheon, 1980).

CHAPTER 9. DAYS OF INFAMY

I drew historical and geographic perspectives on the Philippines and Manila from Bobette Gugliotta, *Pigboat 39* (Lexington: University Press of Kentucky, 1984); Robert L. Underbrink, *Destination Corregidor* (Annapolis, Md.: U.S. Naval Institute, 1971); and Frederick L. Wernstedt and J. E. Spencer, *The Philippine Island World* (Berkeley: University of California Press, 1967). Admiral Hart's ascendancy to command of the Asiatic Fleet is from Barnes, *United States Submarines;* Blair, *Silent Victory;* Gugliotta, *Pigboat 39;* and Roscoe, *United States Submarine Operations in World War II*. Background on Japan's situation is from Paul H. Clyde, *The Far East* (Englewood Cliffs, N.J.: Prentice-Hall, 1958); Ienaga, *The Pacific War;* and Stanley, *Prelude to Pearl Harbor*. Admiral Yamamoto's prediction of a U.S. triumph in a protracted war is from numerous sources, including Hoyt, *Submarines at War*, and David A. Thomas, *The Battle of the Java Sea* (New York: Stein and Day, 1969).

The message broadcast by the *Sailfish* concerning Mumma's breakdown is from Blair, *Silent Victory*. The "skipper problem" is discussed in detail in Blair, *Silent Victory;* Richard Compton-Hall, *The Underwater War, 1939–1945* (Poole, England: Blandford Press, 1982); Cope and Karig, *Battle Submerged;* Hoyt, *Submarines at War;* and W. J. Holmes, *Underseas Victory I and II* (New York: Kensington Publishing, 1966). The Japanese bombing of Manila and Cavite Naval Station is described vividly in Gugliotta, *Pigboat 39,* and Underbrink, *Destination Corregidor.*

War patrols of the *Sailfish* and *Sculpin* are described in patrol logs on file at the National Archives. I illustrated the experiences of both boats in Java from personal interviews and the following sources: Blair, *Silent*

Victory; Gugliotta, *Pigboat 39;* Samuel Eliot Morison, *The Two-Ocean War* (New York: Little, Brown, 1963); Thomas, *The Battle of the Java Sea;* and Underbrink, *Destination Corregidor.*

CHAPTER 10. LOMBOK NIGHTMARE

Conditions on the *Sailfish* and the *Sculpin* were derived from the patrol logs of the two captains. Additional background on the effect of depth bombing on submarine crews came from many sources, including Bernard A. Bastura, ed., *History of U.S. Submarine Veterans of World War II* (Middletown, Conn.: Submarine Library and Museum, 1981); Edward L. Beach, *Dust on the Sea* (New York: Holt, Rinehart and Winston, 1972); Beach, *Run Silent, Run Deep* (New York: Henry Holt and Co., 1955); Lothar-Gunther Buchheim, *The Boat* (New York: Bantam, 1976); Compton-Hall, *The Underwater War;* and National Research Council, *Human Factors in Undersea Warfare* (Washington, D.C.: National Research Council, 1949). My characterization of Lombok Strait is from interviews with veterans of both boats and from James Casing, *Submariners* (London: Macmillan, 1951). The plight of Corregidor is from Underbrink, *Destination Corregidor.*

CHAPTER 11. SANCTUARY

Lockwood's experiences in Perth-Albany are from his books, *Sink 'Em All* (New York: Dutton, 1951), and *Down to the Sea in Subs.* My summary of the command shakeup after the Battle of the Java Sea is from Blair, *Silent Victory;* Thomas, *The Battle of the Java Sea;* and Edward Young, *Undersea Patrol* (New York: McGraw Hill, 1953). My descriptions of Australia, Perth, and Albany are from interviews with submarine veterans; correspondence with residents of both cities; research done for me by Australian author Michael Talbot who resides near Albany; and the following books: David Creed, *Operations of the Fremantle Submarine Base, 1942–1945* (Silverwater, NSW: Naval Historical Society of Australia, 1986); *Fodor's Australia, New Zealand, and the South Pacific 1983* (New York: Fodor's Travel Guides, 1983); Donald S. Garden, *Southern Haven, The Port of Albany* (Albany, Australia: Albany Port Authority, 1978); Mrs. Aeneas Gunn, *We of the Never Never* (Hutchinson of Australia, 1908); Elspeth Huxley, *Their Shining Eldorado* (New York: William Morrow, 1967); Underbrink, *Destination Corregidor;* and Young, *Undersea Patrol.* The war patrol reports of the *Sailfish* and *Sculpin* provided the narrative for their missions in 1942, as well as Rear Adm. Corwin Mendenhall, *Submarine Diary* (Chapel Hill, N.C.: Algonquin Books, 1991). My exploration of the torpedo problems comes from Lockwood's memoirs; Holmes, *Underseas Victory;* Hoyt, *Submarines at War;* Roscoe, *United States Submarine Operations in World War II;* and Wheeler, *War under the Pacific.*

CHAPTER 12. GOING HOME

In illustrating the monotony and humor of long patrols, I drew from my interviews with *Sailfish* and *Sculpin* veterans; the war patrol reports of both subs; and the following sources: Casing, *Submariners;* Compton-Hall, *The Underwater War;* George Grider, *War Fish* (Boston: Little, Brown, 1958); Lockwood and Adamson, *Through Hell and Deep Water;* Richard H. O'Kane, *Clear the Bridge* (Chicago: Rand McNally, 1977); Norman Polmar, *American Submarine* (Annapolis, Md.: Nautical and Aviation Publishing Co. of America, 1981); Sterling, *Wake of the Wahoo;* Robert Trumbull, *Silversides* (New York: Henry Holt and Co., 1945); John Winton, *Down the Hatch* (New York: St. Martin's, 1962); and various issues of *Polaris,* the monthly newsletter of the U.S. Submarine Veterans of World War II association.

My portrait of midwar America is from interviews with submarine veterans and A. A. Hoehling, *Home Front, U.S.A.* (New York: Thomas Y. Crowell, 1966), and Wheeler, *War under the Pacific.* References to San Francisco and Mare Island are from Bastura, ed., *History of U.S. Submarine Veterans of World War II;* and Lt. Cdr. Arnold S. Lott, *A Long Line of Ships* (Annapolis, Md.: U.S. Naval Institute, 1954).

CHAPTER 13. EMPIRE WATERS

Material for this chapter is from interviews with veterans and the patrol logs for both the *Sculpin* and the *Sailfish.* The problems aboard the *Sailfish* on her ninth patrol are detailed in Blair, *Silent Victory.* Torpedo duds are discussed in Blair, *Silent Victory;* Maas, *The Rescuer;* and Wheeler, *War under the Pacific.* Biographical backgrounds on Captain Ward and Captain Connaway are from the Military Records Center, St. Louis. The *Sculpin's* firefights with Japanese sampans are detailed in Adm. I. J. Galatin's *Take Her Deep!* (New York: Pocket Books, 1987).

CHAPTER 14. CONTACT

Wolfpack tactics developed by Admiral Lockwood and Cromwell's role on the *Sculpin* are discussed in Blair, *Silent Victory;* Holmes, *Underseas Victory;* Hoyt, *Submarines at War;* Lockwood, *Down to the Sea in Subs* and *Sink 'Em All;* Morison, *The Two-Ocean War;* Roscoe, *United States Submarine Operations in World War II.* Information about the Gilberts invasion comes from Edwin P. Hoyt, *Storm over the Gilberts* (New York: Van Nostrand Reinhold, 1978). I also drew on Charles A. Lockwood and Hans Christian Adamson, *Battles of the Philippine Sea* (New York: Thomas Y. Crowell, 1967).

CHAPTERS 15–16. THE LOSS OF THE *SCULPIN*/TERROR ON TRUK

My sources for the engagement between the *Sculpin* and the *Yamagumo* include interviews and correspondence with *Sculpin* survivors; editors of *Navy Times, They Fought under the Sea* (Harrisburg, Pa.: Stackpole, 1962); and a statement by George Brown on file at the National Records Center, Military Archives Division, Suitland, Md.

CHAPTER 17. THE *SAILFISH* STRIKES

In addition to my interviews with *Sculpin* survivors, primary sources include Blair, *Silent Victory;* Cope and Karig, *Battle Submerged;* and Hoyt, *Storm over the Gilberts.*

CHAPTER 18. DELIVERANCE

The quote from Admiral Miwa is from *U.S. Submarine Operations of World War II.* Other material is from veterans of both boats; the *Sailfish* log; and Holmes, *Undersea Victory.*

CHAPTER 19. ASHIO

Most of my material is from interviews and correspondence with *Sculpin* survivors; POW depositions, particularly that of 1st Lt. William Frederick Harris (USMC), on file at the National Records Center in Suitland, Md.; and editors of *Navy Times, They Fought under the Sea.*

CHAPTER 20. AN ENEMY IN RETREAT

My account of the *Sailfish*'s honors after the tenth patrol is from interviews with boat veterans, the patrol report, and from Admiral Lockwood's memoirs. My depiction of what preceded the attack on the *Chuyo* is from Lester Bayles and corroborated by other vets. The quote from Admiral Nimitz is from two newspaper accounts of the ceremony provided to me by Billie Ward, Captain Ward's widow. The debate over tactics between General MacArthur and the U.S. Navy is addressed in Blair, *Silent Victory.* My portrait of Captain Ward is from interviews with men who served under him; correspondence with Mrs. Ward; Blair, *Silent Victory;* and Ward's official biography from the Military Records Center in St. Louis. Information about Midway is from Cdr. Edward L. Beach, USN, *Submarine!* (New York: Henry Holt and Company, 1952);

Eugene B. Fluckey, *Thunder Below!* (Chicago: University of Illinois Press, 1992); Grider, *War Fish;* Hoyt, *Submarines at War;* Charles A. Lockwood and Hans Christian Adamson, *Zoomies, Subs and Zeros* (Philadelphia: Chilton, 1956); O'Kane, *Clear the Bridge!;* Sterling, *Wake of the Wahoo.* The account of what happened to the *Sailfish* on her eleventh and twelfth patrols is from her war patrol reports. Additional information on U.S. submarines rescuing pilots is from Blair, *Silent Victory,* and Lockwood and Adamson, *Zoomies, Subs and Zeros.* Detailed analysis of the submarine role in the pivotal battles of the Philippine Sea is drawn from Hoyt, *Submarines at War;* Lockwood, *Sink 'Em All;* Lockwood and Adamson, *Battles of the Philippine Sea;* and Wheeler, *War under the Pacific.* Conditions in Japan at the time are explored in Guillain, *I Saw Tokyo Burning,* and Wheeler, *War under the Pacific.*

CHAPTER 21. THE VALLEY OF DARKNESS

Material for this chapter is from interviews with *Sculpin* POWs; correspondence with others, including Bataan captives who were imprisoned in Ashio; and depositions on file at the National Records Center in Suitland, Md. Background on the Ashio mine is from Mayumi Narabu, Ashio correspondent of *Japan Today,* who provided me with "Traveler's Guide to Tochigi Prefecture," a historical guide to the mine and Tochigi Prefecture. Her attempts to contact surviving guards and mineworkers for me were unsuccessful. I also referred for general background to *Fodor's Japan 1983* (New York: Fodor's Travel Guides, 1983).

CHAPTER 22. BACK FROM THE DEEP

Most of the material for this chapter is from interviews with Ashio POWs and depositions on file at Suitland, Md. Additional deep background on prisoner-of-war camps is from Ronald H. Bailey, *Prisoners of War* (Alexandria, Va.: Time-Life Books, 1981); A. J. Barker, *Behind Barbed Wire* (London: Batsford, 1974); Gen. W. E. Brougher, *South to Bataan, North to Mukden,* ed. D. Clayton James (Athens: University of Georgia Press, 1972); Christopher Burney, *Solitary Confinement* (New York: Coward-McCann, 1952); Christopher, *The Japanese Mind;* James Clavell, *King Rat* (New York: Dell, 1983); John Fletcher-Cooke, *The Emperor's Guest, 1942–45* (London: Leo Cooper, 1972); Donald Knox, *Death March* (New York: Harcourt Brace Jovanovich, 1982); Geoffrey Pharaoh, *No Time for Geishas* (London: Leo Cooper, 1973); and Albert Rupp, *Threshold of Hell* (Long Beach, Calif.: Almar Press, 1983). The attack on Tokyo by firebombers comes from William Craig, *The Fall of*

Japan (New York: Dial Press, 1967). Japan's plans for defending the islands and U.S. plans to invade are explored in Craig, *The Fall of Japan*, and Lockwood and Adamson, *Zoomies, Subs and Zeros*.

EPILOGUE: FOREVER A VIGIL KEEP

Emperor Hirohito's address to the nation is recounted in Craig, *The Fall of Japan*. The battle to return the *Sailfish* to Portsmouth for decommissioning is documented in a number of press clippings from the *Portsmouth Herald* newspaper. My recap of the submarine war is from numerous sources including Blair, *Silent Victory*, and Roscoe, *United States Submarine Operations in World War II*. The decommissioning of the *Sailfish* and the preservation of her conning tower are from press clippings from the *Portsmouth Herald* and *Periscope*, the naval shipyard's newsletter. Shipyard records also note the sale of the rest of the submarine as scrap. The trial of Shigeru Numajiri and his guards is covered extensively in the POW depositions section of the National Records Center in Suitland, Md. The funeral service for Captain Ward is from an account in the *Washington Post*. In addition to attending the fiftieth memorial to the *Squalus* rescue, I corresponded with Oliver Naquin and briefly interviewed him in Portsmouth at the ceremony. Additional information is from Edwards Parks, "The Death Dive and Brave Rescue of the *Squalus*" (*Smithsonian* 19, no. 2 [May 1989]: 102–10).

OTHER SOURCES

Additional sources include the pamphlet by the American Society of Mechanical Engineers, "National Historic Mechanical Engineering Landmark" (Portsmouth: Portsmouth-Kittery Naval Shipbuilding, March 22, 1975). Dr. Albert R. Behnke provided me with "Medical Aspects of Submarine Rescue and Salvage Efforts," which is the report of the *Squalus* disaster by the Medical Corps, U.S. Navy.

Depositions of American POWs held in Japan during World War II and the disposition of war crimes trials are available to the public through Modern Military Field Branch, Military Archives Division, Washington National Records Center Building, Suitland, Md.

Videotapes of the *Squalus-Sailfish-Sculpin* national reunions and other pertinent film footage were provided to me by *Squalus* survivor Carl Bryson and *Sculpin* survivor George Rocek. They are as follows and are in my possession:

Reunions: Portland, Ore., August 1985; Baltimore, August 1986; Milwaukee, Wis., August 1988; Reno, Nev., August 1989; Orlando, Fla., August 1990; Anaheim, Calif., 1993.

50th Anniversary Memorial to the *Squalus,* Portsmouth, N.H., May 23, 1989.

"Silent Victory—Story of the Sculpin Scuttle" (A 1950s TV dramatization of Captain Cromwell's decision to sacrifice his life aboard the submarine).

Original footage of the salvage of the USS *Squalus,* 1939.

The war patrol diaries, "Sculpin (SS-191)" (microfilm roll number NES 1979-9) and "Sailfish (SS-192)" (roll number NES 1976-66), can be found at the Navy and Old Army Branch, Military Archives Division, GSA, National Archives and Records Service, Washington, D.C.

Index

About the Author

Carl LaVO was born at Oak Knoll Naval Hospital in Oakland, California, in 1944. He earned a bachelor of science at the University of Florida. In his twenty-five years as a journalist, he has won numerous writing, editing, design, and photography awards while working for newspapers in California, Florida, and Pennsylvania. He is currently associate editor of the *Bucks County Courier Times*.

He is a frequent contributor to a variety of magazines, including the U.S. Naval Institute *Proceedings*, *Naval History*, *National Wildlife*, *Philadelphia*, *Sierra*, *Down East*, and *Travel-Holiday*. He resides in Levittown, Pennsylvania, with his wife, Mary Anne, and daughter, Genevieve.

The **Naval Institute Press** is the book-publishing arm of the U.S. Naval Institute, a private, nonprofit society for sea service professionals and others who share an interest in naval and maritime affairs. Established in 1873 at the U.S. Naval Academy in Annapolis, Maryland, where its offices remain, today the Naval Institute has more than 100,000 members worldwide.

Members of the Naval Institute receive the influential monthly magazine *Proceedings* and discounts on fine nautical prints and on ship and aircraft photos. They also have access to the transcripts of the Institute's Oral History Program and get discounted admission to any of the Institute-sponsored seminars offered around the country.

The Naval Institute also publishes *Naval History* magazine. This colorful bimonthly is filled with entertaining and thought-provoking articles, first-person reminiscences, and dramatic art and photography. Members receive a discount on *Naval History* subscriptions.

The Naval Institute's book-publishing program, begun in 1898 with basic guides to naval practices, has broadened its scope in recent years to include books of more general interest. Now the Naval Institute Press publishes more than seventy titles each year, ranging from how-to books on boating and navigation to battle histories, biographies, ship and aircraft guides, and novels. Institute members receive discounts on the Press's nearly 400 books in print.

For a free catalog describing Naval Institute Press books currently available, and for further information about subscribing to *Naval History* magazine or about joining the U.S. Naval Institute, please write to:

Membership & Communications Department
U.S. NAVAL INSTITUTE
118 Maryland Avenue
Annapolis, Maryland 21402-5035

Or call, toll-free, (800) 233-USNI.